This book is dedicated to the memory
of my friend, Gordon Allison

Published by Little Toller Books in 2017
Lower Dairy, Toller Fratrum, Dorset

Text © Carol Donaldson 2017

The right of Carol Donaldson to be identified as the author of this work has been asserted by her in accordance with Copyright, Design and Patents Act 1988

Photography © Mark Loos 2017

Jacket artwork © Ffiona Lewis 2017

Typeset in Garamond by Little Toller Books

Printed by TJ International, Cornwall, Padstow

All papers used by Little Toller Books are natural, recyclable products made from wood grown in sustainable, well-managed forests

A catalogue record for this book is available from the British Library

ISBN 978-1-908213-50-1

ON THE MARSHES

Carol Donaldson

LITTLE TOLLER BOOKS

CONTENTS

County of Essex

Sou

River Thames

Cliffe Pools

3

5

4

Northward
Hill

River Thames

Gravesend

2

1

8

6

7

26

9

13

12

Ranscombe Farm
Nature Reserve

10   11

Chatham

Riverside Country Park

15

16

14

M2

M2

M20

M20

Maidstone

1. Lower Higham
2. Cliffe Woods
3. Rye Street
4. Cooling
5. Northward Hill
6. Hoo St Werburgh
7. Upnor

8. Frindsbury
9. Strood
10. Rochester
11. Chatham
12. St Mary's Island
13. Darnet Island
14. Rainham

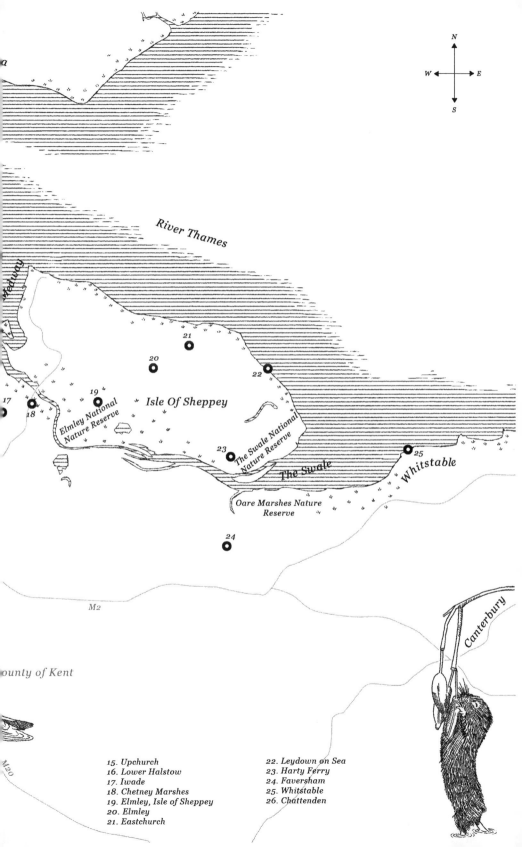

N

W   E

S

River Thames

Medway

Isle Of Sheppey

21

20

17

18

19

Elmley National
Nature Reserve

22

The Swale National
Nature Reserve

23

The Swale

25

Whitstable

Oare Marshes Nature
Reserve

24

Canterbury

M2

ounty of Kent

M20

PROLOGUE

THE PLACE WAS LONG FORGOTTEN. Whatever claims it had once had to commerce and industry were surrendering beneath a sheath of vegetation. Here and there, the skeleton of a walkway appeared beneath the fleshy leaves of stonecrop or a crumbling kiln emerged from ferns, but the site was slowly being consumed by undergrowth. I was glad I was with my friend Will. It was raining and the dark tangle of blackthorn hung with raindrops, catching the light of a wet summer's day as they fell, disappearing into puddles on the concrete. In the distance we could hear the mosquito whine of mopeds, and pockets of human detritus showed that we were not entirely alone.

This place was not Will's natural territory. He was from a well-to-do village outside Canterbury. He had not been brought up in a world of landfill sites and scrublands as I had – half places, not the countryside, not quite human owned. Will had brought me here to show me the island. The River Medway, carving in a loop around the edge of the site, had left behind an isolated hummock of land.

'Untouched for hundreds of years,' he said excitedly.

Will was a writer of spooky horror stories. He imagined lost civilisations on the island. It was an enticing thought, but what had really sparked my interest was the bit of information that Will had casually mentioned as an afterthought.

'A woman is living on a houseboat in the creek. I reckon she's been there for years and no one knows.'

We found the houseboat, but some local teenagers had got there first. The person who had lived in this semi-wilderness had suddenly abandoned her home. It was a sorry sight. The contents of the boat had been strewn around the surrounding land, the windows of the wheelhouse were broken, the rain was soaking the jumble of bed linen, and clothes and utensils lay scattered on the floor. It was not a picturesque retreat, rather a scene of squalor.

Will hung back. Around us the knot of vegetation dripped and rain hissed on the grey river, but still I was drawn to it. Still, after all these years when I had thought I had settled down and no longer needed this life. When I thought I had accepted the bricks and mortar and mortgage, and had rid myself of the thing which had made me feel trapped by them. Still, I wanted to reach out and touch this place and make contact with the person who had lived here and ask, why? Why did you choose this life? Why shun the twenty-first century and choose to live in a houseboat hidden away on a back creek of the Medway?

'Hello,' I called out.

Will stepped back.

Slowly, I approached the boat, picking my way through the scattered belongings, expecting a Doberman to come charging towards us having slipped its chain or, worse, some scraggly haired woman who had lost the art of greeting visitors. There was a gangplank leading onto the boat; I walked towards it.

'I wouldn't,' Will said.

I stepped on board and looked down into the hull. Black mud filled the boat; a trip into that world would be a hellish end.

I walked the length of the deck while Will hovered on shore. The dock wall, which would once have been busy with barges delivering raw materials to the workers, bent away, capped by an impenetrable barrier of blackthorn. Opposite the boat, the island that Will had wanted to show me hid the boat from the main river. The light of the open river glowed in the distance. Out there, pleasure boats passed, riverside flats were developed, roads were ever-widened and no one knew of this boat tucked away. For a moment I entertained a fantasy of taking it over while its owner was gone: tidying the place up, installing the guard dog to keep the kids away, coming here to write and regain what I had lost when I had finally been evicted from my home on the marshes.

The caravan on the north Kent marshes, which I had lived in six years previously, had been the last in a line of inside/outside dwellings which I'd occupied since I was nineteen. Back then, I had spent my summer volunteering in Canada, renovating houses for Native American families and living by a lake in Northern Ontario in a trailer tent which had no running water or electricity.

I loved the simplicity of this world with nothing but the essentials. I loved that I had everything I needed for a happy life: food, shelter, company, things to read and things to write on and no extras. I loved having a lake as my bath tub and washing machine. I was amazed afresh each morning, as I stepped from the trailer, that I was living in a clearing in the Canadian woods. Living in this way you were never really inside. There was always the smell of the trees, the scratching of branches on the canvas and at night the clamorous racket of bullfrogs and whippoorwills and parties of wolves howling down from the hills.

Something clicked into place within me that summer. I felt a rightness, a wholeness, as if my whole life until this point had been out of sync and suddenly I had fallen into step with a person who had always been walking alongside me, just out of reach.

When, inevitably, I returned to England out of duty to my parents and the belief that I had to be sensible, I found that I hated all the trappings of modern urban life. I couldn't get used to carpets and curtains and turning on light switches.

I got over it of course; after all, I was only nineteen, and my passions and energies ran off in new areas. I went to university, met a boy and, afterwards, got a job with a wildlife charity and moved into a flat with the same boy. Or, you could say, I got on with things rather than got over it; the truth was I never stopped searching for the feeling I had that summer.

The caravan on the north Kent marshes was a flash of inspiration. In 2004, I had been offered a job with the RSPB (Royal Society for the Protection of Birds) in Kent and had nowhere to live. Connor, the boy I'd met at university, was in London studying to be a teacher and this move would be on my own. My new boss, AJ, suggested I move into the farmhouse occupied by the two wardens, guys in their forties who had lived in the house together for a LONG time. I had lived in enough shared houses to imagine the scenes of washing up in the sink and wet towels in the bathroom. It didn't appeal. I saw my opportunity.

'Is there any chance I could bring a caravan to the reserve and live in that?' I suggested. I thought I was being cheeky but, with no one but myself to please, I realised that this was a chance to regain, if only for a while, the life I really wanted and, after all, my new boss could only say no.

AJ was a laid-back guy with a philosophy of 'if you're happy, I'm happy'.

'I can't see any reason why not,' he said. 'One of the digger drivers lives in a caravan on site during the week. I'm sure we could find room for another.'

He hadn't quite bargained on the thirty-foot Steeple Oaklands static caravan bought from a site in Jaywick-on-Sea and chosen for its 1970s wood-panelled dining area and extra-large living room (which I figured would make an excellent dance space).

AJ took it well. We parked the caravan under the willow tree in the garden of the farmhouse and connected the electrics and plumbing. With no option for waste disposal, I bought a caravan portaloo and pickaxed my own drains for the sink and shower. At £3,000, I worked out that if I only managed to live in it for six months, I would make my money back on the caravan with the saving on rent.

But those first six months were harder than I had imagined. The marshes seemed oppressive: a vast, bleak flatness with nowhere to hide. My new colleagues appeared silent and serious and, for hours each day, I was stuck on my own while they went out to do 'men's' jobs on the reserve, leaving me to answer the phone and work on the computer. Everyone I loved seemed to be on the other side of the water. One evening, in the autumn twilight, I walked up the hill, which was the epicentre of the reserve, and looked out across the Thames twisting away towards London where Connor was living. There, on the opposite bank, across the churning, mud-coloured river, were the blue hills of Essex, my much maligned home county.

The marshes on that side of the river appeared blighted by oil-storage depots and industry, but across the river were also my family and childhood friends. Just a boat ride would get me there. To have that offer of warmth and company so close made the loneliness more acute. The eye of the marshes glared at me, the grazing meadows appeared harsh and scruffy and the wind pouring out of the North Sea battered everything which dared to stand upright in this land of flatness. Down on the fields, great, black gangs of crows bustled together, waiting for a signal from the light and the season, before making their move into the wood where they roosted in their thousands. Six curlews flew across the sky and the silhouettes of fieldfares and redwings plummeted into the valley. Blackbirds chinked metallically, sounding too much like the computer I had sat at all day. It was not a comforting, friendly landscape. In the openness of the marshes there is nowhere to hide from yourself.

I disguised my unhappiness and dislike of the place well. Local people I met through work would say 'I can see you're in love with this place'.

But I wasn't, not at all.

Caravan living was also proving difficult. My summer by the lake in Canada had not prepared me for winter on the marshes. Living in a metal box in winter is cold. The water in my washing-up bowl froze; my house plants died of frost damage. The electricity blanked out in every storm, forcing me to fight my way across the lawn to the farmhouse and rouse the ever sleepy wardens into letting me in to fiddle with the fuses. Mice invaded through microscopic holes and lived on a diet of food labels, while shredding my clothes for their nests.

By the end of the winter I had earned the grudging respect of my colleagues and I began to see moments when, if only I could get on top of all the problems and breakdowns, maybe that feeling I had once had in Canada could also be found here.

One morning, I snuggled under the blankets on my bed and read *Great Expectations* as fog wrapped around the caravan and muffled the sound of fog horns blowing out on the river. Even in the twenty-first century, the marshes were still a place of mystery. You walked through the villages and had the feeling that things were going on behind closed doors. The packed pews of the churches contrasted with rumours of swingers' clubs in the villages. It was a place where Halloween was frowned upon, but riots took place at the village fete. It was an area where the ghosts of the past were close beside you, where the remnants of shepherds' cottages rubbed up against the lights of the oil refinery.

The estuary had begun to seep into my pores and I realised that beauty could be found here if you looked for it. There were the twisting rivulets which wound their way out across the vast muddy bays as the water made its way to the sea; container ships that seemed to float across the land as they sailed on the hidden river. Beauty was in the boundless sky and private chatterings of rooks gliding across it, in the bubbling aria of a curlew, in the sound of church bells coming across the water from Essex, amplified by the river fog.

To many this was a wasteland, not an area of outstanding natural beauty, but a landscape where man had seen a blank canvas to dump unsightly industry. The remnants of these industries littered the bays: bawley boats rotting in creeks, cranes collapsing into old gravel pits, forts lost and lonely on islands. The estuary had sucked these human fingerprints in the mud. Broken houses and sheepfolds, whole villages had been whipped into submission by the wind from the sea. 'Bring it on,' the estuary seemed to challenge, 'I will take you too'. The estuary was a rough-edged beauty, but it had begun to get under my skin. Six months passed. I survived the winter. Spring came and I stayed.

At the end of the first year I knew I did not want to leave my life on the marshes for a tiny flat or house with a postage-stamp garden close to Connor's new teaching post in Essex.

'Move into the caravan.' I urged him. 'Just for now. It's rent free. We can save for a deposit.'

It was all very logical, to me. Connor saw through it.

'I want to get on with life,' he said. 'Not waste my time with these ideas of living in a shack with no conveniences.'

I knew this. Connor had spent the last year training for a sensible job. I could feel the life he wanted descending on me and, like a rabbit waiting for the blow of an onrushing truck, I was frozen, unable to think of what to do. I kept pretending that it was what I wanted too.

In the end we settled for an uneasy compromise. Connor moved into the caravan but decked it with technology, iPods, laptop, Freeview TV. It made neither of us happy.

By the time of the eviction, two years later, I was holding on too tight, resisting the urge to get a mortgage and buy a house with Connor, resisting changing a job which had stagnated, resisting moving on in life at all because of the caravan, because I wanted the life under the willow tree, a life of little owls yodelling love sonnets outside my window, and mice living in the flowerpots outside my door. The life of lying in bed on an autumn morning with the blackberries ripe in the hedgerow and the willowherb flaming on the reserve, watching the rooks and jackdaws skydance across the fields, batting the wind, revelling in the joy of flight. Cracks were appearing all around – in my job, in my relationship – but I was clinging to the caravan as if it were a lifebelt keeping me afloat.

Clinging to anything this tightly is never good. The eviction happened. But it was in those last few weeks that I discovered that I was not alone in wanting a life close to nature, with few possessions.

The caravan was advertised for sale and people came to visit. There was an ex-traveller who gave me advice on avoiding planning permission, a houseboat owner who let me spend a weekend living aboard her boat while I considered new places to live, the warden of the nearby reserve who lived in a condemned house on the marshes of Sheppey, a former scrap-metal dealer turned sheep farmer who eventually bought the caravan for his daughter to live in. The estuary, it seemed, had become a shelter for these people, and I began to wonder if the two were linked: the landscape in its unconventional beauty, and the people it attracted. Did this landscape, which continued to defy the modern world, attract people who also resisted the urge to be tamed?

Now, with that whole world of the caravan on the marshes swept away, I notice them still. These people. These dwellings. The little huts and houseboats, the caravans and chalets, the people who are still hiding out in the creeks and bays of the estuary.

As I stood on the deck of the wrecked houseboat, with Will pacing on shore, I realised that here had lived another renegade, trying to live in a way contrary to the expected norm, and I had missed my chance to ask her why? This woman would not be returning to her home. Her home would soon go the way of my own and I feared that before long things would change for us all.

In 2013, the estuary was under threat, not only from Boris Johnson's desire for another airport, but from the Lower Thames Crossing and housing estates which threatened to obliterate colonies of nightingales, and a myriad other plans to concrete over the marshes and bay with progress and growth. There was another threat that was sweeping across the marshes like sea fog: the desire to tame, to sanitise and smooth away. This creeping twenty-first-century miasma was a sickness which would wipe away the rough edges and the people hiding out here.

I wanted to understand this place before it was lost. I wanted to walk the estuary from Gravesham to Whitstable and meet some of the people bound up in it. I wanted to celebrate this world before it was gone and find out what it was that bought them here and, in doing so, I hoped to answer the endless questions within myself.

Why am I drawn to this landscape? What is it about modern 'normal' life I find so hard to reconcile with myself? And, once you are on the outside, can you ever come in again?

For the last few years, I had staunchly followed the mantra 'don't look back'. Now I wanted to walk a songline into my past, peeling back the layers to touch the places which had been important. Not to bring that life back, but to understand whom that life had formed. It was also a journey to uncover the stories of those others, those dwellers, living on the edges of the modern world; people who had chosen the estuary to create a life which meant something to them. It was their songline too, a route between plotland and boatyard, island and hermit's home, chalet and shack. By meeting these people, by putting my finger on each place, I wanted to sing this world into life. If there was a common thread, a reason that united them all, then maybe I would find it. Maybe, in finding it, I would make sense of my own story.

I saw the journey as a pilgrimage and these people as my pilgrim sites. They represented something of importance to my own beliefs, that there are more ways to live in this world than the one that society dictates is acceptable. I had made sacrifices because of this belief and now I wished to visit others who had embraced this path. Footfall after footfall, I would walk these two parallel lines between my past and those of the people I met.

ONE

Lower Higham – Cliffe Woods

SPRING IS A BEAUTIFUL time of year on the estuary, a time of the first sun warming the hedgerows, flowers appearing in the woodland and sweet violets and primroses with translucent petals which look too delicate to survive the more ferocious heat of summer. It's a time of rescuing dozy bumble bees and overwintering butterflies from outhouses and experiencing that momentary happiness which comes from showing kindness to another creature. It is a time of the winter tracery of twigs against skies the colour of rosy tellin shells, of the rook city springing into raucous life and of herons sailing back to their ancestral nests.

It is a beautiful time of year on the estuary and I had missed it. After one of the wettest winters the country had ever known I was at home, waiting for the land to dry out so I could begin my journey. Since my visit to the houseboat with Will I had not been idle. My weekends had been spent feasting on local history, sailing the river along with Mr W. Coles Finch while tucked up in bed with a hot water bottle and a 1929 copy of his book, *The Medway River and Valley*. Outside the window, rain fell and gales destroyed the neighbour's fence panels while I would sip my cocoa and see in my mind's eye the remains of man-of-wars lying in bays along the river and the country as he had seen it at a time when Gillingham could still be described as a rural village and the valley had not yet been ravaged by urban sprawl and traffic jams.

During days off I had visited the local studies centre and spent long hours surrounded by newspaper clippings, history pamphlets and microfilm, tracking down stories of long-forgotten plotlands, men living undetected in the woods and spots where generations of Gypsies had camped. As I talked to people about my plans, other stories began to emerge: modern tales of friends or neighbours who had once lived in a bus, a tent or a caravan. By the turn of the year, I had stuck on the wall of my cellar a map of the estuary littered with post-it notes of the route I wished to take and who and what I might find there.

My plan was to walk across the Hoo Peninsula to Rochester, head on to the river, then back to shore, cross the marshes from the Medway to the Swale, walk around the Isle of Sheppey, hope that providence would provide a way back to the mainland, and finish in Whitstable. Altogether the route was around eighty miles. I wanted to see the estuary in all its colours, so I decided to spread the walks out across the course of a year. I also wanted to give myself time to absorb the lessons I suspected I might learn en route.

Now it was the end of May, the footpaths were drying out; after months cooped up in my house, with the sounds of the neighbours echoing through my paper-thin walls, I was itching to get out. I had spent all winter driving back and forth along the M2 to work, stuck in traffic jams or within the walls of the office. I was looking forward to striding out across the estuary under wide skies which allowed the mind to open up and roll with its own thoughts.

There is a freedom to be found in walking. The human pace of footfall, the rhythm and repetition of an instinctual action, like breathing, which lulls you into a state of calm. On the long walks I took as part of my job, across the marshes of Kent, surveying the network of water channels which gridironed the fields, I would experience this calm. On the way out, I would walk the ditch edge, studying my map, diligently filling in forms, noting plants and water depths and nitrate enrichment; on the way back, my mind would talk, not with the daily chatter of timetables and to-do lists, but with a new-found clarity. It was then that I would hear the voice below the surface, the slower, more confident voice telling me the things of real matter. Walking out as a way of walking in. Richard Mabey, in his book, *Nature Cure*, quoted the Roman expression *'solvitur ambulando'* – 'you can work it out by walking'.

But it was years since I had really walked any great distance – and then never alone. In our twenties, Connor and I would set off regularly at weekends from wherever we happened to be living. We would walk to the nearest long-distance footpath and head off for a few days, camping where we stopped. Connor had been a good egg, willing to join me on these unorthodox rambles, although he would probably have preferred to spend his weekend reading the paper in a café before watching the footie. He was always a bad sleeper, and we often had to give up when his feet developed so many blisters he was unable to walk on. But still, I had loved these trips. They felt like an adventure, the chance to step out of modern life for a few days, walk the parallel world of green lanes, and pilgrim routes, sleep in woodlands beneath 'Keep Out' signs. I liked going to a café for morning coffee and looking at the other people and thinking that none of them knew that I had spent the night sleeping in the woods on the outskirts of their town.

Both in minimum-wage jobs, camping was the only way we could afford to explore the area we lived in. B&Bs were out of our reach, so many youth hostels had been closed. Camping was a necessity rather than a choice, but images from those days, sleeping in private woodlands and tucked away in field corners, will stick in my mind forever. A hare coming down a path early in the morning to within feet of our tent, its ears backlit against the sun. Woodlands whitewashed with wild garlic, a tawny owl alighting above us and gazing down with more curiosity than fear. I also remember the nights of hunkering down with the wildlife and the woods suddenly becoming a danger ground of night shooting, and the constrictive fear clutching at your throat as feet stopped outside your tent at 2am in the morning.

Sleeping rough had brought me these experiences and although I wanted to relive the good, I knew that on my own there was no way I wanted to face the bad. In the end it had all become too much for Connor. He had watched the *Blair Witch Project* and professed that he could no longer camp in the woods. I think it was the beginning of him standing up and saying, 'Look Carol, this just isn't my thing'.

My other memory was that carrying a tent, sleeping bag and camp cooker over stiles and hills and rutted country lanes was hard going. I had images of Connor literally hauling me over stiles, and well remembered the momentary loss of humour from exhaustion at the end of the day when you could find nowhere safe to camp and were so tired you wanted to weep, and this was with Connor carrying the bulk of the weight. I knew in reality there was no way I would be able to walk ten to fifteen miles a day carrying a heavy pack and still be in good humour to converse with people I met along the way. I had to pack light.

The night before I left on the first of my planned estuary walks, I emptied out the contents of my work bag, casting aside my diary and work phone with satisfaction. Empty, the bag looked big and roomy; however, once stuffed with a change of clothes, a waterproof jacket, some high-energy fruit and nut mix, a water bottle and micro medical kit there was surprisingly little room left for frivolity.

I put the camera and notepad to one side; after all, I had shoulders and hands to carry such things. I halved the oversized bar of Bourneville Dark, but couldn't bring myself to leave it behind entirely. 'Good for morale,' I argued. I attached a camping knife to my belt, primarily for sharpening my pencil and spearing my food but, I figured, it would also act as a deterrent for any would-be assailant. In sharp contrast, I also squeezed a lipstick into a side pocket. I had long learned that, if in a tight corner, caught trespassing, illegally camping, or generally mildly breaking some unknown bylaw, it helped if, while playing the innocent, you looked halfway decent. I appreciate that this will not earn me any 'feminist of the year' points, but I had been raised by a woman whose answer to all life's problems was to 'put some lippy on', so wasn't quite prepared to face even the sheep on the marshes bare-faced.

While the lipstick I considered essential, I discarded any reading matter other than a pocket tide timetable bought from the local fishing-tackle shop. My waterproof trousers were also left to one side. The forecast for the bank holiday weekend was reassuring, sun on Sunday, followed by a grey but generally dry day on Monday.

I was carrying no camping gear and precious little food; instead, I would be relying on the age-old tradition of hospitality offered to those on a pilgrimage. For each leg of the journey I would throw myself on the mercy of old friends, recent friends, casual acquaintances and people who had never met me, people who thought I was crackers, or that my plans were weird and confusing, but were still willing to put me up, feed me and talk to me. So, as a final touch, I packed a scallop shell, the symbol of pilgrims travelling on the Way of St James to Santiago de Compostela in Spain. The scallop, as well as being the emblem of St James, had a rather practical use for the pilgrim, who could present himself at houses along the route and ask for one scoop of food. This traditionally allowed everyone to give charity without being overburdened, though looking at my own small shell, pink, ridged and fitting neatly into my palm, I felt I would need to knock on a lot of doors and receive a lot of scoops if I were going to receive enough sustenance to keep me going.

The idea of pilgrimage was also the reason I had chosen to begin my journey at St Mary's church in Higham. In the weeks prior to setting off, I had pictured myself strolling from Lower Higham Station down the lane, through orchards and wheat fields to the church, the sun on my back, a tune on my lips and noble thoughts in my head. Unfortunately, I had forgotten to consult Southeastern trains about my vision and, instead, on a Sunday morning at the end of May, having walked purposely from my home to Rainham station, I discovered that 'planned engineering works' would see my twenty-minute train journey take two hours. Forced to backtrack and pick up the car, I had then been obliged to take a long diversion to avoid a lorry which had shed its load and search in vain for some non-restricted parking in the village. I gave up and drove down the lane to the church, abandoning the car against the church wall, hoping it would still be there, unclamped when I returned to it in a few days' time.

Finally, away from the car, Sunday morning peace descended. The hamlet of Lower Higham was made up of about ten cottages, some still thatched, tucked away at the end of a lane which nowadays leads nowhere but the marshes. It is the kind of place in which sparrows dust-bathe undisturbed in the middle of the road and house martins still nest under the eaves.

Once, this place had been better known, notorious even. The road used to lead to an abbey populated by a group of Benedictine nuns of the order of St Sulpice. The nuns acted as gatekeepers and were responsible for a causeway that once led across the marshes. They guided travellers through this dangerous, sodden district of mists and mosquitoes to the ferry at Cliffe, which carried people across the Thames. It is hard nowadays to imagine sleepy Lower Higham as a tenth-century Dartford toll booth, but back then, the causeway was an important thoroughfare.

In those days, the Thames at this point was an unpredictable beast, not the fixed and straight river we know today, but a place of constant change, with multiple channels, dangerous sandbanks, extensive marshlands and in-river islands. With no flood embankments to contain it, the river drowned the land at regular intervals, sweeping away animals, people and buildings. In 1293, a flood swept across the marshes and part of the causeway was damaged. The cost of its repair crippled the abbey financially, and both its fortune and its population of nuns began to fall away.

By 1508, when Edward Steroper became the new vicar of St Mary's, there were only four nuns remaining, among them the fabulously named Anchoretta Unglethorpe. Soon after Edward's arrival rumours began to circulate that Edward was 'keeping company' with Anchoretta, obliging the bishop of Rochester to send a written warning. Edward not only ignored the warning but, dissatisfied with just one nun, wanted more. In 1519, an inquiry was held, in which a local woman gave evidence that three of the four nuns had fallen for Edward's charms and two had borne his children. The fourth must have had a will of iron or just a really efficient chastity belt. At the inquiry there was evidence that the women had tried to reform and fend off Edward but, in the end, the scandal was too much; the nuns were dismissed and the abbey closed.

St Mary's Church was not a place of much happiness for women. Here the nuns would have first met Edward, and here they may have prayed for the will to resist him. Here Kate Collins, Charles Dickens' daughter, had been married, and Dickens, according to his housekeeper, had been found later that evening crying 'what have I done?' into Kate's skirts. As I stepped inside the quiet cool of the building, I could picture the nuns in the aisles, the rails polished by the thousands of hands that had rested there. I could imagine Edward in the pulpit, carved with buttons of flowers and long-columned archways. I could picture Dickens, maybe wracked with guilt that his divorce had driven his daughter into an inauspicious marriage, leading her down the aisle hung with red oil lamps. But the walls of this building did not resonate with sadness, they resonated with sanctuary. Some places are holy and some are not, and it doesn't matter if they are grand and beautiful and built in the name of God, some places just don't have it. St Mary's does, at least to me.

I had come here many times on dark days and good, when the roads were heavy with puddles, when the skies were full of swallows; pushing open the latch of the wooden door carved with animals and green men and women who looked remarkably like nuns; kneeling before the statue of Jesus on top of the medieval rood screen while rain splattered the windows and the floor was cold beneath me. It was unheated, unlit, always open, always silent, always empty and I wanted it always to be that way for me. It was a place that my mind turned to when I was in towns, a place of thought and meditation and answers. I make no apology for having faith; it works for me.

I had come here in the midst of losing the caravan and Connor and had wept endlessly without shame, knowing that no one would find me. Now, seven years later, I was back, a different person. Suffering changes you. I had thought for a long time that sadness had become ingrained in me like dirt beneath the fingernails, but in the last year or so it had begun to fade. I was confident. I was hopeful. It had taken a long time, but I had a life in Kent once again. So, as I sat in the pew my thoughts were lighter. I asked the traditional pilgrim plea: for a safe journey, free passage, no illness or injury, for all those I loved to stay safe while I travelled. For all to go well.

I stepped from the cool darkness of the church into the sun and set off along a footpath through the green shoots of the wheat field opposite. The morning was fresh after a day of rain and the village sang with the bank holiday sounds of hammering and sawing. There was a flippity cold breeze blowing and I was grateful for the fleece I had brought, despite it being pockmarked by burn holes from winter bonfires. The sun baked my neck and I stopped to fish in my bag for my hat, complete with mosquito netting, bought for the express purpose of surviving aerial bombardment by daddy-longlegs, my most feared nemesis, of whose clacking wings and freaky dancing no amount of common sense could prevent my terror.

Blackbirds chinked in alarm as I walked between hedgerows of elm and hawthorn. The smell of waterweed and peaty mud reached me from the ditches lining the path, a smell, which, after years of surveying wildlife on the marshes, was a good smell to me, the smell of a day out of the office. Chiffchaffs and strident cettis warblers called from a stand of wet woodland, the cettis shouting road-traffic instructions at me. 'Stop. Look. Listen. Wait until you cross the road'. I emerged into an open field with a tractor ploughing in the distance; the breeze picked up and my hat went flying off into the wheat field, trailing its veil of mosquito netting behind it like a heavy-winged moth. I climbed furtively through the crop to retrieve it, imagining the ploughman muttering 'bloody ramblers'. I jammed the hat back on, but it made a bid for freedom again and, on the third attempt I gave up and stuffed it back in my pack. The sun beat down on my brains.

I passed a ménage; a girl on a tall black horse was practising riding in patterns I knew only too well from a pony-obsessed childhood. Cross at C, stop at B, serpentine.

'Good morning,' I called and got a nod in reply.

I strolled confidently across a meadow of long grass and, by the time I reached the other side, my trousers and non-waterproof boots were drenched with dew. The air was rich with the sweet woody scent of hawthorn, a thick and heady mixture. The surrounding scrub was full of baby-pink dog roses and the scratchy squeals of whitethroats. Common blue butterflies rose up from the wet grass with the warming air, their underwings an abstract mosaic of tan and silver, with droplets of black speckling the surface. I climbed a stile and there was Cliffe Woods before me.

TWO

In Cliffe Woods

CLIFFE WOODS WAS ONCE a community of shack dwellers set amid the woodland, a plotland settlement of the type which sprang up between the wars, particularly around London when the city was smog-filled, the slums crowded, land was cheap, travel became possible and many people headed for the countryside to escape.

The plotlands were a product of agricultural decline. From the end of the nineteenth century, bankrupt farms were broken up and sold as cheap plots. These plots were initially bought by people attempting to scrape a living by keeping chickens, growing vegetables or taking in laundry. In this way, poor people could often keep themselves afloat and stay out of the hated workhouses.

By the 1920s, land sales were regular affairs across the South East, with special trains put on to take Londoners to view the plots. The possibility of owning a weekend house in the country was particularly appealing to those living in overcrowded rented accommodation in the city. After the Second World War, thousands of Londoners, made homeless by bombing, were camping in fields around the city or taking over empty Army and Air Force bases to form new communities.

By the time author Lena Kennedy came to the area in the 1950s, the community of plotland shacks was well established. The car had arrived and the working class still had no money, but at least they had won the right to weekends and holidays.

In her book, *Away to the Woods*, Lena describes how she and her husband arrived for a few days' break from city life. Lena's husband Fred remembered the area fondly from the time he had visited as a child with his boys' club, part of the movement to give East End kids a taste of the countryside. They drove down from London in their old Austin 7 with two squabbling kids and a dog in the back and ended up camping at Allhallows-on-Sea. Lena loved the fresh air and watching the kids and dog play on the beach and persuaded Fred to return the following year with a larger tent. They kept the tent erected on site all season and furnished it with tables, chairs and a double bed, brought down from London tied to the top of the Austin. This became their first holiday home.

The couple fitted right in with the other people at the camp: a mixture of working-class families and Irish immigrants who had arrived looking for work in the oil refinery on the Isle of Grain. Lena and the children began to stay down there all week while Fred worked in London. But, when polio hit the area and several of the camp kids got ill, she decided to move her family to safety.

So, on a hot afternoon in the 1950s, the children and the dog were put back in the car and they toured the lanes once again. It was during a stop for a drink at the Merryboys pub that they first heard about the shacks in the wood. Following a man they met in the pub, they ploughed along a muddy woodland track and came to a view across the estuary. Below them they could see what Lena described as 'tiny matchbox buildings each in its square of garden'. With their savings they put down a deposit for a piece of overgrown land and a dilapidated caravan. The plot cost them £75.

Lena's journey from weekend camping in Kent to owning her own plot was typical of many others. Two wars and much sacrifice had made the survivors feel they had as much 'right' to own a place in the country as anyone. They, too, wanted a piece of England, even if their holiday home was hand-built from scrap, and so the plotland communities began. To many the plotland was a weekend escape; to others it was a permanent retreat from city life, a smallholding where the kids could enjoy fresh air and they could 'make do' and use many of the self-sufficient skills that had got them through the war.

From my vantage point on the stile outside the village, Cliffe Woods had become what Lena most feared, a place of 'small modern houses all the way over her lovely green hill'. Except that now the houses had grown, spawning double garages and vast, paved driveways. On the map, I could still see the skeletal outline of the plotlands: long, thin pieces of land with dwellings set well back.

I headed down a path into the village and along the busy main road, passing bungalows called 'Tresco' and 'Glenlea'. View Road, which had been a muddy track when Fred and Lena had visited, was now paved and the other shacks were long gone. The drive to 'Little Orchards' was tarmacked, 'Orchard Cottage' was three storeys high, but then I came to a plot which, in sharp contrast to the security gates and entry systems all around, appeared to be a just patch of scrub surrounded by a picket fence.

Lena Kennedy's daughter, Angela, greeted me at the garden gate, one of those iron scrollwork gates which were so popular in the days before everyone turned their garden into a car park. I followed her down the garden path to the bungalow that her parents had built after the world of little shacks had been brushed away. Angela still lived in London, as her parents had, but came to the plot on weekends. She hadn't been down in weeks and rushed around the little kitchen making me a cup of tea, while alternately unpacking the car and remonstrating with her grandson who was meant to be helping her.

We drank tea in the living room, the walls of which were covered in brightly coloured paintings, clippings of newspaper articles about her mother, certificates commemorating family achievements and photos of a young Angela looking every bit the cool, blonde, Sixties girl, who would be sitting next to John Lennon in a Beatles biopic. Finishing our tea, we clambered through the garden, with Angela's black Labrador, Acorn, at our heels.

Much of the plot had become overgrown, but Angela had found

herself a team of both willing and not-so-willing helpers. In the garden Kevin and Alan were hard at work, chopping logs, fixing tools and clearing the brambles from her mother's roses. They were staying for a few weeks, living in the caravans tucked away behind the bungalow, earning their keep by working on the land. Angela's grandson, recovering after a night out with friends, found his enthusiasm for chopping logs quickly giving way to an enthusiasm for falling asleep on the living room couch.

On the way through the plot I passed a narrow wooden shed, which had once housed the outside dunny, and the big metal tank where Angela's parents had collected rainwater. 'It was an unusual childhood, I guess,' Angela said. 'We washed our hair in rainwater and collected drinking water from a standpipe at the end of the road, using a yoke with two buckets attached. No one thought of it as a hard life, it was just the way things were.'

The enterprise of the plotlanders somehow makes me want to weep. Dennis Hardy and Colin Ward in the book *Arcadia for All: The Legacy of a Makeshift Landscape* tell how one man cycled down from London carrying the tools, timber and glass to build his house strapped to his back. Another couple borrowed a pound from a neighbour to put down a deposit on their land. They bought a First World War army surplus tent which they rented out to other people on their London estate. With the earnings they bought the materials to build their house.

Many people's holiday home began life as a makeshift shed but, slowly, over the years the sheds were embellished with architectural styles as varied as their owners. The plotlands, according to Ward and Hardy, represented the opportunity to 'create a world of one's own choosing'. The local authorities offered the plotlanders nothing in the way of water or sanitation and soon people began to realise they could get by without these amenities. Other people arrived on their land carrying all their own drinking water or strained rain water through an old stocking. They worked out ways to help each other; what skills they lacked they learned. Building their own houses, being self-sufficient gave them a sense of pride and satisfaction.

I understood this pride in self-sufficiency. During that first cold winter in the caravan, my pipes had burst and I could find no one to fix them. Plumbers, I learned, were none too keen to come out to caravan-dwellers who, in their opinion, were obviously 'Pikeys' and unlikely to pay. Eventually, I found a man willing to look at my boiler. He charged me £80. I watched him very closely and the next time the boiler broke I took it apart myself. I found a spider living in one of the gas jets, blew him away, put the boiler back together and turned it on. Flames whooshed up to the ceiling; not quite right. I tried again, tightening the nuts, re-jiggling the screws. Next time things worked perfectly. Soon, with the help of a book from the library, I was digging soakaway drains and mending the leaky shower. I knew the satisfaction to be found in self-reliance, that feeling of being a capable woman able to take on a problem and solve it.

Now this power, this autonomy, was eroding. We were losing the skills that kept us free men and women. Nowadays, when the boiler breaks, no one thinks of looking at it themselves. It is dangerous. Your pipes and plumbing are a mystery to be feared, not something to tackle with a spanner and common sense. We work long hours to pay for the things we could do ourselves. The equation between our labour and our lives has got dark and misty. In the plotland days it was more transparent. In Lena's day your dreams were achievable. Lena and her husband had been free people; now, somehow, we are all owned, and it is hard to pinpoint when or how this changed.

When I had mended the gas boiler I began to see a glimmer of possibility. If I could fix things, I wouldn't need to pay others to do this and, even better, if I could build things, maybe I could get by without buying so much stuff and if I didn't need to buy so much then I wouldn't need so much money, and if I didn't need so much money, didn't that mean I could work less and actually stop and enjoy the world around me? It was an idea that excited me, but I knew that if I mentioned it to Connor it would be snatched away as nonsense, an unrealistic fantasy that wasn't possible in twenty-first century Britain.

In their day, Lena and Fred weren't considered crazed radicals for mending and building things; that was just what poor people did. Nowadays, it seems that making do, patching up old things to keep them working, using your ingenuity to create the things you can't afford is looked down on, particularly by the poor. Now, it seems, if you can't afford the things you want, you get out a loan and buy them anyway. But was Connor right? Is it impossible in the modern world to change our mindset, to rediscover a little of the self-sufficiency of the plotlanders and take back some autonomy over our lives?

Back in the caravan I bought Connor's philosophy and had waited for my *Grand Designs* moment. Connor argued that the only people who built their own homes were Kevin McCloud protégés, moneyed, middle-class bankers and, if I wanted to build my own house, then I'd better get a plan to become one of them. I tried, buying magazines called *Build Your Own Home*, full of adverts for underfloor heating and plots costing five years' salary. I knew that this was not the kind of house building I wanted; I also knew that, if Connor were to be part of the equation, it was the only kind that could be entertained.

Lena Kennedy died several years ago, but as I walked through her garden I felt that this was a woman who would have understood what I had really been looking for all those years ago. When Lena and Fred first arrived, the plot at Cliffe Woods had been a jungle. Lena loved the tall trees and the wild rampant nature of the land but Fred was more practical. The summer of their arrival they erected a tent and began clearing the land while the kids played on a rope swing or in the woods. Later, Fred bought an old railway hut from *Exchange and Mart*, transporting it through the Dartford Tunnel in pieces and then rebuilding it on site with the help of a friend. It was to become the family's first proper home. Angela remembered the Tilly lamps, which they lit in the evenings, her mother calling at her to stand well back as the flame burst into life with a swoosh before dying down. 'The brightness would grow slowly,' she said. 'There were also the oil stoves, terrible smelly contraptions, whose fumes gave everyone headaches.'

The railway hut had been added to over the years and now the shack resembled a rambling summer house in the garden. Ivy clambered up the peeling paint and hazel trees overhung the glass-panelled door. Nature had reclaimed the garden, and in many ways it now looked as Lena had first described it, with wild roses and waist-high grass. Angela pushed open the doors. I stepped in and back into a half-forgotten memory of neighbours' houses full of dark Victorian furniture, crochet blankets, knick-knacks collected from holidays and country walks.

On the table, next to a display of pinecones and a half-drunk bottle of wine, stood an ancient typewriter where Lena had worked on many of her bestselling novels: stories of romance and saucy East End girls come good. She hadn't been published until her mid-sixties, but afterwards she and Fred had been unexpectedly thrown into fame and wealth. There was a photo of Lena accepting the *This is Your Life* book from Eamonn Andrews, another with her and her husband aboard the *QE2*. My favourite was one of her wearing a fox-fur coat, not very PC in today's world, but I understood it. A fur coat for an East End girl was the symbol that you had made it. My own grandmother, also from a tough East End family, had lusted after one.

We toured the house: the tiny kitchen with its ancient gas cooker where Lena had cooked up huge dinners and batter puddings for visiting family, the little bedroom which had once been Angela's, the room her mother had written in, plastered with newspaper clippings and fading posters advertising Lena's books. Angela apologised for the mess and the spider webs, but all I could think was that I would be very happy here, with the sound of rain on the roof and the morning birds and the scratchy twigs against the single-paned glass. I could see myself here, in this shack in the woods, on dark winter days with the woodburner on, wrapped in blankets, writing. Here in this self-contained, hand-built, self-sufficient world I could be myself.

Later, over lunch in the bungalow, we were joined by other plotholders. John Howes had played with Angela when they were children. The shack girls and the village boys still keep in touch, meeting regularly to talk about the old days. They remembered the roads, so thick with mud that they had to walk in wellingtons and pick up their school shoes from the village shop, leaving the wellingtons outside in rows to await the return of the school bus. Angela remembered the road to the Merryboys pub. It was a shady path lit by glow worms; she would collect these green glowing lights and place them in her hair.

The thing they talked about most was the feeling of community. 'It's not like the old days,' John and Angela agreed as we ate our way through buttered potatoes, cold ham, boiled eggs and salad washed down with gallons of tea. 'Then, people were always popping around with a pot of jam, or a cabbage from the garden. The community has all gone; now everyone texts or emails, no one speaks.'

Throughout lunch, people came and went. Kevin and Andy joined us at the table, Angela's grandson reappeared to grab a handful of cheese, a neighbour dropped by to lend Angela a saw. We all sat around the table and laughed and talked and I was reminded of family parties when I was a child. It was ironic that these very people who felt that the community feeling had gone were in fact surrounded by it.

I sensed that for the people who grew up here as children that community of shack-dwellers would always be present. It is not the texts and emails that keep us apart so much nowadays as the fact that we move around so much. Our childhood friends are lost to us, we don't see each other's children grow up and get married. The plotlanders had bucked this trend. They had kept those links from their childhoods. Despite the loss of that world, the plotlands lived on in them. The sense of community which John and Angela talked about was still bouncing around that table.

John admitted that he liked to feel that link to the past. He liked to go to the part of his plot which was still covered in trees and look up through the branches. 'This is Cliffe Woods', I say to myself. John had bought land on the marshes, further away from the village where he could go. 'To shoot, I tell myself,' he said. 'Except nowadays I've gone all Peter Scott-ish and just like to watch the ducks and geese. I prefer it there, I don't put much store on a house.

A house is just a shed, somewhere to go when it's raining.'

I am reminded of Henry Thoreau's saying: 'Most men appear never to have considered what a house is and are actually needlessly poor all their lives because they think that they must have such a one as their neighbours.' Thoreau was the original plotlander, taking to the woods in 1854 to build his own house, write his book about Walden Pond and live 'simply and deliberately'. He felt that the cost of a thing was measured by how much life he had to give for it; consequently, he did not wish to work all his days in order to pay off the mortgage on a large house, but instead was content to live simply and spend his free time enjoying nature. Thoreau, I had no doubt, would have applauded the plotlanders' self-sufficiency.

I asked John if he felt that many people nowadays could do what Angela and his own parents had done, buy a piece of land, build their own home? 'People don't seem to be able to do anything without money now,' he said. 'My granddaughter wants a tree house and my daughter pays £500 for it. I say to her husband, "Why don't you build it?" and he looks at me like I'm mad.'

When did we change? When did we stop believing that we could do things for ourselves and instead gave the reins of our lives over to others? Was it when we became wards of a nanny state and lost our self-sufficiency, or was it when we became greedy for all the shiny things on the TV set and luxuries became essentials? Through building their own house the plot-owners had escaped the mortgage trap which Thoreau claimed forged gold and silver fetters. 'For when a man has got his house,' he warned, 'he may be not richer but poorer for it and it be the house that has got him.'

The majority of the plotlanders hadn't chosen their simple life for a higher cause but from a need for thrift and enterprise caused by poverty. 'No one had any money, so you had no choice but to build the house yourself,' John told me. 'There was no looking down at anyone, we were all in the woods.'

Lena and Fred would find it much harder to create a home in the country today, no matter how thrifty and enterprising they were. Even if they could afford to buy a piece of land with planning permission, they would never be allowed to build a makeshift structure, live in it and add to it as time and money allowed. Today's market benefits big building companies, not small-scale enterprise. These days, a self-builder has to produce a fully finished, fully serviced house from the very beginning in order to pass the multiple rules laid down by planners, building inspectors and mortgage companies. If they were to flout the rules the law would step in and demolish their efforts, much as it did the original plotlanders.

Angela and John's families arrived one summer in the 1960s to find a compulsory purchase order placed on the hill. Lena feared the invasion of 'little boxes, no doubt filled with town dwellers, who would desecrate our woods, ruin our lovely orchards, kill off our wildlife.' The former East Enders now saw themselves as the guardians of the countryside, protecting it from people who didn't understand, much as the rural communities had thought when the East Enders first arrived.

From the very beginning, the plotland shacks had caused outrage among traditional users of the countryside who accused the plotlanders of urbanising the country. Patrick Abercrombie, a city planner who co-founded the Council for the Preservation of Rural England (now the Campaign to Protect Rural England), suggested: 'The preserver of rural amenities cannot allow any sort of old junk cabin to deform the choicest spots'. Many of the preservationists' fears were well founded. If unchecked, many of our beauty spots would have been turned into a giant suburb. But beneath the desire to protect the countryside, there appears to have been an equal desire to protect it from the 'wrong sort'. The fear that the working classes were arriving in places they were never meant to be persists in much of the rhetoric. Plotland homes are described as 'squalid little huts' and 'ugly shanty towns'. It was OK, it seemed, for the right sort to build a second home in the countryside, but there was something outrageous and dangerous about a working man wanting the same thing.

In the end, many of the plotland developments were acquired through stealth. In Cliffe Woods the land was compulsorily purchased at agricultural prices and then sold on to builders for development. The money offered to the plotholders was far too low for them to buy another house and many were forced to emigrate. 'People didn't want to leave,' John told me. But, as in many other places, the shack-dwellers of Cliffe Woods were ill equipped to fight a legal battle against the council. 'It was different in those days,' John said. 'People didn't argue with authority; they were all-powerful.' Many of the shacks were bulldozed into rubble as families watched. The last to leave was a grandmother, forcibly evicted from her home. She was seen walking down the road with her grandchildren trailing behind her.

Angela and John's families were lucky. By some twist of fate Lena's shack lay just outside the land earmarked for development. John's family managed to apply for planning permission just before the axe fell. 'They chucked out one set of residents and put in a new set,' John said. 'Maybe the new set were more of the right sort.' I asked Angela about the future of the shack in the woods. 'I always want to keep it the way it was,' she insisted, 'but who knows what will happen after I'm gone?'

THREE

Cliffe Woods – Rye Street

ULL OF TEA and with a bellyful of potatoes, I left Cliffe Woods behind and crossed a meadow jewelled with the bright, pink flowers of grass vetchling. I stopped to pass the time of day with a mare and foal and was rewarded with a whiffling snort from the mare's moustachioed lips. I lost the footpath and found myself back on the roads, but it hardly mattered; I saw more cyclists and walkers than cars. A young guy and girl passed me and said hello. They were carrying shopping bags full of bread and Bakewell tarts. A giant holm oak and black poplar spread shady arms across the road outside the gates of a former mansion and the sweet, rotten scent of horse dung and hay permeated the air.

The Merryboys pub, where Lena and her husband had first heard about the plots at Cliffe Woods, was now a stables, of the type where I had learned to ride. A vast wooden hay barn looked close to collapse and the former grand stables and outhouses of the manor had seen better days. The air was a cacophony of zinging swallows and cheeping goldfinches.

At the junction with Rye Street I was greeted by a sign: 'Stop Estuary Airport'. I would see many more as I made my way across the peninsula, a reminder that this place was continually fighting a war for its survival. That spring, Boris Johnson, then Mayor of London, was planning his island odyssey for the Thames Estuary.

If Boris had his way, the Hoo Peninsula would become one big ring road serving his dream to replace Heathrow with an all-singing, all-dancing four-runway airport on one of the busiest bird-migration routes in Europe.

Some 300,000 birds make their way down the Thames Estuary every year. I am not an aviation expert but 300,000 birds and a jet engine don't mix. It would mean that an aeroplane taking off from here would be twelve times more likely to experience bird strike than any other airport in the UK. I, for one, would not wish to select this as my airport of choice.

This wasn't the first time the area had been threatened with an airport. When I first came to the peninsula in 2004 there was a palpable sense of battle fatigue. Local people and the RSPB had successfully fought another airport proposal for the Hoo Peninsula. The people I met in my first weeks here were relieved, but also war weary, exhausted from investing every ounce of their lives and not insignificant amounts of money into fighting for something they loved. Now, they were being asked to pour themselves into it again.

Corn-bunting calls jangled like unwinding springs as I walked along the lane. The mega-cranes of Thamesport rose in the distance. The industrialised Essex Coast looked like another world, another age, a Futurescape, not in the way the RSPB would have it, as an interconnected world of marshland and hedgerows making up one giant reserve for wildlife, but in the way Westminster would have it. The government wanted this land paved with progress in a bid to make it profitable and sanitised and serve the needs of London. It seemed to think of progress in terms of money, with little thought for the quiet pleasures that enrich life, such as villages where sparrows can dust-bathe in the road or the precious jewels of grass vetchling found in the meadows.

A man with a metal detector and a lurcher scoured the fields, a reminder of other battles which had taken place here. The Romans fought across this land almost two thousand years ago, pursuing the Britons across the peninsula from Upnor. Many soldiers drowned in the pools and mud of the marshes, unable to find their way out of the wastes which covered the area.

I walked down the road, past the orchards of dwarf pear trees and dusty hawthorn hedges, drawn out of my way by the chance to catch a glimpse of the thing I knew lay behind the hedge.

It could be one of a million other static caravans which lived on the marshes but it wasn't, it was mine. Despite the fact that Keith, the farmer I sold it to seven years ago earlier, had phoned that morning to say that its current occupant wasn't around and I couldn't get in, I was here anyway. What sort of pilgrimage would it be if I wasn't?

I could only look at it from the other side of the hedge but that felt OK. Maybe it was too early in this journey to go inside. Maybe by asking Keith if I could visit I was trying to fit things into a neat box but, if the caravan years had taught me anything, it was that life was not a neat box, and if you try to force it that way it doesn't work. I looked at the caravan, its dirty white sides and fading green stripe and I couldn't feel what I wanted to feel. It was just another caravan after all. I made to leave, but at the gate to the farm I bumped into Keith. He was tanned as only a farmer can be and wearing an open-necked shirt and a leather drover's hat. 'She's in now,' Keith said. 'I'll knock on the door and you can have a look inside. It's been decorated,' he said apologetically. 'It will look different.'

I was sure Keith thought I was bonkers for wanting to look inside a ratty old tin box that I had sold years ago and I felt a bit of a fool. It was that old thing of me on the marshes, trying to look tough, trying to be one of the lads. Keith was the hardest man on the marshes, a former scrap-metal dealer who came out here to be a sheep farmer. We didn't ask why. He was quietly spoken and cool beyond words. I did not want to look soft in front of Keith.

We walked towards the caravan and I felt a bungy cord in my back wanting to bounce me away again. I thought 'bloody hell, I'm not ready'. Up close the caravan looked more run down, moss growing in the window frames, the little wooden steps that my dad had made me to reach the door nowhere to be seen. No longer under the willow tree, but stuck in a concrete courtyard next to a house, it both was and wasn't my caravan. My caravan had vanished as that life had vanished. I didn't know if I wanted to step inside and see something – a cupboard handle, the wallpaper, the kitchen table – something which would remind me that I once had that life and that the person I shared it with, was, in reality, still alive too, not dead as I sometimes told myself, but maybe, like the caravan, just a shell, with the man I knew gone from the insides.

Keith knocked and I was mightily relieved when we got no answer.

'I'll come back another time,' I told him and scurried away, not so sure that I would.

I was walking faster now. In truth I was running away.

The year I lost the caravan Connor and I were getting married. It wasn't exactly what you'd call a snap decision. We had already been together twelve years. Why hadn't we done it before? The bottom line was that he had never asked me. I think at the beginning of our relationship, in our early twenties, we had been too young but, at thirty-three, I still didn't feel adult enough and wasn't so sure if that was a good thing anymore.

The truth was, I had never wanted to be married. I felt that once I became Connor's wife I would be expected to play some domesticated role I just didn't and couldn't fit. It wasn't that I didn't love him. Loving Connor was never something I questioned. From the first days of our relationship I felt that he was the person I had been waiting for. We could talk all night and, in the early days, often did. In the early days, Connor had been willing to follow all my ideas and adventures and I couldn't imagine not having him at my side.

For years our arrangement had worked. We were happy, we were moving around for work, living sometimes apart and sometimes together. My sister and friends got married but Connor and I were, to the outside world, still the peachy couple, still in love, still the best of friends and I still believed we were together forever.

Although this situation still worked for me, it had ceased to work for Connor. At the age of thirty-two, Connor retrained as a teacher and everything changed. He wanted 'normal', he wanted 'to get on with life'. He wanted, I guess, though he never said it, a nine-to-five job, a suburban home and kids. I wanted to write and travel and live in a cabin in the woods. We were clearly heading for trouble.

Connor asked me to marry him on 13 January on a windy beach in Norfolk. I believe 13 January is the least auspicious day of the year.

Though I had never wanted to be married, over the years I had occasionally wanted to be married to Connor. I had occasionally had glimpses of wanting to be committed to This Man, to be This Man's wife. I wanted to have some official status in his life, to be joined to Him. I'm not sure I ever told him that. Still, I was shocked. The timing seemed all wrong. We hadn't been getting on that well. It struck me as odd that he would choose now, but what could I do? I said yes.

On our return, we told our parents and our closest friends but I didn't mention it to anyone at work. It didn't seem real. Connor and I talked about weddings, we thought about when and where but did little to move the plan forward, and then Fiona S came into my life and changed everything.

For years the RSPB had worried about the 'Bromhey Gang'. Though membership of this gang was elastic, the basic rule of joining was that you lived, had lived, or sometimes lived in the little world surrounding Bromhey farmhouse on the reserve. At the time, the gang consisted of Connor and me in the caravan, Mike, Mike's girlfriend and Gordon, the warden of Northward Hill, who was an excellent naturalist and a great curry cook, not known for grand displays of emotion – his reaction to most things could be gauged by the level to which his eyebrows disappeared into his hairline.

Mike, the warden of the neighbouring reserve, Cliffe Pools, was a cultured man who used long words without pretence, read endlessly, painted pictures of the marshes and was a master of pub quizzes. Mike was the least embarrassed person I have ever met, neither fazed at being discovered with his mother cutting his hair on the front lawn or in revealing the most intimate feelings about his family.

Until the 'No Airport at Cliffe' campaign, which began in 2002, the reserve at Northward Hill had been a quiet backwater where the staff got on with the business of managing the land, but thought little of visitors. Suddenly, the area had a public profile. There was going to be a suite of 'flagship' reserves. The north Kent marshes was to be rebranded as The North Kent Marshes and this bunch of old-school, scruffy eccentrics, referred to as the 'Northward Hillbillies', didn't quite fit the image. I, of course, as Community Officer, was all part of the rebranding plan; the only problem was I was as scruffy and irreverent as the rest of them.

The RSPB was in transition. The society had long been accused of being elitist and reserves as intimidating to anyone other than experts. I agreed. I well remembered the dark days of the 1990s when I had attended the South West region's AGM only to listen to a speaker pronounce that the RSPB were pitching themselves at Range-Rover-driving claret-drinkers in the A, B & C1 social category. As I was none of these things, I wondered whether I should stand up and leave.

The new drive to make the reserves more open and inclusive was something I wholly supported. But Regional Office were concerned that, far from being the new breed of staff, the Bromhey Gang were a bunch of itinerant birders out there, bending the rules and taking advantage.

Maybe at times there was a little truth in this. Mike did fall asleep at lunchtime on the 'oh so comfy couch' in the back room. I did sometimes park up in a lay-by to listen to the conclusion of a good play on Radio 4. Gordon did turn up to meetings in the same stained and ember-burnt shirt that he worked in all week. But we also got up at 5am to do bird surveys, reported late-night hare coursers on the marshes and dealt with baby birds left on our doorstep in the dead of night. Living on the reserve, we were never not on duty.

The Bromhey Gang were old-school wardens with a dedication and camaraderie born out of living in an isolated place and being, to all intents and purposes, 'your own boss'. It takes a certain kind of person to live on a reserve, one that can handle the isolation, and rarely can that type of person also be 'media-friendly' and sell memberships.

But Regional Office wanted the old culture broken, and Fiona S was there to break it. She arrived mid-winter and installed herself in the farmhouse, which endeared her to no one. 'She's on a good salary,' Mike complained. 'What does she need to move into a shared house for? The house is for wardens not managers.' I was grateful for my decision to buy the caravan. After all, who wants to live with their boss? But, as we were to find out, bumping into our boss in her nightie was the least of our worries.

On her first day she turned up at the creaky portable cabin that was our office and began making changes.

'Can my staff gather together?' she called.

Mike, Gordon, AJ and I exchanged looks. AJ had been the boss until now. He was laid back and we all cheeked him but secretly respected him. With AJ we were all colleagues together, professionals who knew our jobs and were motivated to do them. 'My staff' was a new one on us.

'Things are going to change round here', she said. 'From now on you will pay for tea and coffee.' She shook a jar at us. 'Your money will go in here. I will bring my own separate supplies in, which you are not to touch.' Before we could digest this news she carried on. 'I also want you to remove all the works vehicles from under the awning outside the office.'

'Into the rain?' I said, watching the drops streak down the broken windows of the cabin and imagining the open trucks filling with water.

'Yes, the space outside the office will be used for the manager's car only.'

Gordon's eyebrows shot up and Mike snorted into his tea.

A few days later she asked us to start reporting our whereabouts on the reserve, and when I got back a few minutes late one day she went into meltdown. 'I didn't know where you were,' she screeched. 'I didn't know what to do. I phoned HQ to report you missing.'

I was bemused. Perhaps, I thought, she's just a little unstable – she took to carrying a pat of butter around with her all day, between the farmhouse and the office. 'It will never melt,' she wittered. 'It is so cold here that butter will never melt.'

For the first few weeks of her reign we all went about trying to avoid eye contact with Fiona S, keeping our head down, but still turning circles trying to abide by her new rules. Then in early January a big storm blew in across the marshes – in the early hours of the morning I lay in bed while 70-mile-per-hour winds rocked the caravan onto two legs, listening to the noise of the wind fighting with the tin roof. Twigs rained down from the willow, cracking against the windows while the wind shrieked across the top of the chimney pot. At 6.30am I got up to make a cup of tea only to find that the gas had run out.

I went out into the storm and tried to wrestle with the nut which connected the canister to the caravan, wielding a giant wrench while the willow whirlpooled around my head and smacked me repeatedly across the face. The wind was tearing across the reserve and roaring overhead. I gave up fighting with the gas and instead raced across the lawn to the office to make breakfast using the microwave.

Fiona S arrived at 8am.

'Why are you in this early?' she asked.

'I couldn't sleep. I thought I might as well come in and work.'

'You should have asked my permission to come in early.'

What, at 7am? I thought.

Fiona S marched across the room and loomed over me. 'There is too much fluidity between your home and your office,' she said. She spotted the remains of my breakfast in a bowl by my desk.

'From now on you are not to use the microwave to cook your own food.'

She walked up to me, unplugged the only heater in the room and carried it back to her office, slamming the door behind her.

No one was left unaffected by Fiona S. Mike's girlfriend was told to move out of the farmhouse; I knew that Connor would be next. And outside the reserve her influence was little better. Soon we were receiving phone calls from members, community leaders and council officers, complaining about the demands Fiona S was making and the bad feeling she was generating.

However, not everyone saw her as a bad thing. Trevor, our long-term handyman, felt differently. As a lifetime member of the RSPB he felt angered by our laid-back approach.

'You all treat this place like it's a social club and work gets in the way,' he said. 'Why should my membership fees pay for that? Fiona S told me there was no way that people would get away with this in a commercial organisation or a council office.'

He was right of course, we wouldn't have, but reserves were not these places. Rightly or wrongly, at that time they had a culture of their own. You lived on site, you lived the job, and sweeping away that culture overnight, as Fiona S wished to do, was wrong.

I began to dread going into work in the mornings. Often, I would feel her standing behind me and turn to find her glaring at me for no reason. Mike, Gordon and AJ could escape to the reserve on the pretence of checking fencing or counting birds, but my job involved few escape routes and I would find myself stuck alone with her in the office.

In the middle of February, when she took a few days off, we finally cracked en masse.

'I'm not having much more of this,' AJ said. 'She's got to go or I'm resigning. I've asked for work pruning in the orchards.'

'So have I,' I confessed.

We looked at each other. This was crazy, AJ had been with the RSPB since he was a teenager. We couldn't both resign and become pruners. That afternoon we drafted an email to AJ's boss, James Brightwell, laying out the whole sorry tale of Fiona S and our unwillingness to work for her.

James turned up at the reserve the next day. I was sceptical about his arrival, expecting one office-bound bureaucrat to support another. But I am not the best judge of character. 'I want to apologise to you all,' he said. 'I am sorry if my actions have put you under stress. I take full responsibility. I was short-sighted and should never have put you all in this situation.'

You would have thought that would be the end of Fiona S. After his visit to the farmhouse, James sacked her. But two days later she returned and refused to leave, hunkering in the garden, claiming our evidence was 'too anecdotal', talking of an industrial tribunal, and when lawyers were brought in I had to provide written evidence of everything she had ever said to me.

Eventually, one day in March, when I was out on the reserve, Gordon sent me a text: 'She has gone'. I experienced a brief moment of feeling sorry for her. Spring was arriving, the orchard would blossom, lambs would be born, the willow was coming back into leaf, the barn owl was patiently hunting the reedy ditches, the air was full of birdsong and the lawn full of bunnies. Fiona S was not going to experience all of this but, thanks to James, I would.

In celebration, Connor and I headed up to Yorkshire. Since his marriage proposal, life had become all work and worry and we seriously needed to get away and spend some time together. Two days into my holiday I received a phone call from AJ.

'I'm sorry to call you on holiday,' he said, 'but there may be a problem with the caravan.'

'What sort of problem?' I asked, fearing the pipes had burst again.

'I don't know yet but we need to discuss alternative places for you to live.'

I looked out over Whitby Harbour and felt a lead bubble drop into my stomach.

'There are no alternatives,' I said. 'The caravan is my home.'

'What about the farmhouse with Gordon and Mike. You could have Fiona S's old room.'

I thought of the farmhouse, the sticky carpets, the washing up in the sink, seeing my colleagues twenty-four hours a day.

'That's not an option,' I said. 'I want to stay in the caravan.'

'Let's hope it's your choice,' AJ said.

I arrived home to a letter from the council. *We have been informed that you are living full time in a caravan on a nature reserve. Our records show you have no planning permission. You must apply for planning permission within 28 days. If you do not apply for planning permission you will be served notice and we will begin action against you.*

In disbelief I phoned AJ.

'How can they do this?' I said. 'When I first moved in we talked about planning permission and head office said I didn't need it.'

'Seems we were wrong,' AJ said. 'Anyway things have changed. The RSPB are fighting a battle with an illegal developer next to Cliffe Pools. They are trying to get the guy evicted for not having planning permission and now it seems their own house isn't in order.'

'That man's built an industrial estate,' I exploded. 'I live in a caravan. It's hardly on the same scale.'

'It's still an embarrassment,' AJ said. 'The message from head office is that you're to move out as soon as possible. You're not to apply for planning permission. They don't see what the big deal is. They don't see why you can't move out immediately. You can move into the farmhouse. I don't see why you are so bothered about living in a caravan.'

I guess to AJ and the rest of the staff it did seem crazy. No one knew that the caravan was the thing that gave me most happiness and made me feel that I was still, for now, being true to myself.

I carried the letter across to Connor.

'We're going to lose our home,' I said, unable to believe it was happening. I had spent so long thinking about ways to keep living in the caravan and suddenly it seemed my time was up; the decision had been taken from me.

'I should phone the planning department,' I said, 'see if I can reason with them or buy some time.'

'Yes, more time would be good,' Connor said, but his thoughts seemed elsewhere.

'Maybe we should visit them,' I continued.

'Yes, maybe *you* should,' he said and put up the barrier of the *Daily Mirror* between us. It seemed that the home we had both lived in for the last two years was now my home, my problem.

I ventured back to the office and dialled the number on the letter, finally getting put through to a planning officer.

'It's not like I'm squatting on the reserve,' I told him. 'I work here. I have permission to live here. Being on site is an important part of my job.'

'That is of no relevance,' the officer said. 'We have been told that you live in the caravan full-time and have done for years. You have a simple choice, fill in the forms for planning permission or be evicted.'

'But I'm not allowed to apply,' I said, my voice beginning to wobble. The hostility seemed to emanate in waves along the phone lines. I imagined the planning officer in his office, and imagined him imagining me living in a caravan on the marshes, thinking to himself 'what sort of woman lives like that?'

Overwhelmed, I could feel tears start in my eyes and wiped them away angrily not wanting to cry in the office in front of the men. 'If you do not intend to apply,' the voice said, 'then I suggest you move and quickly. In twenty-eight days we will begin proceedings to remove your caravan.'

'But I've nowhere else to live,' I shouted, slamming the phone down. I charged across the lawn to the only place there was shelter and privacy and burst into tears. Connor stood there as I blubbed and cursed the council, his newspaper hanging loosely in one hand and a cup of tea in the other. This was not the Easter holiday he had imagined.

In the middle of the howling and ranting, my work phone rang. It was James. 'I just heard what has happened,' he said. 'This is terrible. I want you to know that you are not alone. You are an excellent member of staff and I am going to do my absolute best to make sure that the RSPB support you.'

I stood in the doorway of the caravan looking out at the willow tree, the phone pressed against my ear to combat the terrible signal. I took a deep breath. He had said I was not alone.

'I'm sorry, I'm sorry to be crying.'

'Don't be,' he said. 'I totally understand why you feel like this. How could you not feel like this?'

'I know it's only a caravan,' I cried, the last vestiges of professionalism gone.

'For God's sake Carol,' James interjected. 'Stop saying it's only a caravan. It's your home.'

If he had been there at that moment I would have flung my arms around him. Relief washed over me that someone, not my partner, not my friends, but this man, understood, that it wasn't just a scrubby, 1970s, Jaywick-on-Sea caravan, but my home that I loved and was losing. How was it that of all the people who should have understood, only this man told me it was OK to feel this way?

'Now, you don't have to do anything,' James continued. 'I will go to the RSPB lawyers and the planning department. I don't think I can stop this,' he warned. 'The RSPB will not let you apply for planning permission. We can't stop this but I can buy you time, maybe six months. Would that help?'

'Yes,' I said. 'Yes, thank you.'

I returned to the office that afternoon but couldn't work. I had six months. Six months in which to get married, find somewhere to live and possibly another job. Unable to focus, I scribbled combinations of these three things on paper: marriage, home, job; home, marriage, job; re-juggling the order as everything came crowding in.

A few days later James phoned again. 'I have some bad news,' he said. 'My boss is being very bullish about this. He's told me not to involve the RSPB lawyers or to speak to the council on your behalf.'

My heart sank as the twenty-eight day deadline loomed onto the horizon again. 'So you can't help me?' I asked.

James paused down the end of the line. 'I am telling you that my boss has told me not to help you. But I would also like to tell you that my boss goes on holiday in a few days time.'

James' boss went on holiday. In his absence James went to the lawyers and the council. He bought me six months.

FOUR

Rye Street – Cooling – Northward Hill

L EAVING THE CARAVAN and its memories behind, I pushed open a field gate into a meadow full of red clover and felt better. I crossed over a stile and headed for the road which wound into Cooling village.

Outside Cooling Castle the jackdaws greeted me. The area is known as the 'home of the heron', owing to the large colony in the woods at Northward Hill, but anyone who lives there knows that the rooks and crows are the real birds of the marshes. Three thousand of these birds roost among the giant twig nests of the heronry, taking over the place in the winter while the herons sit moodily hunkered down in the fields, staring glumly into the ditches and waiting for the spring. I had stood beneath the rookery on a winter's evening, shivering and waiting for the birds to accept me and return from their days foraging. Underneath the rookery the sound of their calls was like a sonic boom, revolving in waves, crashing overhead and rolling out across the marshes. Birds spiralled above, raining down on the wood like black petals, the wave vanishing as the birds tilted their wings and the gathering darkness momentarily swallowed them. It was both thrilling and frightening to stand on the edge of a wood on a winter's evening and be faced with an organism so much larger than yourself. It was a rare privilege for one moment to feel your vulnerability to nature as your ancestors would have done, to know your true place on the earth as one small creature, not the God of creation that humans nowadays imagine they are.

In the summer, the birds are not so obvious, but their sound still forms the backdrop to the everyday – the clacking of jackdaws, nesting in holes in the castle meant for shooting arrows and pouring boiling oil through; young crows drifting across the wide plain of the marsh, sounding unsure and desirous to please as they chat, click and squeal a conversation and follow older, cooler friends across the sky.

The crumbling ruins of Cooling Castle were hidden behind a giant hedge, through which the occasional drunken car driver would crash and end up in the moat beyond. The outer towers had long, widening cracks snaking their way up the sides. I was sure they would collapse any day, though no one seemed to do anything about them.

I passed the impressive gatehouse, which had held off a siege by Thomas Wyatt. It was like a children's drawing of a castle gatehouse, with its machicolated towers and plaque in old English, telling the peasants that the castle was built for their protection. One of the castle's famous inhabitants had been John Oldcastle, rumoured to be the inspiration for Falstaff in Shakespeare's *Henry V*. He believed in Lollardry, which preached that the Catholic Church had been corrupted by greed and was too concerned with secular matters. These were dangerous times for such outspokenness and Sir John met a suitably grisly end, unlike his wife, the rather marvellous Joan de la Pole, who had five husbands, inherited all their estates and outlived them all.

The 'Stop Estuary Airport' signs were more numerous now. Cooling with its castle and St James's Church, the supposed location for 'Pip's Graves', as described by Charles Dickens in the opening pages of *Great Expectations*, would have been obliterated under the original airport plans. It was proposed that the graves, visited by Dickens fans from around the world, could be removed and displayed elsewhere. In the airport foyer maybe? I could imagine the politicians and architects in London crowded around the boardroom table discussing the plans: 'A tasteful exhibit, interactive perhaps, with a backdrop showing a film of how the marshes looked, all situated within Charles Dickens International.'

Great Expectations opens with one of the most evocative descriptions of the 'marsh country' ever written. Anyone who has stood by these graves on a 'raw afternoon towards evening' and looked out across the stone-walled churchyard and the flat fields, where the raspberries are grown in the summer, can well imagine the 'small bundle of shivers' that is Pip, and knows all about the 'savage distant lair' from which the wind rushes. In winter, this land is as governed by the sea as if it stood on the coast. The marshes are so flat that nothing breaks the winter storms. It is a land of boats going to sea and boats coming from the sea and fog horns muffled in dampness.

I visited the graves while I still could and parked my bottom on the steps of the Comport Family tomb. In truth, the thirteen little lozenge-shaped graves, lined either side of the headstone in front of me, belonged to the children of the Comport and Baker Families. All the children died in 1770 of the ague or marsh fever, a form of malaria.

The Hoo Peninsula had never been a desirable place to live. Floods swept regularly across the land and, after the building of the first sea wall in the twelfth century, pools of stagnant water were left behind which provided ripe breeding grounds for the anopheline mosquito, which carried the ague. I had seen the mosquitoes of the north Kent marshes; they were, to my reckoning, the largest in the Western Hemisphere, so it was small wonder that they carried away much of the local population for hundreds of years.

The general perception of the Hoo Peninsula as inhospitable and unhealthy was a factor in keeping the population down. Villages remained small and only the most hardy or desperate would choose to stay in the isolated farmhouses dotting the malarial marshes.

As I looked at the tombs, it struck me as slightly disturbing that anyone would think this sad little monument to the deaths of so many children could be transported elsewhere as a tourist attraction. The marshes, Dickens and the sadness of this ague-haunted district were entwined. Dickens may well have sat in the same spot as I, resting on one of his famously long walks from his home at nearby Gad's Hill, contemplating the opening scene to the novel. The tombstone I leant against could very well have been the one over which he imagined the escaped prisoner Magwitch holding Pip upside down over while he demanded 'wittles'.

I was in need of some wittles myself and headed to the Horseshoe and Castle pub down the road from the churchyard. Kevin the landlord greeted me as he always did, as if I had left the area yesterday. The bar was lined with locals, the walls with stuffed animals. The restaurant was full of bemused tourists trying to decipher the 'gastro pub' menu. I bought a pint of pale ale and some crisps and ventured outside to sit beneath the hanging baskets.

At the next table a bunch of locals were involved in a discussion about mad dogs in Cooling. Despite only having forty-five houses, Cooling seemed to have an ample share of 'mad dogs', some so notorious that even I recognised their descriptions. I finished my pint and, feeling perkier, strolled towards Lipwell Hill.

It was bank holiday, the sun was out and everyone was having a barbecue. The smell of chargrilled burgers and the sound of low-key rock music drifted over garden gates. The breeze had stiffened again and the pale ale had gone to my legs.

The green lane that climbed Lipwell Hill was a jungle of nettles with daddy-longlegs waiting in ambush. Splay winged and spider-legged they sat, dark and menacing, in the shadows, hooked hands clinging onto leaves. They are the embodiment of all my nightmares. Don't try to tell me 'they won't hurt you', my primeval lizard brain knows better. En masse, I had heard, they contain enough cyanide to wipe out the human race (they have no mouth parts, so no way of injecting it). I am convinced that these long-legged dancers were dangerous once and could be again.

While I lived in the caravan, autumn was a misery for me. The lawn between the caravan and the office would become a rippling surface of leapfrogging bodies, the walls outside the office were coated with ornate studs, every bush and weed had a layer of transparent rustling wings. Even in the caravan I was not always safe. Occasionally, they would find their way in, dancing in the mist above the shower, making me emit piercing spectacular 'Hammer House of Horror' screams into the night, frightening Gordon as he leant from the windows of the farmhouse. Gordon undoubtedly would have raised his eyebrows momentarily in surprise and then, imagining it to be a fox screaming on the marshes, gone back to contemplating the stars.

Throughout early autumn I would pray for frost or October or whatever would rid me of the object of my fears, but know that I still had weeks of being surrounded by these creatures as they indulged in an orgy of bottom-to-bottom loving or fighting among the grass, wielding their spindly arms with surprising ferocity.

This year, after the rains of winter, they had arrived two seasons early. This seemed unfair, below the belt even. Was I now to be traumatised twice a year? I knew that the shady, damp, holloway up Lipwell Hill would be ideal daddy territory, but it had to be done. I put on a brave face and tried not to think or feel as I made my way up the path. The black, oozing mud of the path was dotted with millions of star-like elderflowers, their musky, lemon scent cloying the air. I grabbed dock leaves as I marched along to cope with the nettle stings erupting on my legs, but didn't dare stop for fear of the daddies. I burst out into the sun and stopped to rub the welts on my ankles with the dock.

A panorama of the marsh spread below me, just as Dickens had described, with 'dykes and mounds and gates with scattered cattle feeding on it'. Shade House, a square, block building broke the skyline. Once a lookout point and storage place for smugglers, its single eye blinked, Cyclops-like, back across the fields. The 'low leaden line' of the Thames was today placid and benign.

This area had always been a haven for those willing to flout authority. The North Kent Gang of smugglers operated along the coast in the early nineteenth century, bringing goods into the isolated bays on the Thames and ferrying them inland along the creeks. There, many local people were willing to help out, for a price. Everyone, from the farm boy to the local vicar, hid goods, kept an eye out for revenue men and provided horses and carts for transport. It was rumoured that tunnels ran beneath the marshes, linking Egypt Bay on the river with Shade House and onwards to Cooling Church where smuggled goods had been hidden beneath the pulpit.

Was the geography of the marshes, which had provided a hideaway for law-breakers, also a reason that it attracted those wishing to live in alternative ways? In this sparsely populated backwater was it easier to follow your own rules? Could you live as you chose here because there were simply fewer neighbours to complain, more space to stretch out and, unless you stuck your head above the parapet, as I had done, less chance of being spotted by authority?

If so, what would happen to us when the Hoo Peninsula became the Thames Gateway and we were overtaken by waterfront apartments, leisure complexes and the watchful eyes that would surely come with this 'regeneration'? Would any of us survive this onslaught? How would the houseboat yards, chalet parks and caravan-dwellers fair with this change? Would we, in fact, be considered part of the problem, something to be swept away and out to sea?

Though it was getting late and I was tired, I took a diversion along a grassy track. In a hollow, out of view of any house, I cut off past a line of walnut trees to visit my land. It was still my land, even though technically the local farmer owned it and wouldn't sell. I didn't entirely blame him. I was that thing the preservationists who protested over the plotlands feared: someone who wanted to buy a small plot of land for recreational use. Opposite was the evidence of where that could lead. The once beautiful rolling valley around Buckhole Farm had been sold off into plots, subdivided into horse paddocks by ugly electric fencing and was now littered with sheds. Here, I was with the preservationists; a beautiful view had been spoilt for the benefit of a wealthy few. How was I different? The difference maybe was only in my head, but it was also in the situation of my land, tucked away, out of sight, down the track I now followed. The grassy path opened up into a meadow of buttercups. Rabbits, with ears backlit by the sun, and squat, surprised partridges scurried away. The meadow was surrounded on three sides by high embankments, backed by a strip of coppice woodland which hid the freight railway from view.

On winter nights in the caravan I was always surprised to hear the whistle of a train. The railway was so tucked away in a deep embankment, it was easy to forget about it. Once it had been built to ferry Queen Victoria to her yacht at Grain, now it was goods to the power stations.

The view from 'my land' was one of the best on the peninsula: a little unspoilt sliver of marshland and woods rolling down to the Thames. The RSPB had owned this bit of land and when they decided to sell it I had tried to buy, but some obscure rule decreed they couldn't sell land to staff. Instead, it was sold to the rich farming family who owned the land next door.

'Why do they want that tiny bit of meadow?' I had wailed to Connor. 'They own half the marshes already. What do they need it for?'

My meadow, it turned out, offered 'good partridge cover', and the farmers wanted it to indulge their love of shooting. I tried to buy the land from them, shining the full beam of any charm I possessed at the farmer's son; it was no good, they had seen my type before. They owned the land and had no need to sell off bits of it to a girl like me. What they didn't, couldn't realise was that the land was already mine. I had willed it to me. I had focused on it and it would be mine... one day. Like a Jack Russell that had got hold of a rabbit, I would worry away at it until it gave. The farmers, rich though they may be, knew nothing about the willpower of the Donaldsons.

I walked to the back of the meadow where the buttercups grew thick and touched the ground where one day I would have my cabin and then I did something macho and primeval and correct. I peed on the spot, marking my territory, in case the farmer forgot who owned it.

It was a small act of defiance with a noble tradition, taking back that of which I felt I had been robbed. Movements such as the Diggers and Levellers of the seventeenth century had sought to advance the idea that all men had a right to the land. Prior to the Norman Conquest, the Diggers asserted, land had been held in common by the people, and the culture of land ownership, imposed by William the Conqueror, was quite foreign to Britain. In a period when food prices were at an all-time high, the Diggers had occupied enclosed common land and planted their own vegetables, encouraging others to join them and find 'true freedom and nourishment in the use of the earth'.

The Levellers saw it slightly differently. 'God created all men equal,' they said, and 'the land belonged to all people as a right.' They wished to create a 'Commonwealth', in which ordinary people would be in control of their own destinies without the intervention of the Government. Oh to live in such radical times, when ideas like these were seen as even possible. The Levellers and the Diggers are the forebears of all sorts of anti-authoritarian movements, from squatters to communes; people who seize land and property, which is often unmanaged, and occupy it as a community.

When I had camped with Connor under 'Private Keep Out' signs, I had been very much on the side of the Levellers and Diggers. It had felt like a two-fingered salute to the owners. You can't take this land from us, it belongs to all. In Scotland, of course, this right already exists: the 2003 Land Reform Act gave everyone the right to camp on unenclosed land. Would I be happy, though, for a modern-day Leveller to occupy my land? I didn't think so. If I'm honest, I was no more up for community ownership of the land than the farmers. I didn't want gangs of hippie children with names like Badger and Rainbow running round, scaring the wildlife and growing organic vegetables, and I suspected that they would be the least of my worries. What if I turned up at my land one day and found it had been taken over by some scrambler bike club or a group of paintballers? I was pretty sure that the Diggers hadn't foreseen these issues.

I didn't want to plough the land and grow corn either. I just wanted to enjoy the view and camp there. I didn't want to share it with everyone, I just wanted it to belong to me and not the neighbouring farmers. I wasn't sure what the answer was. I wanted private ownership, but I also wanted some right for everyone to enjoy the countryside without harm. Maybe if, in the future, I found young Badger and Rainbow cooking an organic stew in my field I would just let them be, as long as they moved on the next day and took their rubbish with them.

Possibly, I should have camped in my meadow to assert my right to it, but the truth was I was rather more frightened of the farmer, or at least his father, who hung dead crows from his fruit trees, than I was of the RSPB wardens.

I left the land behind and walked down the hill to the RSPB's Northward Hill Reserve and Bromhey Farm. The view had changed since I had lived there and not for the better. The willow tree beneath which my caravan had sat was gone. Why was a mystery, perhaps the victim of some health-and-safety purge. The silos where the little owl had nested and which had provided the wintry soundscape of clankings and squeakings had met a similar fate.

I could see the spot that my caravan had occupied; my vegetable patch and garden was a bed of nettles. I remembered how long it had taken to dig those nettles out of the veg patch, labouring in the sun, with Gordon alongside, digging his own plot. I remembered how I loved sitting in my hidden garden behind the caravan with a glass of wine, surrounded by the fragrance of my tomato plants ripening in pots against the sun-beaten metal, the sound of the woodpeckers tapping on my nut feeder, the rustling of the woodmice who took up residence in the flowerpot outside my door after I barred them from the inside of the caravan. I liked sitting there and hearing the noises of the farmyard, the clanking of the barns, the sound of Eric the Bull in his pen occasionally bellowing at his lady loves away in the fields. I liked listening to the conversations between Keith and his workers in the farmyard, hidden from view by the silos and the yellow branches of the willow tree springing back into life.

It wasn't always so rosy. I also remembered the winters when I would walk around indoors, wrapped in a blanket in a cloud of my own breath, when life was reduced to living within a circle in front of the gas fire. I had cheered myself up during those dark months by hanging fairy lights from the ceiling of the caravan and dancing myself into a spinning frenzy in the living room. That first year, when I lived in the caravan on my own, I felt as though I'd been boiled down, like heroin on a teaspoon, reduced to the most concentrated version of myself through spending so much time alone. I spent too long drinking whisky and reading *Hamlet* and playing mind games until I was one step away from madness but, despite the craziness, I liked this version of me. I felt edgy, capable. I felt that if I stepped out of myself and looked back I would look like an interesting woman.

Down in the car park I bumped into Trevor. Trevor had been the reserve's plumber and builder as well as a passionate naturalist.

'Christ Almighty,' Trevor said as I appeared from behind the hedgerows. 'What are you doing here?'

I told him I was planning to camp in the cherry orchard. Trevor liked this idea, one over on the RSPB, of whom he was no longer the greatest fan, angered, as many others were, by the tidying up of the reserve which had swept away ancient barns where barn owls nested and comfy seats paid for by RSPB members in commemoration of former volunteers. When I queried the removal of the barns, an RSPB employee told me that the land was theirs and they could do with it as they wished.

But was it? The RSPB are not private landowners, they are funded by members and public money. The RSPB claimed that the barns were dangerous and had to go, but they also had a badger sett underneath, were a hub of wildlife-watching on the reserve and a prominent and much-photographed feature of the local landscape. When they were removed without consultation there was an outcry. So whose barns were they? The community's, the members', the visitors' or the RSPB's to do with as they pleased with no warning? Who did own land which was bought by and whose upkeep was paid for by many people? Did, as Trevor asserted, all these people have a right to a say?

Trevor was happy to help me ferry my bags to the orchard. My friend Karen had agreed to join me in this slight trespassing and had brought with her all the camping gear I couldn't carry. She arrived and the three of us carted it down to the orchard in Trevor's car and hid it under a tree to join the sleeping bag, bed roll and breakfast food wrapped in bin liners which I had furtively carried across the reserve the previous morning, looking for all the world like someone about to bury a body on the marshes.

I had hidden my stash among the nettles hoping that the badgers wouldn't sniff it out and, when I came to fetch it, I wouldn't find shredded sleeping bag mixed in with the porridge oats. I had no beef with the RSPB. They do many great things when it comes to land management and birds. They may be our one hope in the fight against rampant development and corrupt politics, but I couldn't deny that I had a secret satisfaction at being back, camping, without permission, under their noses, on the reserve.

Trevor left, and Karen and I set up camp at the very back of the orchard where we were unlikely to be discovered. In recent years I had not had many opportunities for wild camping. Instead, Karen and I had become glampers; staying in yurts and shepherd huts, packing long dresses, bottles of wine and board games. It was camping, but not as I had known it back in the days with Connor. That night I found myself in some weird fusion between the two: eating lukewarm pasta off Karen's *Carry on Camping* dinner set and drinking slightly iffy Babycham from the bottle before heading out for a walk.

It was a beautiful evening, the kind that I had seen so many of when I lived on the reserve and never forgot how blessedly lucky I was to be there. Every evening in the summer I would walk the reserve between 9pm and 10pm, my favourite hour. It was then that the little owls would hurtle overhead like flying Christmas puddings, all intent and purpose, when the barn owl would hunt, floating softly along the reed-fringed ditches like a giant butterfly before wheeling in mid-flight and plummeting into the grass after a vole. Down by the old barn I would sit with my back against the wall, trying not to slap at the mosquitoes, and wait in anticipation as the sounds of grunts and slurps grew louder and two white ears appeared from the badger sett. I had known young badgers to clamber right up to me and sniff at my foot and, with their poor eyesight, not realise what I was.

'It looks like Africa,' Karen said, looking out from the viewpoint across the marshes. It was something I had often thought myself. The vast stretch of the grassland down to the river with clustered shapes of moving animals and sky filling sunsets was how I imagined the Serengeti might be. Only the Wizard of Oz-style Emerald City at Canvey Island was out of keeping with this vision. The cranes and storage depots looked like a twinkling Disneyland over the water.

'Essex looks so developed from here,' Karen said, 'but then, when you stand at the end of Southend Pier, you would never guess that all this countryside was across the water either.'

She was right. From Southend pier the Hoo Peninsula looked like an industrial estate.

'It's a place I never would have come to explore if you hadn't moved here,' Karen said. 'It's such an unknown place.'

This was of course both a blessing and a problem for the Hoo Peninsula. It was beautiful, untouched, a little lost in another century and all the better for it, but if it was unknown, even for those just across the water in Essex or the Medway towns, no one would know why it was unthinkable that the place could be destroyed to make way for an airport, a housing estate, another Dartford Bridge, or all the other things that threatened it. The place was like the grass vetchling in the meadow, a jewel, which should be valued just as it is. You had to go there to see its beauty, you had to walk there to understand why it was precious.

Encouraging more people to visit the marshes, however, had to be thought about carefully if wildlife was to be protected. The proposed England Coast Path, for instance, a long-distance National Trail following the entire coastline of England (due for completion in 2020), would potentially thread its way alongside fields where lapwings and redshanks breed. Numbers of these birds have plummeted because they struggle to find suitable land on which to breed, and the birds would simply abandon their nests if faced with an influx of dog-walkers. Access for recreation often meant bad news for wildlife. I wanted people to see this place and value it, but maybe not feel they had a right to explore every inch of it.

Karen and I sat in Gordon's Hide. Gordon had died 'in the saddle' one wintry night two years previously and the hide was a fitting memorial. We watched a hobby hawking for dragonflies across the pools, skimming low across the buttered water. Avocets sifted their beaks through the mud, searching for insects, scattering droplets which caught the dying light.

Outside, darkness had come on and we walked back to the orchard, my head full of memories. I imagined for one moment that I could turn and walk towards the farmhouse and across the lawn and there would be my caravan, its windows giving out a welcoming glow, with Connor inside making a milky drink, and for one moment I wanted that more than anything.

I remembered how good he had been when we were young and I had carted him on endless nature walks across bleak reserves, but I also remembered how, after he came to live with me, he would never join me on my evening walks. How instead, on evenings when the sky was aflame and the night-time melody of marsh frogs would ring from the ditches and badgers were abroad, he would sit inside watching the news or reading the paper. Connor had an early start and, so as not to disturb him, I too would be forced to be in by 10pm and tucked up in bed while a huge moon hung in the sky and the evening had only just begun.

When had things changed? I couldn't name a day or a date when things had stopped being so good, just a gradual eroding, a corrosive drip of two people trying to reconcile their differences. Connor needed reassurance, I needed freedom. Connor needed someone who orbited him, who could reassure him that he was the centre of their world and I was a rogue asteroid always on the verge of a flight into space. We did what any two human beings do in those circumstances, we tried to change each other. We told the other that they were wrong for wanting the life they did. I rolled my eyes as Connor lay back in the caravan on a sunny day with the sports pages. I would make him feel boring for wanting to watch *EastEnders*. Connor scraped away bit by bit at the competent woman who had lived in the caravan on her own. That woman was too full of pride, the things she wanted were all wrong, her dreams were childish, she needed to grow up and embrace the world of mortgages and children. Drip, drip, drip, we destroyed each other's confidence and lived in frustration.

With six months left to find a new home and arrange a wedding, Connor and I did nothing. We talked, we toured wedding reception venues in a listless manner, but slowly Connor vanished. He had done this before, this vanishing act. He climbed down a ladder into himself and could be found nowhere.

'Let's go for a walk on the reserve?' I would suggest, but Connor would struggle out of his work suit into jogging bottoms and flop in front of the telly. I would walk alone. I would tell myself that this was ok. Maybe it was a good thing. After all, didn't I want my own space?

As the summer wore on, we spent less and less time together. He began spending his evenings and weekends back in Essex with his fellow teachers. Without a car, I was trapped on the reserve. 'Wait for the holidays,' I told myself. 'It's just the end of school, he's busy, things will be better in the holidays.' But I began to see my life ahead. How could we live like this, ignoring each other all year and only really spending decent time together on holiday? In the year that we were getting married surely we should be doing things together. Walking the reserve alone at night was suddenly not such a good thing, it was a lonely thing.

As the darkness grew, I walked back across the reserve with Karen. In the orchard we settled down in the tent. Outside, I could hear the distant bubble of a nightingale among the willows. After the day's walk, my thoughts did not keep me awake. I was soon asleep.

FIVE

Northward Hill – Hoo St Werburgh

I AWOKE EARLY next morning to hear rain pattering on the tent and an infernal jackdaw calling overhead. The night had been cold and punctuated by the continual calls of damn crazy nocturnal cuckoos who, I now remembered, had always kept me awake in the caravan – a fact which, through my rose-tinted spectacles, I had curiously forgotten. Karen and I emerged furtively from the orchard carrying our camping gear and surprised a heron, who wheeled away in alarm. I tidied myself up in the reserve's toilet, brushing my hair and cleaning my teeth using the tiny wash basin and oversized mirror that Trevor had installed many years ago, before Karen ran me into the village of High Halstow, dropping me off at Bradford's.

Bradford's had been my garage since I lived on the Hoo Peninsula. On my fridge was a notice: 'Only go to Doug at Bradford's', a necessary reminder after I had made the mistake, a few years earlier, of using another garage. I sometimes thought if I were to move to Scotland I would still make the drive to Bradford's for my MOT. They were that rare thing, a garage you can trust.

Inside I found Doug, a true gentleman and excellent mechanic.

'Where is it?' he said, peering through the window for my ancient Nissan Micra, which he tended as if it were a priceless classic.

I told him I was walking.

He laughed. 'Want a coffee?' he asked.

The garage had been in Doug's family for generations, passed from father to son. Now Doug and his son, Ralph, were keen to carry on the tradition. Doug and I sat amid canisters of motor oil and brake fluid, sipping our coffee, chatting about Ralph's GCSE prospects and the price of season tickets for Spurs.

I followed the footpath round the side of the garage and fought my way through the same 'impenetrable brambles' which Alan Sillitoe had encountered when he came this way. Sillitoe's account of his walk along the Saxon Shore Way in the early 1980s evokes both the feel of a decade, characterised by high unemployment, class division and the last gasps of traditional British culture, and the brittle edge of this area where beauty and decay rub against each other. I was going to be following in Alan Sillitoe's footsteps for most of the day.

The path led through a plantation of ash trees and onto a road passing a travellers' camp. The track leading away from the camp was deeply rutted and covered in dog shit. I encountered a man with a pork-pie hat, a roll-up and a bull terrier on a rope. The dog barked but looked more scared of me, as I came pounding out of the woods. The man shrugged and looked slightly embarrassed that his dog was not meaner.

On Ropers Green Lane I left the Thames behind and a view of the River Medway opened up away to the left at the foot of the gently sloping wheat fields. Unlike the Thames, the Medway was still a place of low-lying islands, saltmarsh and sandbanks covered by the high tide. Skylarks called overhead with electrical energy, seeming to mimic the crackle of power lines which littered the skyline. Plantains flowered along the track, each one a planet with its own celestial body of orbiting moons.

The modern, red-brick ugliness of the village of Hoo St Werburgh perched on a ridge leading down to the river. The village had exploded in recent years, every meadow and playing field sacrificed to the relentless drive for more housing. I crossed the main road and walked down the track to Angel Farm, feeling watched. Security cameras and lights surrounded the compound. A Harley revved up outside the farmhouse, belonging to one of the members of the Hell's Angels chapter that used the house as their base.

I followed another track down to the river. The ground underfoot was made up of small handmade bricks. Thousands of tons of brick from Kent brickfields would have in the past been loaded on barges heading for London, destined to build the capital's houses. After the slum clearances and the Blitz, many of them would have made their way back here to surface country roads.

I climbed up onto the sea wall and sat down, shouldering the heavy pack off my back and fished around through the tightly packed contents for the emergency supply of Bourneville dark chocolate. It was high tide on the Medway. The water rolled in like creased silk, its wrinkles ironed out as it reached the shore. The cranes and long pier of Kingsnorth Power Station walked their way out into the channel. An egret circled the bay, trying to choose a spot on which to land. Two brent geese, smart in their charcoal dinner jackets, swam among the eel grass calling to each other. I struggled up, my legs still aching after yesterday's miles, and hauled my bag onto my shoulders again.

I passed Thames barges decomposing in the mud of the estuary, the skin of their hulls peeling away, their ribs picked clean by each tide. I tried to imagine the river as it once was, thick with the sails of the barges, bawley boats and Huffler skiffs. Once these barges would have sailed this way carrying London's waste of horse dung, straw and broken crockery to be churned into the fields for nutrients. Now oystercatchers picked over their bodies, while in the background, along the jetties, other barges were being restored by new owners. This was the world of the boatyards; old boats came here and were either reborn or laid to rest. It seemed unfair, almost indecent; the rust-red sails and freshly painted black bodies of the lucky barges seemed to gloat over the remains of the dying.

Down at Whitton Marina I climbed a set of rickety metal steps to a makeshift walkway hanging precariously over the mud ooze, like the wooden planks linking the London slums in film versions of

Oliver Twist. This was the reality of houseboat dwelling: a scrapyard, a working world of half-finished boats, with bits lying across decks which might one day come in useful, and washing lines swinging from masts. It was a far cry from the glossy, executive-pad images I had flashed in front of Connor when I had tried to persuade him to consider houseboat living. He looked at the pictures of the houseboats I downloaded and began to get enthusiastic about the idea of living in St Katherine's Docks. This was more the world he could see himself in: high-tech, blond wood and down lighting. It was only when we visited the local boatyards that the reality hit him.

I reached Alex's boat and climbed down wooden steps into the cabin. I had first met Alex back in January when I had come to visit another houseboat owner and had arranged to drop by when I was passing.

Alex was out back on the deck. Beneath us a beautiful marquetry floor formed a sunburst, mirrored above by a series of wooden spokes; these radiated out and supported sailcloth, which cracked in the wind and made up the ceiling and walls. Alex, now seventy-eight, created all of this himself, in his younger days.

When I arrived, he was poring over an old map of the estuary, leaning forward, threatening to spill the little red hat which sat on top of his shoulder-length grey hair. The hat was ringed with small mirrors which danced light across the outline of dwellings, moorings and slipways that had long since disappeared into the mud. We bent over the old chart. Alex pointed to Milton Basin, now a waterfront development of flats.

'We learnt to swim in the old canal basin,' he said. 'It used to be green with algae, but us older lads would work the sluices, drain the water out and give it a good scrub down before letting the fresh water in so the younger kids could swim.'

Alex folded the map away and led me to the living room.

When I first came to visit Alex in the winter, the woodburner had been blazing and we had sat surrounded by homemade blankets. Today, the wooden windows and door of the boat were thrown open. A friend of Alex's was helping with some DIY and traipsed in and out, collecting screws and bits of timber from below. Alex made me coffee and we sat on squashy couches surrounded by a jungle of spider plants. Twenties jazz was blaring out of the CD player; the group, Alex told me, had the marvellous name of Rigor Mortis and the Deadbeats. It was a homely place to be on a Sunday morning. The wood panelling and funky music reminded me of the caravan. Alex ran his hand along a shelf of seafaring objects and picked up a faded black and white photo of his parents' boat, a stow boat, the *Loratta*. It sat reflected in the calm water of a dock full of barges in full sail ready to head out and trade along the coast.

Alex had boats in his blood.

'My grandmother was from a wealthy family,' he told me, 'a boat-building family, but then she met a strapping Scotsman, a cooper. In those days the coopers moved about with the fishing. He wasn't what my grandmother was meant to fall in love with but her mother took pity on her and gave her the money to go south with him.'

The boat builder's daughter and the cooper bought a piece of land at Swanley in Kent in 1880.

'But they always had boats,' Alex said. 'My dad was in the Navy during the First World War and my mum was a top swimmer. In those days, kids who lived near the water had to be good swimmers. For the mudlarking,' he explained. 'They would swim round passenger ships and dive for coins thrown by the tourists.'

He put the photo back on the shelf, next to a picture of his mother who died when Alex was two.

'Where is the *Loratta* now?' I asked, fearing she may be one of the derelict barges which littered the bay.

'She's in Zanzibar,' he said. 'Ferrying passengers across to Africa.'

I wondered how Alex found this out, but he may well have been to Zanzibar; it wouldn't surprise me.

Alex was one of those people who had lived many lives in one life. He was a man with plenty of stories, which slipped into one another like the tides. For years he worked on the pirate radio ship, Radio Caroline, and showed me pictures of tight-shorts-clad, curly-headed DJs climbing onto a boat with a giant antennae swaying overhead. The photographs were populated by slippery young women of the type that used to beam from *Top of the Pops* album covers. Alex remembered all their names.

'Frieda was the first,' he said. He had met her after he became 'afloat'.

Alex's working life on boats had begun by accident. 'I had a friend who was working on a barge. He wanted to take a holiday so he asked if I could cover his job for a week.'

Alex had been on boats as a kid and knew how to work one. After a week he asked the skipper when his friend was returning and the skipper had shrugged.

'I don't know,' he said 'but you're better.' So he'd stayed.

When Frieda had come into his life, he had followed tradition.

'The waterfront was strict,' he told me. 'When you were serious about a girl you bought her a pair of horseshoe earrings and when you were earning enough to support her you both pierced your ears and soldered one into your ear and the other into hers.'

'What happened to Frieda?' I yelled above the jazz, but here Alex's memories became cloudy.

Alex had been introduced to me by another of the houseboat owners whom I had come to visit on a raw winter's day. I had pulled up in the wind-blasted car park on a Sunday morning and emerged to the lost-soul howling of wind through rigging. A man emerged from a static caravan and stared at me silently.

'I'm here to meet Martin Simpson,' I said, feeling, however silently, he was demanding to know my status.

'You're here to meet Martin Simpson,' he repeated, eyeing me in a way which made me feel I was dressed to kill, not in jeans and a duffle coat.

He stomped away through the puddles.

Thankfully, Martin arrived; he was tall, with spiky grey hair and a beaming smile, full of jolly breeziness despite the bleak weather.

'The site manager,' he told me as we made our way along wet gangplanks between rusted railings which I daren't hold onto for fear they would give way and send me toppling into the mud below. Drooping wires flipped around over our heads in the wind, carrying electricity to the outermost boats. We passed giant, metal poles embedded in the mud. Loops of steel wire attached these to the boats so they could rise and fall with the tide and not drift out to sea in a storm, should the anchors give way. It was a world of rigging and ropes and rotting timber, the stuff of nightmares for a health and safety inspector, but the boatyard was a separate country, which made its own rules and where the twenty-first century didn't quite apply.

At the end of the walkways we boarded Martin's tanker, painted a sunny yellow and topped with a gravel beach.

'The neighbour's cat thinks it's a giant litter tray,' Martin laughed.

He led the way onto the deck which looked out towards the squat fort on Hoo Ness Island and along the coastline to the industrial cathedral of Kingsnorth.

'You have the best view on the whole marina,' I said as widgeon paddled beneath us in the shallows and oystercatchers piped along the bay.

Martin had looked at it sadly. He knew he did, but still he was planning to move.

He opened a metal door with a porthole and we descended down steps to the living quarters. Here was the world that Connor had wanted: wooden floors covered in furry rugs, a dark-purple wall that ran along one side displaying a Gustav Klimt painting. We settled down with cups of tea on the leather sofa and Martin told me the story.

The site owner had been making his life increasingly difficult. Martin ran a social club.

'He doesn't like the fact that women from the club come out to visit the boat. They're just friends,' Martin emphasised, 'but now he's told me I'm not allowed to have more than four people on the boat at once.'

A rule, it turned out, that was applied only to Martin.

The previous summer, Martin had used his prime position on the estuary to take others out kayaking, wanting to share the beauty of the area, but recently friends had turned up in the car park to find a sign telling them that 'Martin's event is cancelled.'

'He's jealous,' I suggested.

Martin shrugged. Another boat owner had given it to him straight, but without malice. 'Your face doesn't fit.'

To tell the truth, it probably didn't. Martin had come to living on a houseboat from owning a waterfront property in the ritzy village of East Farleigh in Kent. Here he had owned a cruiser which he used for trips to the continent. A sticky divorce had left him financially on his uppers.

'Poverty brings a lot of people here,' he said, 'but they choose to stay.'

Martin loved the way that living on the river confronted all your senses, the way the tide rose and fell and the light changed, the noises of water hitting the boat in the storm.

'The water gives me energy,' he said. 'It affects me, the tide changes and so does my mood.'

Martin had built his life back up, from living on what had once been his pleasure boat. He had bought an old tanker for the price of scrap metal and renovated it using his skills as a builder and architect. Now he owned a portfolio of properties and went on luxury holidays to far-flung destinations. He spoke proudly of being a Bargee, a river gypsy, but I could see why maybe he didn't blend with the other boat owners.

When I visited him, Martin was planning to move the boat to an upmarket marina where he hoped his face would fit better. He was days away from the move and trying to be positive.

'It's time to change, maybe sell the boat and create something new,' he said. He looked out of his windows across the expanse of the estuary and wistfully said, 'I'm going to have boats six foot away from me on either side in Rochester.'

I sympathised with Martin. He spoke about the community spirit among the boat owners, but it was still a community where one man's mean spirit could drive another away from his home.

I was planning to visit Martin later that evening at his new yard and had a long walk ahead. I reluctantly told Alex that I had to be going.

'We need to give you something to warm you up, help the walking,' he said.

He went into the galley, a tiny space. Pots and pans hung neatly on the wall, two apples in a basket dangled from a candlestick light, the wire trailed overhead, looking none too safe. He fished in a cupboard emerging with a tall dusty bottle stoppered with a cork and poured me a glass of blueberry brandy.

'Do your kids worry about you, Alex?' I asked. 'Living out here on the boat.'

'Why would they worry about me?' he said.

'Because you're getting old,' interjected his friend as he wandered through to pick up more tools. 'Would they want you to live in a house?' I suggested.

'You don't get a view like this from a house,' Alex said, gazing out of the galley window. 'And if you don't like the view then you wait for a bit and it will change with the tide. What do I want to be living in a house for? I have everything I want here. If I'm cold I put on a jumper or in the summer I put the sides up, let the sun in. It's fantastic. The only time I lock my door is when the wind blows. In a house you worry about things. Here, I water my plants and that's it. What do I want a house for?'

I left Alex, the sounds of jazz ringing in my ears and walked through the boatyards, laughing all the way, despite the fact it had begun to rain. It may have been the effects of the brandy, but it was also the warmth of that community spirit Martin had spoken about.

Not long after the final split with Connor I had visited the houseboat office in Hoo. It was an estate agents' where I had stopped many times to gaze in fascination at the boats for sale: former fishing boats, and metal tankers, 1930s yachts, canal barges and bright-red lighthouse ships with towering beacons. Eventually, I had plucked up the courage to go in.

Inside, the room was sparse and dark, the only furniture a wooden desk, filing cabinet and sagging couch. The man behind the tatty desk looked up; he had greasy black hair which needed a cut and a pair of large glasses. He looked happy to see me.

'Sit down, sit down,' he said.

I sat on the sofa, sinking into the gap between the cushions. He pulled up a wooden chair opposite, so close our knees were almost touching.

'I'm interested in living on a houseboat,' I told him, 'but I'm worried about what's involved.'

He pulled out a plastic file and flipped through a number of adverts for boats in Swan Marina, the smartest boatyard on this part of the river, a place with wi-fi connection and security.

'It's a friendly place,' he said. 'My wife and I lived there. I met her on the internet,' he confided. 'She's Romanian, I brought her over here. When we lived there people were always popping in and out of each other's homes. It was one big community.' The man shuffled closer. 'Are you single?' he asked, looking at me with growing interest.

'Yes,' I said warily. After fourteen years in a relationship, it still felt odd to say it.

He patted my knee. 'You won't have any trouble getting company,' he said. 'They are going to love you in the boatyards.'

I made my excuses and quickly left, my head swimming with images of middle-aged men, down on their luck wandering into my boat offering to paint my deck and then staying to tell me their troubles. I was not ready for this future, but in some ways the boat salesman had been right. Part of me – the sociable Essex girl side – would have slotted in at the boatyards, but another part of me craved isolation, the ability to shut one's door and think solitary thoughts. I wondered if this would have been harder to find.

SIX

Hoo St Werburgh – Upnor – Frindsbury – Strood – Rochester

I SAT DOWN at Upnor beach on a washed-up log and watched the tide flip around, trying to work out if it was coming in, meaning I would have to scurry along the beach, or going out, which meant I could stroll. It seemed to have a life of its own, waking up without warning and riffling its way towards the shore with little choppy waves. I tried to imagine the river as Mr Coles Finch had described it in the book I had pored over during the winter, with the rotting hulks of the man-of-war ships anchored at each end and turning with the tide to block the channel. I pictured the prison hulks, looking as Dickens had described them in *Great Expectations*, 'like a wicked Noah's ark, cribbed and barred and moored by massive, rusty, iron chains'. In Dickens' day boatloads of tourists would row out to these permanent floating prisons to gaze upon the emaciated prisoners and buy the beautiful carved trinkets produced from the bones left behind after their meals. I thought of the young Francis Drake, who lived on a hulk on this river with ten brothers while his father was vicar of the nearby church. It was here that Francis started his maritime career. Apprenticed to a hoyman, he went to sea aged nine.

The river, however, had changed so much that it was hard to even remember how it had looked when I had first come here in the 1980s with my school class to spend a week at the Arethusa Centre, a children's camp upstream. Then Upnor had seemed like a wilderness, the opposite shore a jungle of scrub, the muddy beach deserted. Now the far side of the river had sprouted the regulation sprawl of urban flats and the beach was busy with dog walkers. As a child I had searched the beach for clay pipes, collecting a bag of broken pipe bowls and stems. Now the strand line was littered with cigarette butts.

I worked my way along the beach, past the crumbling ruins of Cockham Wood Fort, each brick picked out in relief from the next by the action of the tide nibbling away at the mortar in between. A long line of broken dragon's teeth showed the remains of a former walkway that would have allowed people to cross the beach even at high tide. Eventually my search paid off and I found one fragment of clay pipe. I carried it with me for a while before leaving it behind; after all, there had to be something left for future children to discover.

I could still see a remnant of the sand which had brought thousands of tourists flooding here during the 1920s. Back in the local studies centre I had found a newspaper from the time which read, 'When the weather is fine the whole beach is alive with joyous merrymakers revelling in the many delights which nature bestowed on this favoured spot.' A picture with the article showed the beach jam-packed with women in long skirts and men in boaters. The 'gay hordes' were wedged in like sardines, and I imagined them turning to face the warmth of a spring day like a field of sunflowers. Unfortunately, some time after this photo was taken, the Navy built a concrete structure just out from the shore, which raised the level of the beach and meant that the entire place became covered in silt.

It was a familiar story of competing interests co-existing unsuccessfully in an overcrowded corner of the country and, as always, it seemed, it was the interests of those with the most might that took precedence. I wanted the north Kent marshes as a place of sanctuary for the wildlife but also for people to come and experience the peace and the dark skies and the sound of lapwings in the spring; to forget for a moment their urban cares and twenty-first-century stress and remember that life wasn't always like this and didn't have to be. Who's to say that people didn't 'need' that far more than they 'needed' another airport or Thames Crossing?

The steep banks of the cliffs leading to Cockham Wood were eroding at a rapid pace, the sandstone washing away in every storm, the rabbits and miner bees doing the rest. I searched one particularly eroded section of cliff for fossils, hoping to find something a little more portable than the straight-tusked elephant skeleton found beneath Upnor Castle. Fearing the castle guard would claim the skeleton as their property, the excavators broke the bones into pieces and smuggled them past the sentry.

Outside Lower Upnor three teenage boys in dirty jogging bottoms with mullet haircuts passed me, debating their recent algebra exam.

'What does E equal?' one asked.

'Fuck knows,' the others said. 'How can you even ask me that?'

It was a philosophical question. They marched on and I entered Upnor with mud on my boots.

From Lower Upnor I walked through a dark tunnel of foliage and climbed a series of stone steps fringed with the bright-blue flowers of green alkanet. I headed down the steep cobbled high street of Upper Upnor passing weatherboard cottages and a pub full of bank holiday laughter and the smell of pie and chips. I tramped along an alley running beside the Royal Engineers boatyard. The air throbbed with the thrum of traffic as it headed beneath the Medway Tunnel. I emerged at Whitehall Creek, once home to a thriving community of houseboats. Alan Sillitoe had commented on one of the barges when he passed this way in the 1980s – a black, wooden barge with a smoking chimney and washing line. 'The barge is snug in the mud,' Sillitoe wrote, 'well away from the town, an almost perfect habitation for these overpopulated days.' Now the creek was lost behind a roundabout and McDonalds, and the population had exploded.

I continued uphill through an overgrown meadow and found myself in a country lane, an unexpected delight on the outskirts of Strood, with a view of the river. The rain was beginning to fall in fat drops, but I took a detour to visit All Saints Church at Frindsbury.

The church sat on the edge of a quarry high above the river, a little snippit of the past surrounded by urban sprawl. The Medway from this spot opened out in a wide sweeping bend towards Rochester Bridge. Once this bend of the river would have been full of sailing ships waiting for the services of the hufflers. The hufflers waited in the 'hards' which stood either side of the bridge. As a ship approached they would scurry out to meet it and help lower the sails and masts so the ship could 'shoot' the low arches of the bridge.

The churchyard at Frindsbury was a ramble of toppling headstones surrounded by a red-brick wall into which generations of people had carved names and dates and historic facts about the scene below, like a grassroots interpretation panel. I walked the length of the wall, trying to read the inscriptions, half lost beneath foliage, moss furring into the lettering, revealing names like lemon juice on invisible ink. The wall grew dark with rain. I left the church and tiptoed carefully down a steep slope leading from the ridge to the river.

The rain was coming in harder, hissing on the mud and vanishing into worm holes. The river was a furry dead tongue winding its way into the city. It was a day to be holed up, in a pub, on Alex's houseboat, in Lena Kennedy's shack, but teenagers were out here, doing their bank holiday thing, crawling over the wreckage of old industry, throwing bricks, yelling, jogging bottoms and hoodies coated with mud. It was what boys have always done on a wet bank holiday and long may it continue. Far rather they're out here, forging alliances, testing their strength, taking risks, than sitting at home, lost in Facebook.

I walked along a crumbling esplanade past weedy planting boxes and outdoor gym equipment. The river was foaming and unhealthy-looking. Mud melted from the banks and seaweed hung from old piers.

I arrived in Rochester, just as the rain became torrential, and crossed the bridge behind a party of teenagers who kept stopping, blocking my path, spitting on the ground. The girls had a marvellous capacity for screaming and did so with much hilarity at everything the boys said. I reached Rochester and walked a short way along the

High Street, thinking of hiding out in a pub until the rain subsided, but every pub was packed with drunken bank holiday revellers. Unable to find a seat and not feeling in the mood to perch at the bar and fend off comments from inebriated locals, I marched on.

On the far bank I could see through the grey mist the houseboat yard where Connor and I had once stayed. I could just make out the outline of the little blue boat called *Marmite* that I had borrowed from a friend for a few days. The boat was moored opposite Rochester Castle and had its own beach garden made up of shingle and shells, salt-baked driftwood sculptures, wind chimes and mirrors. Unfortunately, the yard also backed onto a scrap-metal dealer, the railway line and an industrial estate but, as even Connor had to admit, the boat had a great view.

On our first evening we had lit the barbecue, poured a glass of wine and sat by the driftwood table watching the sun go down, diffused by the mist from the river. I fell asleep to the sucking sound of the mud and woke at 3am to the sound of the drawbridge scraping against the jetty. I crawled out of bed and climbed up onto the deck to find a watery world had slipped in all around, just a line of saltmarsh marking the start of the main river channel. Rochester lay opposite, the castle dark and secret at this closed-in hour of the morning.

I had hoped that the few days on the houseboat would bring us closer, but if anything the stay seemed to convince Connor all the more that this wasn't the life for him.

Back at the caravan I tried to talk to Connor about the wedding, a holiday, the not insignificant matter of where we were going to live come September, but he showed no interest. He began to spend as much time away from the caravan as possible and, when he was there he acted as though I was invisible. At night, when I came to bed, he would turn his back on me and feign sleep. I was not ninety, and even if I was, I hoped I would still want the man I wanted to want me. This man, the one I was engaged to, treated me like an unfortunate inconvenience in his life.

I had tried so hard to stay in control of my life, to keep some semblance of myself amid the roaring tide of opinion that told me that everything I felt and thought and wanted was wrong, but now my world was slipping from me and I could do nothing to stop it. I knew I could no longer cling to the caravan. I had promised James Brightwell I would be off site by the end of August and I owed it to him to keep this promise.

I put a postcard in the window of local shops advertising the caravan for sale and people began to call. The first to arrive was a farmer wanting an extra caravan to add to the fleet of vans which housed his orchard workers. He poked around my tiny space and left, dissatisfied. Then a flamboyant woman arrived. She wanted something she could live in while building her luxury house. She looked at my wood-panelled dining room with distaste. It was depressing, people coming in, getting mud on the carpets, judging my home. I trailed behind them resentfully, wondering how it was that they could keep my caravan while I couldn't.

Then, one evening in June, there was a knock at the door. I opened it to find a man and a woman standing there. The woman had long, wild hair, the man, a shirt split to the waist, muttonchop whiskers and a boozer's nose.

'Hello,' I said warily. They looked like travellers.

'We saw a card in the shop window saying the van was for sale,' the woman said. 'I hope we're not disturbing you, just dropping by like this, but I wondered if we might pop in and have a look.'

I invited them in.

They took their shoes off in the kitchen. 'I know what it's like, living in a van,' the women said. 'You don't want to get mud on the carpets.'

I smiled.

'This is Connor,' I said.

Connor looked up from the corner of the couch and went back to watching the news. He'd made it pretty clear that selling the caravan was my problem, not his.

I showed them around. It didn't take long. You could pretty much stand in the kitchen and open the doors to the bedrooms and bathroom without moving from the spot. The couple made appreciative noises.

'It's a beautiful spot you're living in,' the woman said. 'Such a fantastic place, how comes you're selling?'

So I told them about the eviction.

The man's face darkened. 'This is outrageous,' he said. 'You work here. You've got a job to do with the countryside. They can't do this to you.'

'It's done,' I said. 'We've only got a few weeks left.'

'No, you have to know how to play the system. What you do is get twelve geese and tell the council that you have to live on the site and look after your livestock. Make sure it's twelve geese, mind.'

I thanked him for the advice, but explained that it was a bit hard to defy the landowner; after all, I was employed by them. I could end up out of a job.

The man scratched his whiskers, looking more upset than I was. 'Life on square wheels isn't easy,' he said.

The women clapped me on the shoulder. 'I'm sorry for your troubles. I can see you love it here. You're a girl after my own heart.'

Connor looked up from the couch and saw me standing in between these two whiskery, travelling characters. He half shut his eyes in despair. The last thing he wanted was for someone to encourage my notions, but for one moment I looked back at him with defiance, feeling a confidence that I hadn't felt in a long time.

'See?' I wanted to say. 'I am not stupid. I am not childish. I am not alone in seeing the value of a simple life.'

A few nights previously, I had told Connor about a book I was reading. It was about a couple who lived in a cabin in the woods and brought their child up in a simple way without a lot of fuss and baby gadgets. When I had enthused about their lifestyle Connor had said, 'How irresponsible. Why would you struggle with a simple way of life when you no longer have to?'

To me there were so many reasons why you would do this, but it seemed pointless to explain them when they would all be dismissed as nonsense. Instead I pocketed my excitement along with all the other ideas that inspired me but couldn't talk about and wrote one line from the book in my diary. 'Only dead fish swim with the stream'. It felt like a secret defiance against everyone who told me that the only way to live was to get a get a sensible job, a mortgage, settle down and conform.

I knew that I should stop and look at the implications of this, try to talk to Connor, but the tide of wedding preparations swept on. Our parents arranged to meet in London and I arrived at Embankment Station only to find my name being announced across the tannoy. I knew immediately that it was my dad, who had suffered from heart problems for many years. He had collapsed on the train on the way to meet us. Connor and I rushed to the hospital and found him connected to wires and on oxygen. The doctors told me his heart had become worse. They talked about valve replacements and bypasses. Suddenly, life seemed too short. Over the next few days, in between hospital visits, I shopped for wedding dresses and pretended everything was ok. My dad recovered.

With a month left until the eviction date, Connor came home from work one evening and told me that he was planning to spend Friday night in Essex with a young teacher at his school. There had always been these women in Connor's life: female 'friends' who I never met, whose names would be dropped into conversation once too often. Occasionally I would find out he had met these women for drinks or gone to a hotel with them or told them he would leave me for them. This time, he and the 'friend' were going to a party, a teachers-only party, so I couldn't come. Besides, he told me, she was going through a hard time and needed his support. The row went on and on. In danger of flinging the kettle at Connor's head if I stayed, I slammed out of the caravan and walked across the reserve in the dark. I walked to the viewpoint and sat on the bench, on the hill, listening to the sounds of marsh frogs cackling in the ditches and nightingales jazz-scatting in the wood. A fox appeared on its midnight hunt and crossed the brow of the hill, all pointy-eared alertness, silhouetted against the moon. I walked back to the caravan, feeling a little calmer.

Inside, Connor was making a cup of tea.

'I'm sorry you're upset,' he said.

'It's no good being sorry if you don't understand why I'm upset,' I told him.

Connor stood there, looking down at the floor, teaspoon in hand. I thought this was to be it, the usual response, looking helpless, hoping I would forgive him, but suddenly he mumbled, 'I know I have been acting like a jerk recently.' He looked up. 'Partly it's losing the caravan. It feels like we're at a crossroads. I want one thing, you want another and I wonder if this is it. The end of the road. For us,' he added. 'Maybe we just need a fresh start.'

I was stunned. 'No,' I wanted to shout. 'I love you. Don't do this.' But I didn't. Before, I always had. When I sensed him dissolving through my fingers I had always grasped tighter, but now I wondered if I really did love Connor, this Connor, or whether I was just in love with the Connor I had once known, the hopeful boy who had never experienced much of the world and was consequently surprised and delighted by it all. I loved that Connor, but deep down I knew he was lost to me. Ever since taking the teaching job, a new Connor had emerged. A man who wanted no more talk of travel or alternative lifestyles, who saw only one way to live, the way everyone else lived, and in that there was no room for negotiation. I was either with him and willing to live that life or I was against him. We stood facing each other in the little kitchen as the steam from the tea misted the windows and tick, tick, tick went the countdown clock to our wedding.

We called it off. The church and reception were booked, my dress was bought and paid for, my sister had booked her flights over from Australia, but still we called off the wedding. Everyone was angry at us.

'You are the ideal couple,' people complained. 'The only really good couple I know. You don't just jog along like everyone else. You are the real thing. Why are you doing this?'

I didn't have an answer. I was in a daze, unable to think.

Connor was resolute. 'We have to spend six months apart,' he declared, 'scratch our itches, and then see.'

Connor spent more and more time in Essex and I couldn't think about this either. I had one month until I lost my home and I had no idea what would happen next.

In the end, I did three things. I booked a long holiday to Russia. I felt if one were going to be a tragic, jilted figure then one might as well go the whole hog and do it in a Russian winter. I sold the caravan to Keith, the farmer, and I agreed to move into the farmhouse with Gordon and Mike. As much as I liked my colleagues I hated the thought of moving in with them, dreading the lack of privacy when, in my current state of shock, privacy was the thing I craved. Having never told my workmates I was getting married, I now felt it would look stupid to reveal why the girl with the Essex banter had vanished and been replaced by a pale, red-eyed woman who drifted around in a daze.

While at work, I tried to look normal. I ran events, organised the annual country fair, spent the budget but, at the end of the day, all I wanted was to shut the door of the caravan, draw the curtains and fall to the floor in despair. I felt the protection of the caravan more and more. It was my shell into which I could retreat and hide, but any day now I was going to lose it. Moving in with Gordon and Mike, I would be on display, all of it; the inside and outside of me were going to be exposed. With so little time left, the farmhouse seemed the only option.

August drew to a close. I sat in the garden that I had created behind the caravan. It was wildly overgrown. There had seemed little point in tending it that year. I closed my eyes. I could feel the summer evening heat radiating off the metal sides of the caravan. I could feel my home behind me, still, still there. Maybe, I thought, after it is gone, I can come and sit here and close my eyes and still feel it. That night I slept hardly at all, dreading the morning.

I burst into tears over breakfast.

'I can't bear it,' I said. 'I don't want to move into the farmhouse.'

'You'll hardly be spending any time there,' Connor said. 'You can go and stay at your parents, whenever you want.'

Connor had fallen on his feet and had found a two-bedroom bungalow to rent half a mile away in the village of High Halstow.

There had been no suggestion I could stay.

I stepped out of the caravan with the first box of my possessions in my arms. Outside, the reserve was in full swing, preparing for the annual Wildlife and Countryside Fair. The staff, volunteers, stallholders, seemingly the whole population of the bloody Hoo Peninsula were there, running around, marking out the site, erecting marquees. They stopped to watch me cross the lawn. I had heard the whispers in the office.

'Why was I choosing today to move? Why couldn't I have done it a week ago?'

On closer inspection, the farmhouse was worse than I had imagined, the kitchen caked with grease, the carpets thick with dirt. The bed, which I had found hidden in one of the barns, was musty and damp. I carried my life across the lawn, doggedly shifting my possessions until my whole life was spread across the room in boxes.

At one o'clock, while I was scrubbing the caravan floor, Keith and his family arrived. Their daughter, excited about acquiring her first home, rushed around the rooms deciding how she would redecorate. Burly men appeared to cut the electricity and pull out my carefully constructed drains. Keith's son, Jamie, arrived in a digger and ripped a hole in the garden fence.

'We'll mend it later,' he said. 'We need to get the thing out of here somehow.'

I stepped out of the caravan and then was panic-stricken at the thought that I would never step inside it again. I wanted to claw my way back in, lie on the floor and refuse to leave, but I couldn't. The second I had stepped out, it was no longer mine.

Jamie and Keith hitched a tractor to the tow bar and heaved. The wheels, which had been wedged in the ground for three years, moved, the caravan jolted forward. Keith's daughter came to shake my hand and I managed not to cry. The caravan was pulled through the gap in the fence and vanished down the lane. I was left standing on a tiny patch of bald earth which had been my living room, surrounded by the remnants of a garden with no home to cling to. I could feel everyone watching me and was reminded of a line I had once read from a Jack Kerouac novel: 'They will crucify him here on the streets of this city and every eye shall see.' You may think I was being melodramatic and maybe I was, but if so then I hope you never see a day when your life is wrenched from you in full view of your colleagues and you have nowhere to hide.

That night Connor and I retreated to a hotel. Connor was reluctant to spend the money. 'We can sleep in your new room,' he said.

'Where?' I asked, looking around. There was not a single inch of available space. Something was beginning to niggle at me as well. It seemed that Connor thought he was entitled to share my living space until the very last moment, but that this arrangement was clearly not reciprocal.

'I want one final night in a clean bed,' I said. 'Before I accept that this is now where I live.'

The next day I returned to work, running the fair, smiling and organising.

Connor called. 'I've got the keys to the bungalow,' he said. 'Come up after work and help me unpack.'

At the door he greeted me excitedly. Proudly he showed me round the bungalow with its large bathroom and living room, conservatory and garden. I followed him around and felt my anger grow.

'How can you have all this and not help me out,' I said, 'just for a few weeks until I go to Russia? I will find somewhere else when I get back.'

'NO, you can't stay here,' he said. 'We have split up.'

'But I didn't throw you out of the caravan when we called off the wedding. I wouldn't have dreamt of it, because I don't hate you and you had nowhere else to go. Why can't you offer me the same?'

Connor looked taken aback by the truth of this.

'I'm asking as a friend,' I said in desperation. 'Please let me stay here.'

Connor sighed, 'I just have no emotional energy to discuss this,' he said.

Sharply, the fog of the last few weeks lifted. Why was I doing this, begging this man? I stood up to go, knowing at that moment that the old Connor was dead, our relationship was dead and the only self-respectful thing to do was to walk away.

Back in the rain of a bank holiday Monday in Rochester, I left the houseboat yard and its memories behind and began the walk along the esplanade to Martin Simpson's new boat yard. Martin had been happy to let me stay. His new boatyard, he'd told me, was smarter and much more him. The rain grew heavier and I stomped along the tarmac as cars whizzed through puddles and drenched me. I was dog tired and hungry and cold and grumpy. I pounded along through an overgrown alley, wet cow parsley overhung the path, slapping against my legs and rain dripped down my neck.

I reached the boatyard and sent Martin a text. 'I am here, I am drenched'. Martin met me outside carrying a large umbrella. He was a gentleman and only did a slight double take on seeing that the somewhat glamorous girl he had met earlier in the year had morphed into a dripping rat. Once down in the cabin I stood on one of the furry rugs dripping onto the parquet floor. I was exhausted beyond politeness.

'Bloody hell, that was horrible,' I belted out. 'Jesus, I am frozen and knackered.'

'Would you like a drink? Something to eat?' Martin said helpfully

'A bath,' I said, 'a hot bath, then tea.' I was not being a good guest, but couldn't help it.

I emerged from the bath half an hour later, human but only just. I flopped comatose onto Martin's couch in front of the telly and watched fish swim across the *Blue Planet*, too tired to make chatter. The water slipped in, the lights on the Medway Bridge began to shine, I crawled into a makeshift bed on the couch and sank into oblivion.

SEVEN

Rochester – Chatham – St Mary's Island – Darnet Island

A FEW WEEKS' LATER on a blistering day in June, I caught the train to Rochester with my bicycle fully laden with camping gear. I planned to spend the next two days camping on the river island of Darnet, and the amount of equipment needed was way too heavy to carry on my back.

I had visited Darnet Island years earlier on a trip which had ended in near disaster but had been pivotal in my decision to 'be sensible' and buy a house. Being 'sensible' had never been my natural position, so maybe it was time to revisit an episode in my past which had made this course seem like a good idea at the time. I set off along Rochester High Street in the direction of Chatham, passing the weather-boarded houses and Victorian street lamps.

At Bath Hard Lane I took a diversion to rejoin the Medway. The stretch of river here looked like a thing abandoned; tying-up posts for houseboats lay dormant, wharves remembered only in name. Chatham lay across the river. From a distance it appeared peaceful and stately, the spire of the naval memorial looking down upon a town of military buildings. Chatham Dockyards were hoping to get World Heritage Status for their naval history. The dockyards, lining the river a mile below the town, had once been busy with the building of Tudor warships and Nelson's flagship, HMS *Victory*.

The Docks had closed thirty years ago and the town had struggled with high unemployment and dereliction ever since. When I first moved to the area I had taken one walk through Chatham town centre, seen the early morning drunks and the teenage mothers puffing smoke over their children's heads and thought 'my God, and they say Romford's bad'. Chatham needed status.

The Medway towns are great in many ways. Rochester is beautiful with its cathedral, castle and high street of antique and designer clothes shops. Rainham, where I live, is a homely place which still boasts a fishmonger's, greengrocer's and baker's as well as second-hand book and record shops. This, along with the addition of some marvellous town eccentrics – a man who stands on street corners performing exercise classes and a 6ft 2 inch transvestite with a voice like Barry White – had sealed it for me as a place to live.

Medway has beautiful countryside, a thriving arts community, a lot happening, but you can't hide the fact that parts of the towns are rough as all hell.

I turned back onto the High Street towards Chatham. Closer to the town, I cycled past shops selling rugs, fishing tackle and 'adult' services. The High Street was an artery linking Chatham and Rochester which bled commuters who, having exhausted the possibilities in one town, strolled bored and restless, or purposeful with trouble-making, into the other. A man yelled at me to 'get on your bike and cycle', and, when I ignored him, invited me to join him in an act of carnal delight. A grubby man picked up discarded cigarette butts from a shop doorway while passing teens bellowed 'you skanker' at him. I mounted my bike to escape and wobbled downhill on the heavily laden cycle, which proved a little hard to control. I swerved into Chatham Bus Station and was forced to leap from the saddle to avoid colliding with a railing, spraining my wrist in the process.

I had no desire to linger in the town centre, so pushed the bike uphill in the blazing heat. On the outskirts of Chatham, I stopped at St Mary's churchyard, under the shade of a knobbly trunked plane tree. Memorials for sailors who had died aboard their ships were set into the church wall. Every window of the church was boarded up, the stained glass never more to shine while youths and drunks were around to throw stones at it.

I continued uphill past the barracks of the Royal Engineers and Fort Amherst, outside which General Kitchener stood guard. Young men in army fatigues jogged by in the heat. I free-wheeled down to the bottom of Dock Road and onto St Mary's Island.

At the island, an elegant bridge separated the two basins of the marina. A sign greeted me, 'Welcome to the Fishing Village'. The maritime-inspired houses fronting the harbour were clapboarded in pale blue. It had been built a few years ago to look like the sort of place which would once have echoed with the sound of hammers and shouts of men mending sails and rudders.

I followed the clearly delineated cycle path around the island, feeling a growing need to break the rules and leap from the path onto the road, but neat, trimmed borders prevented such reckless action. The streets were empty, shiny cars circled the roundabouts and turned off into places called Samphire Road and Sea Aster Court. The cul-de-sacs looked like the perfect place for kids to play out, but there were none. 'Maybe they are all in the community centre,' I thought, but the kids' playground outside was empty. I began to feel like I had become lost in a David Lynch film, a polished world hiding an evil secret.

Finally, after cycling through a warren of fake fishing cottages, I found a boardwalk with a fine view of the river. Cockham Woods lay on the opposite shore. I could see the beach I had walked along in the rain to Upnor a few weeks' earlier. The leaning pillbox and tumbled remains of Cockham Fort looked tiny, like commemorative Lego bricks of British battles.

I cycled along a causeway beside the river. There, people were out walking their dogs or kids; teenagers were practising cycle tricks, leaping the walls of an old slipway. I began to like the island more. At the end of the boardwalk I came across a silver sculpture called 'The Mariners' with an inscription by N. S. Jenkins. 'Salt worn and weary eyes, cast back, sea hard lives carve proud history, sailors, traders, whores or heroes. Kin of a rivers family. Strong lithe and young she's sailing on. Horizons unseen, glories grow. Future floods in, past ebbs out. A city's story far to flow.' I liked it. I liked the line about the past ebbing out and the future flooding in. It seemed a fitting epitaph for my journey.

Connor and I didn't end after I walked away from the bungalow. We limped on for another eighteen months. I went to Russia, had a flirtation with a much younger man, got drunk in Moscow with a bunch of Australians and came back feeling more confident than I had in years. Connor maybe sensed this and wanted me back. He had been lonely and asked me to move into the bungalow where he had refused to let me stay. I was furious. It seemed typical that he would drag me and everyone who knew me through the trauma of calling off a wedding and then, a couple of months later, claim he was feeling perkier and it was back on. I had seen a glimmer of a future in which I would make new friends, reach for the things I wanted, be made to feel attractive, and I wasn't ready to be sucked back into life with Connor until I was sure that things would be different. I suggested counselling but he was reluctant. Then my dad became ill again, dangerously ill. He spent months in hospital. I needed someone in my life. Connor was there. In body he was there and I was grateful, but as a person he just drifted further and further away.

I had said to Connor that I never again wanted to fear another woman's name. He said he understood but nothing changed. All those years I believed that if I told him enough times how his flirtations with those other women made me feel he would finally understand and stop. By the time I discovered his final 'friend' I had realised that Connor knew exactly how much his behaviour hurt me, but he couldn't stop. In the end, I learned it was not the women whose names you hear that you have to worry about, it is the woman whose name is never mentioned. One such woman came into Connor's life and I was finally handed the evidence I needed on Christmas Eve.

It was such a shabby end to our relationship. I threw Connor out of my parents' house on Christmas morning and have never spoken to him again. After fourteen years that is really hard. At the time, I felt that it was the only thing I could do. It was the only way to move forward, but now I'm not so sure if there didn't need to be some final talk, some final something. For a long time afterwards I had felt as if he were a boat tied to my dock. Despite it all, I still felt the need to help him, to shelter him, to support him. It was a hard thing to untie that boat and let it sail forth for better or worse on the course it had set for itself. My 'journey' was helping that boat sail away and hopefully enabling me to set my own course for the future.

Dave Thorpe from Kent Wildfowlers phoned my mobile. The Wildfowlers are part-owners of Darnet Island where I had asked permission to spend the night. I had met Dave only a handful of times many years ago and my recollection was that I was rude to him. I had been working with the RSPB and, despite all the friendly rhetoric, the Wildfowlers were on the other side of the coin. We both wanted decent habitat so that birds could thrive; the difference was the RSPB wanted to protect them and the Wildfowlers wanted to shoot them. Still, when I had phoned Dave to ask permission to go to the island, he had been nothing but helpful and had organised for one of their members to take me across on his private hovercraft. He had, however, reservations about me staying on the island on my own.

'I don't like the idea of it,' he said. 'Anyone could land.'

His fears had amplified my own. In the week prior to this trip I had cycled out to look at the island across the water and had been dismayed to see smoke rising from the shore. It wasn't fear of being on my own that bothered me, but fear of the kind of company I might find there. I didn't fancy a night of fending off the advances of some rum old sea dog. At the same time, the thought of having the island to myself filled me with delight.

Now Dave was phoning to say 'good news, you won't be on

your own. A whole group of hovercraft-owners and their kids are camping out there as well.'

'Great,' I said, thinking the news was anything but. I cycled down to the Strand and found Dave amid a sea of hovercrafters, all men.

'Your protectors,' one of them announced.

Phil Hann, from Outdoor Pursuits, arrived with the Lamborghini of all hovercrafts, covered in a camouflage pattern of a willow woodland, with a bright-orange fan on the back. Phil was a broad, tanned man, who spent all year on the estuary fishing and shooting. It might not have been my cup of tea, but I couldn't deny that this was a connection with the estuary too, a deep connection of love it, kill it, eat it. It was a timeless connection, and, if practised sustainably and without waste, then not one that I, a non-vegetarian, could easily condemn.

'Climb on board,' Phil said, handing me a life jacket and a bright-yellow pair of ear defenders. I sat there like a lady in a sedan chair while Dave and Phil tucked my luggage in around me, making sure all the straps were well away from the fan. They loaded my bike into the back of Dave's van for safe keeping and Phil climbed aboard. Then we were off, on this aquatic motorbike, bouncing across the waves, cutting through sailing boats, passing the slip ways, wooden piers and decaying barges of Hoo Ness, the larger of the two military islands.

In 1860, as a response to rumours that France was amassing troops to invade England, a Royal Commission was set up and concluded that Chatham Docks, the major naval establishment in the east of England, needed better protection and that new defences had to be created. The original plan was to build forts either side of the Medway at Burntwick Island and Oakham Ness, but the commission soon found that the ground in their chosen locations was way too soft to bear the weight of the three-storey forts, so the site was shifted to Darnet and Hoo Ness. However, as soon as building work began, they realised that these islands were also too boggy, so the design of the forts was scaled down to two floors and the land drained. The lower floor of the fort had been purposely flooded some years previously to prevent vandalism, but the top floor and the majority of the island now stayed dry at high tide.

The artist Stephen Turner had lived on both Hoo and Darnet islands for many weeks in 1998 when he was creating a series of large canvases for an exhibition called, 'Tide and Change'. To say that Stephen created the canvases is not quite correct; the river created them. Stephen pegged out the sheets at low tide and waited for the high tide to wash over them, leaving its fingerprint behind.

I had first met Stephen when he came to Northward Hill to work on a new artwork called 'Moon View', for which he camped out on the reserve and recorded the night-time wildlife. Years later, I took a trip out on the Medway with him as part of his 'Sedimental' project. The trip had been full of Arts Council people and students with huge fluffy microphones recording our every word for posterity. We had all been self-conscious, but I remembered that, as we passed Hoo Ness island, something had changed. Stephen stopped being Stephen Turner the artist and instead talked about his love for the island and the rotting hulks in a way which made me think: this man really cares about this place, he feels it within himself, he longs for it.

Stephen had been visiting Hoo Ness island unofficially for years, though when he received his first arts commission he realised that he would have to ask permission if he wanted to stay there. Medway Ports, the owners, were not helpful. They wrote telling him to take his art project elsewhere and if they caught him on the island they would prosecute. Undeterred, Stephen approached the man who had a waste disposal licence for tipping gravel on the island and asked if he could be employed for no wages to guard the machinery. In his new capacity as official night watchman he had permission to stay.

'Why Hoo?' I asked when I visited Stephen in his studio in Chatham Dockyard.

'I had seen a book at a boot fair called *Escape to an Island* and thought, "it's a sign". I've always been drawn to isolated spaces. As a small boy I created a den in some derelict buildings down the end of the road. I've always had that need to escape company. I look for somewhere you can choose to be sociable or not.'

During his time on Hoo Ness, Stephen had been visited by two boys of about thirteen who had rowed across in an inflatable dingy.

'Not a proper one,' Stephen told me, 'but one that you would have bought from Woolworths and used at the beach.'

The boys had read about Stephen in a newspaper article and thought he might like the company.

'The boys had a tent but no tent poles' Stephen said. 'Somehow they managed to fashion one from some driftwood and set up. After a short while one of the boys comes across and says, "I'm cold, we've got no matches. Can I have some of your fire?"'

Ritually, Stephen handed them a burning coal; after a while they were back again.

'"Where's the tap mate?"' they asked. 'I explained that there was no tap,' Stephen said. 'In fact there was no fresh water unless they had brought their own.'

The boys asked if they could have some of his, plus some beans. With limited supplies, carefully rationed for his time on the island, Stephen reluctantly handed over some water and food.

'I settled down in my tent,' he continued, 'but in the night, I saw a dark shape loom outside, then a hand descended slowly and reappeared holding my kettle. I got out of bed and went and confronted the boys.'

'But we have nothing and you have everything,' the boys protested. On an island, it seemed all bets were off and it was dog eat dog.

'The next day the boys left in their dingy,' Stephen told me, 'but two days later they returned.'

'We love it here too,' they told Stephen, 'and we're bringing our mates out here for a party.'

'Did you feel invaded?' I asked him.

'I did,' he admitted. 'So much so that, when a passing sailor realised my predicament and offered to give me a lift off, I readily accepted.'

A more welcome visitor to Hoo Ness had been the writer Roger Deakin. He had swum from The Strand out to the island in September of the same year, a trip he wrote about in his fabulous book, *Waterlog*. Roger had not relished the swim, fearing, and with good cause, the pollution and bacteria in the water, but he had been amazed at the beauty of the island fort, describing it as 'One of the most impressive historical buildings in England, and certainly one of the most neglected.'

I could see the fort on Hoo Ness Island, although, like Stephen, I too had been refused permission to land. Phil and I left Hoo Ness behind and within seconds we were whizzing straight up the beach at Darnet.

Phil carried my stuff up the beach beyond the high-tide mark and shot back across the waves. For a few beautiful moments I had the island to myself, apart from the oystercatchers and redshank piping overhead. A seal appeared in the flat calm of the bay. Its dark eyes checked me out as I stood on a peninsula of land among the sea lavender and purslane; it raised its nose skywards and was gone.

I began pitching my tent, choosing a spot away from the long-established campfire and supplies of the other hovercrafters. I am not an antisocial person, quite the opposite, and it was this tendency in myself that I was wary of. I had come here to be alone and I knew I was too inclined to spend the night drinking whisky and recounting stories around a fire.

So I was dismayed when the gang arrived and began to pitch their tent inches from my own. I watched them for a few moments.

'If you want some privacy,' I said, 'I can move somewhere else.'

'No, you're ok,' they said. 'You can stay there.'

Soon the island was full of men swearing and kids shouting.

It was like a bad holiday camp. I sat in my tent, trying to write while one of the hovercraft owners tested the revving capacity of his engine on the mud beneath me. The roar went on and on. One of the kids approached.

'We're all going across to the mainland for fish and chips. Do you want us to bring you some?'

It was a kind offer but I declined. It was not what I wanted. I wanted inaccessibility, remoteness, not takeaway deliveries.

I grabbed my stuff and headed over to the far side of the island, the windy side, the side with the view of Kingsnorth power station, not the other islands of the estuary, but at least it was peaceful.

'It's not a new thing, this access to the estuary,' Stephen had told me. 'When I was on Hoo a party of fifty people landed in boats. They had done so for years and held their annual party on the island. Another time a group of kids arrived with no boat. I asked them how they had reached the island and they said they had walked across the causeway. The causeway is broken and treacherous and not marked on maps.'

'How did they know where to go?' I asked. I knew the causeway only too well and was amazed the kids had made it to Darnet.

'I asked the kids that,' Stephen said, 'and one of them said, "Me dad showed me when I was little". The difference,' Stephen said, 'is it's more of an invasion now. Before, the people who came were local, they came because they were part of a natural cycle. Their parents had shown them how to walk there at low water; it was a long-held tradition. Now it's different. Everyone seems to zip about at will on noisy jet skis that disturb the peace of the place for other people and for wildlife.'

Back on Darnet, the sun was beginning to set. I foraged for driftwood and, after the winter storms, found plenty of old planks and logs washed down with the tides. Getting a fire going proved harder than I had imagined. The little flame from the cheap lighter was sporadic and the pages from my notebook did not burn well. I leant down to blow on the flames, inhaling the fumes from the woodsmoke.

'Come on, Carol,' I told myself. 'You do this every week in the woods all winter. You won't fail at this.'

I conveniently forgot that it was my volunteer group who got the fire going every week as part of our weekly countryside management tasks, not me. Still, I had seen a good few fires started, I knew the principles and, besides, I had an ace up my sleeve: a little bag of woodchip, oily resinous tinder which would bring a tear even to Ray Mears's eye.

I set the wavering flame of the lighter to the curls of wood and saw the glow as they caught; more coaxing with breath and dried grass and the fire grew. I sacrificed some beautifully sculpted driftwood and the fire began to build. I sat back and watched the sun go down on Midsummer Eve while my little saltwood fire burnt down to ash and my jacket potatoes slowly softened in the coals. The tide rose and receded, the wind picked up. I was sticky from salt spray and my eyes stung with smoke, but at that moment I was proud of myself, feeling like a survivalist chick.

I settled back and thought about the offer of fish and chips. It felt wrong, though I couldn't put my finger on why. Weeks after my return I mentioned this incident to Stephen.

'That's what I mean about the difference with the access to the estuary,' he said. 'Now we have a society of convenience. Everything is within reach and easily available. If you go to Darnet it ought to be special. Before you could only go there at high water, you had to work with the tide, you had to work at nature's speed. It made you pay your respects to where you were. If you can now go off to Gillingham for a beer in the evening then what are you there for? I like to go to remote places with few conveniences,' he said, 'so I can reflect on other ways of living. When you come back from somewhere remote, it makes you more aware of the world.'

Stephen was right. The offer of fish and chips had connected me to the land as surely as if there had been a high-speed rail link outside my tent flap. It had destroyed the remoteness. It was as John Ruskin had said, 'seeing but not looking'. The hovercrafters wanted to say they were spending the night on an island, but didn't want any of the inconveniences that might bring. They wanted the island on their terms. If you came to the island as I had, as Stephen had, bringing all your own supplies, then you were at the will of the estuary. You were not above nature, you were subject to the tides and the weather, and if something went wrong – a storm surge, a hole in your water bottle – then nature could knock you flat. The hovercrafters were not subject to nature in the same way. They were on an island in name only.

At 9.30pm, the oystercatchers stopped mooching by the shore and went on a fly past of the fort. Seven flew overhead in a gang with a lone outrider up ahead. They pipe-piped across the sky, fluttering back and forth across their territory, proclaiming it theirs, protesting at the human intrusion. They circled my head continuously like vengeful angels; a shrieking lament over the growing darkness.

I fished baked potatoes from the coals. They were smoke-blackened and charcoal-tasting and just about perfect. I was dog tired from the heat of the day and the cycle, but my fire still had plenty of life in it and I couldn't bring myself to kill it. Eventually, I admitted defeat, doused it with wet pebbles and returned to my tent by the light of my head torch, through the tufts of sea purslane, trying not to turn an ankle in the muddy crevasses left behind by the tide.

I reached my camp in time to see two rats chasing each other with joy over the sea lavender inches from my tent. When I had told a friend I was going to Darnet Fort for Midsummer, he said, 'You mean Rat Island?' before recounting a story of using his bag as a pillow only to wake in the night and find it full of rats. Remembering this story, I locked all my food away in my heavy canvas cycle bags and barred the door with cooking equipment.

The night was cold and the oystercatchers never really stopped calling. The tone softened a little but they never gave up. At 3am I crawled from the tent for a wee and was surprised to see the hovercraft boys still around the campfire. I hoped I was not silhouetted by the growing dawn.

The gulls were beginning to call out on the saltings, the towns across the water were lit with the gold of street lamps and a hundred traffic lights set to green. The sky was growing light behind the power station, the cranes silhouetted against the blue and dusty pink of dawn. They looked like giant walkers, setting out across the marshes, striding across the landscape at night and returning to their riverside posts at dawn. I returned to my sleeping bag and listened to the gulls until I fell asleep once more.

EIGHT

Darnet Island – Rainham

I WOKE THREE hours later to find the tide seeping in again. The bay was a morning looking-glass shattered into fragments by ducks landing, scattering droplets into the sun. The tide padded its way inland, eating away at the base of mud pillars sculpted into undulating shapes. Broken teeth of lost jetties slipped beneath the incoming water.

I made porridge and sat in the mouth of the tent drinking tea which tasted strangely of TCP and watched two shelduck fly overhead calling 'zhoo, zzzhhooo, zhoooo', like small space rockets. The seal returned. He and I had the bay to ourselves at this early hour before the hovercrafters and the jet skiers and the roar of engines blasted into our morning. I felt, as I often felt, how privileged I was. How bloody well I did for a poor girl from Essex. I had been ferried to an island by some people who barely knew me and who were under no obligation to do anything for me and here I was, sharing a moment of mutual curiosity with another creature. Some people spent their whole lives without moments such as this.

I had a plan: head across the island before anyone was up and go for a swim. I returned to my evening fire spot and was dismayed to see the tall figure of one of the hovercrafters already on the beach. I skulked moodily in the distance, thinking uncharitably, 'Go away, let me have it to myself,' but he saw me and came across to chat.

He introduced himself as Pete and said that he and the fellow hovercrafters had sat around the campfire last night drinking a bottle of single malt and wondering if the 'author was lonely'. I assured him that the 'author' was fine and had come here to write about being isolated on an island, so had taken herself off to cook baked potatoes and commune with the ducks. Somehow we got talking about the delights of home brew and he sat down to draw me a diagram of a Liebig condenser, with which, he assured me, I could turn cheap wine into fine brandy.

He had me now, I was interested. I forgot my vow to be antisocial and asked him if he had been to the island before. It was his first time camping on Darnet.

'I had to sell the hovercraft after divorcing my wife,' he said. 'She thought herself something special, but was just a big girl from Dartford.'

This made me laugh. 'It sounds like a song title,' I said. 'I married a big girl from Dartford.'

The divorce left him broke, he told me. He had to live in his van. 'The experience has changed me,' Pete said. 'Nowadays, I always carry a change of clothes and I can turn my emotions on and off.'

I was beginning to see a pattern. Many of the people I had met didn't consciously choose to live in a houseboat or a caravan. Instead they had found themselves so poor they didn't have a choice. Some of these people had been enjoying fairly luxurious lifestyles before the fall. Martin had once had a big house and a speedboat, and Pete had been zipping around the estuary on a hovercraft and been a member of a private club. I wondered if these stories of riches to rags were a sign of the times, examples of people overstretching their credit cards and aspiring to a lifestyle that was not easy to sustain when something – divorce, redundancy, a downturn in the economy – rocked the boat.

Pete told me that coming to the island allowed him to get away from it all.

'I love waking up and hearing the birds calling,' he told me. 'I love this area. I wrote my dissertation on it.' Now he was three things, he told me: 'an English lecturer, a tree surgeon and a scrap-metal dealer'.

I speculated that the scrap metal paid better than the other two.

Pete disappeared but returned ten minutes later with a fresh fruit salad and two forks. We sat on the shingle and munched our way through strawberries and black grapes. The morning was turning out a little unexpected, but I was going with it.

'Do you want to go for a swim?' I suggested.

Pete looked suspiciously at the brown froth washing against the shore.

'Just mud,' I told him and waded out into the shallows in my shorts and vest top.

A large jellyfish gulped its way through the salty water. I had forgotten about the jellyfish of these brackish rivers which could get as large as dinner plates. I couldn't remember if they stung or not; it floated on its way and I walked out further. The water was surprisingly warm, the mud beneath my feet, silky and fine. I jumped in and swam out towards the tower of Kingsnorth. Pete stripped to his boxers and followed.

'I've never done this before,' he said.

'Neither have I,' I told him. I had never willingly jumped into the Medway, put off by the ever-sucking mud and the stories of pollution. 'Just don't drink the water,' I suggested. Roger Deakin had said that, after his swim, the word 'Medway' would forever be associated with 'the taste of khaki water'. Pete looked wary, but jumped in.

Seaweed wrapped around my feet, warty strands of bladderwrack running between my toes. The seal reappeared, skyhopping to check us out. I was hopeful he would be curious enough to approach, but he stayed offshore. The oystercatchers circled overhead and I rotated onto my back, feeling the sun on my face. Early morning sailors stared curiously at us as we floated around in the bay, treading water and sharing stories. I began to get chilly.

'I'm getting out,' I told Pete, but stayed put, suddenly self-conscious of emerging in just a wet vest top and shorts.

Pete sensed my embarrassment. 'I brought a towel,' he said, 'if you want to use it.'

I scurried up the shore and wrapped myself in it.

Pete emerged.

'I'm going to go back to the tent to change,' I said, beginning to shiver in the breeze. Back at the tent I promptly fell asleep in the sun. The island was having the effect that all islands have on me of allowing me to wind down. The same effect that drew others here, it transpired. Leave the mainland and all your worries and stresses behind. I lay on my back with my head propped up on my cycle bags and dozed and woke and watched the birds come and go.

Pete reappeared with a full fry-up. I crunched on crispy bacon.

'So what's your book about?' he asked.

I told him about the caravan on the marshes and the journey and the people I had met so far. He asked if I lived in the caravan on my own. I told him about Connor.

'That life was for me,' I said. 'But it wasn't for him. He tried, he did try, but it just wasn't him.' I stopped myself. 'I don't know why I'm being so generous,' I said, but I did know. The other women were Connor's fault, the wanting different lifestyles was no one's.

'And are you happier now?' Pete asked.

I looked out across the bay. It was not an easy question to answer.

'Yes and no,' I said. 'Yes, that relationship had to end, Yes, being a single woman opens up a world of adventures and friendships that I could not have if I were part of a couple, this weekend being a case in point. Do I want to be single forever?' I said. 'No.'

Pete nodded. He got it. Anyone who had married a big girl from Dartford would get it. Life was full of yes and no.

Pete and the hovercrafters left just before midday and I finally had the island to myself. I decided to explore the fort.

The fort was reached along a dark tunnel cutting through the dense thatch of blackthorn. I emerged into the sunlight and stepped onto a little circular ledge. A plank of sea-washed wood spanned the moat, where once the drawbridge would have been. It was propped at an angle, only just reaching the other side. It had a large hole in one end where a knot had worn away. It looked none too safe. I stepped tentatively onto it. It felt as if it could easily slide from its precarious perch and send me flailing into the brown and brackish water ten feet below. I was grateful for good balance as I scurried across the expanse and onto the concrete apron that surrounded the circular fort.

I climbed through a metal window which would have once contained one of the eleven guns. Inside, it was far more beautiful than it had any need to be. The ceiling vaulted into cool, grey arches, tiny bricks had been hand-laid into curves, flagstone pillars reached down to the dusty floor. It reminded me of a Moorish cistern I had once seen in Morocco where the flooded floor had mirrored the ceiling above. Alcoves in the wall of the fort dropped into dark wells. Here, the ammunition would have been fed from the floor below to the waiting gunners.

Fireplaces surrounded a central courtyard, which was open to the sky and had once been the parade ground. Tantalising hooks and metal pillars showed where long dead men had worked, slept and ate. The forts had been decommissioned before the First World War, having done their job by acting as a deterrent against French invasion, but had been used again in the Second World War as lookout posts. The building was all pinpoints of light, coming from the gun holes. A swing hung from one of the ceiling hooks. Beside it a slogan read, 'free the weed'. The sign was peeling away, a historical reminder of a different decade. The floor below was flooded, but I could see the flying buttresses supporting the upper floor, and numerous enticing entrances led away into darkness.

Away from the fort, I took a walk to the far side of the island where the high ground petered out into the saltings. As the tide receded, the island became a moonscape of craters, ravines and plains of mud covered in filaments of seaweed. I ate my way across the marsh, trying a nibble of golden samphire, vegetable-fresh with a tinge of aniseed, and marsh samphire, which tasted like sweaty day-old socks. Dry seaweed crisped beneath my feet, herring gulls patrolled, searching for the dead and dying pink crabs that littered the tideline. I ventured onto a firm-looking beach only to find myself sinking into the ever-deceptive mud. I was wary and respectful of the mud and beat a hasty retreat.

I walked across a shingle beach through thousands of years of human history thrown up by tide and storm, washed ashore, melted by water, tossed against pier heads and warships: there were flint scrapers, clay pipes, Roman pottery, glass bottles, Victorian china, all tumbled together and mashed amid the sand.

The strandline was no respecter of rarity or antiquity, no respecter of human history at all. I picked up a bird's leg bone, a glass button, a flint with the edges retouched. My friend Jack had commented on this human desire for collecting. How many thousands of beach finds litter shelves and drawers and boxes in people's homes? He wished to declare a Beach Amnesty Day, when we would all anonymously return our pilfered finds and no questions would be asked.

I liked the idea, but lacked the discipline to deny myself all the many delights at my feet. I decided I would take four items only. If I found something, I lost something. I picked up a pipe bowl, I lost a pipe stem, I picked up a glass bottle, I lost the glass button, I picked up a bone so old it had turned to stone, I lost the flint scraper. The previous day, one of the hovercraft crew had arrived with a human leg bone strapped to the front of his boat like a macabre trophy of war. He had picked it up on Deadman's Island, a place where they had buried plague victims. I was slightly horrified that anyone would take a part of a human body as a trophy to display on their mantelpiece.

My stomach began to groan and I made my way back to my camp, looking forward to lunch and enjoying my last few hours of solitude before Phil arrived to pick me up. The tide was a long way out and I felt safe. No one could get out here now, I figured, not with a sea of soft mud all around. But when I returned to the fort I saw two bare-chested men walking along the beach. Somehow they had made it through the ebbing waters of a small creek in their motorboat. I felt suddenly a little vulnerable. I was alone with no way of leaving the island and any rescue squad many miles and hours away.

I ignored the men as they unloaded deckchairs and cooler boxes of beer. They set up a few feet from where I was cooking chilli on a little camp stove and sat there, drinking beer and watching me.

Why? They had a whole bloody island with a fort and a thousand years of human history scattered on the beach; was I really the most interesting thing to see? A girl cooking chilli and reading a book?

We continued to sit feet from each other, not speaking. I didn't want them here and became cat-like, simply pretending they didn't exist. I gazed into the middle distance and tried to think island thoughts, though it was hard when you had an audience. I knew I was acting rude and weird, like some freaky island hermit, but I hadn't come here to make small talk.

Maybe I had been naive to think I would ever find solitude at Darnet Island on a sunny solstice weekend. The island was blindingly obvious and easily reachable for anyone with water transport. It had the enticements of a fort and seals in the bay. It was both a mystery land across the water and tantalisingly close. It was not just Darnet that was occupied. Across the river I could see a small encampment of tents and canoes on Normarsh, an island leased by the RSPB and an important site for breeding birds. Crowds of Mediterranean gulls and terns circled above their nests, disturbed by the campers, while herring gulls took the opportunity to swoop in stealing eggs and chicks. Out on the main river, it was like a four-lane superhighway of sailing boats, motor boats and jet skis. It seemed everyone wanted a part of the estuary for sport and fun or peace and tranquillity, or fishing, exercise, or exploration. All these human desires were crashing together and there was less and less space for the wildlife.

It was hard to know what the solution was. There was talk of a voluntary code of conduct for users of the estuary, raising awareness of the need to stay away from breeding-bird colonies and not terrify the seals, but the worst perpetrators were not the kind to modify their own behaviour for the good of other people, let alone the wildlife. Protected zones and enforced speed limits were suggested, but who would police these? Even if a waterfront police force was in operation, would this be a good thing? With more surveillance and more rules came less privacy, less wilderness, less chance for those who wanted to enjoy the estuary in a harmonious way to do so.

Many of the people who used the estuary did so in ways which were sympathetic to the environment and caused little harm. It was just that increasing numbers of people wanted to race through it on noisy powerful toys, which, as Stephen Turner had said, imposed their presence on everyone and everything else.

One of the two guys strolled over.

'It's great here, isn't it?' he said, smiling down at me.

I stopped the freaky hermit act, unable to keep it up in the face of his jolly enthusiasm and smiled back.

'I wanted to come here after I saw a film on YouTube,' the guy continued. 'You should watch it, *45 Days on the Island of Beauty*. It's by a guy called Dave Wise.'

'I know Dave,' I said. Dave was a local photographer and filmmaker who had camped out on Darnet for several weeks in 2012.

'Wow,' the man said. He called to his mate. 'She knows Dave Wise.'

I did know Dave. It was Dave who had first brought me out to Darnet.

Everyone had warned us not to go, not to canoe across to Darnet on an October day of powering rain and high winds, but we had planned the trip weeks ago and didn't want to back out. Dave and our friend Jack launched the canoe into the grey waves and we struck out into the wind, 'digging in' and making good time across the open water. For the first few hours things were fine. It was exciting to be on an island in the river. But we soon discovered that the gangplank to the fort was missing and we couldn't find a replacement.

The rain didn't let up. After a couple of hours the adventure had begun to wear thin. It was cold and wet and Jack and I padded around the island perimeter while he entertained me with stories and facts from his vast store of knowledge.

'How soon do you think we can leave?' Jack said, as we wandered the beach, searching among the debris for archaeological treasure in the rain.

I laughed, appreciating his honesty. Neither of us was fooling ourselves that we were action heroes.

'We're stuck here till high tide,' I said.

Jack bent down and picked up a flint. He showed it to me, the tiny flakes chipped away, the bulb of percussion where a hammer stone had once struck it from the core. 'Neolithic scraper,' he said and brightened up.

Dave had brought a two-man tent and as the afternoon wore on, the three of us crawled inside with Dave's dog Juno and sat listening to the wind buffeting against the nylon, drinking hot chocolate and eating giant cookies. The tide rose slowly. Jack began to get worried. He had left his car at the Country Park and without it was going to struggle to get home to the village he lived in on the other side of Kent.

'They lock the gates at dusk,' he said. 'My wife and daughter will worry if I'm late and I don't have a mobile to call them.'

'Neither do I,' Dave admitted.

'I do,' I said. I took it out and looked at it. It showed no signal and precious little battery life.

I looked out of the tent flap. The grey afternoon was already fading away.

'It might be another hour before the tide's high enough to get you back to the mainland,' Dave said. 'There is a causeway linking Normarsh Island to the mainland. I've seen it on a map. I could drop you off and you could follow the causeway and get your car before the park locks.' Dave was planning to spend the night camping on Darnet.

We all agreed that this seemed like the best plan and launched the boat again into the shallow waters surrounding the island. Halfway back across the river I felt the boat run aground.

'This is it,' Dave said. 'The end of the causeway.'

'Where?' I wanted to say. All I could see were a few broken stones sinking into the mud, but Jack climbed out and handed his life jacket back.

I stepped out and sank ankle deep in mud. I clambered onto the broken stones, slick with algae and bladderwrack and felt a flutter of fear. 'This is dangerous,' my mind was shouting.

'Come on,' Jack said. 'If my car gets locked in then I'm buggered.'
I unbuckled my life jacket and handed it to Dave.

'Have a safe journey back,' I said.

I took another step and my foot sank into the mud, my boot disappeared and, as I pulled the boot away it was left behind. My sock sunk into more grey ooze and my foot was held fast.

'Jack,' I shouted, 'I'm stuck.' He came back and hauled me out. I pulled my boot out, it was filled with mud and water, but I tugged it back on.

I stood up. All around, the grey mud of the estuary was slipping beneath the incoming tide. Dave was a distant figure paddling back to Darnet, convinced we would be ok. When Dave had said a causeway, I had imagined a solid embankment well above high tide, but this was little more than a broken line of stones

'Come on,' Jack said. He shot off, transformed into a mountain goat, along the broken causeway. I ran along after him in panic, jumping gaps where the ancient track had long washed away, terrified I would break an ankle and become stuck as the tide rose. I stumbled and floundered across the seaweed. Twice more my boots got stuck and I had to yank myself free from the mud which fought to suck me down and hold me fast in its tight clawry grip.

Finally, we could see the mainland just up ahead.

'Almost there,' Jack shouted. The path bent away to the left. Jack reached it first. 'Shit, shit,' I heard him say. I rounded a corner and was faced with a wide channel of water, pouring through a gap between where I was standing and the mainland. The causeway had been cut. Whatever map Dave had seen it on had not been drawn in this century.

It was growing dark, I was cold and wet and covered in mud. We were standing on a little bit of marshland inches high with the tide rushing in.

'We can swim,' Jack said. 'It's not deep.'

'NO,' I said, suddenly finding my voice. Nothing on God's earth was going to make me step into that grey churning water.

'Ok,' Jack said. 'Maybe not.'

I fished in my pocket and thanked my stars that, despite being covered in mud, my mobile still showed a little battery life and a signal. I didn't hesitate, I knew there was only one way out of this. I phoned 999.

'What service do you want?' the clipped voice at the other end of the phone asked.

'A lifeboat, I think,' I told her, and explained our predicament.

'What is your position?' the woman asked.

I looked around. Darkness was falling, lights glinted on the water pouring through the channel, but I could see nothing on land that would give me any idea of where I was. I had become wildly disoriented in my flight along the causeway, and the Medway was riddled with islands. We could have been just about anywhere.

'Where are we?' I asked Jack.

'Maybe near Horrid Hill,' he said. 'It's hard to tell.'

'We don't know,' I told the woman. 'We ran along a track from Normarsh and now we're somewhere at the end of it.'

I spotted a signpost lodged into the mud and walked towards it. 'Private Property,' it read, 'No Unauthorised Shooting'.

'We're standing by a white sign,' I told the operator. 'We'll stay here and wait.'

I figured, if the worst came, then we could at least cling to the sign and not get washed away. Strangely, this thought didn't scare me. I had gone into that state of calm I always experience in a crisis, when I just become supremely practical.

'We're sending a boat now,' the woman said. 'Sit tight.'

We waited. Widgeon flashed overhead, whistling to each other in the darkness and the lights of the power station began to shine.

'We could walk around, see if we can find another way off,' Jack said.

'No,' I said. 'We'd better stay by the sign. It's the only marker. At least it might show up if they shine a light on it.' Typically, I had now become terribly sensible, probably as a reaction to doing something so foolish. 'Let's have a cup of tea,' I said. 'We might as well enjoy the experience.'

Jack got out his flask and we drank mint tea and waited.

'There are so many islands in the river,' he said.

It got darker. Soon I could see nothing, only hear the water lapping beneath our little perch. My confidence began to waiver.

Suddenly, flashlights appeared on shore. A loud hailer boomed out across the river.

'This is the police. Are you there? Show a light if you are there.'

I flashed the light on my mobile phone.

'Don't worry, the coastguard are on their way,' the disembodied voice shouted.

A flare shot into the night sky and burst overhead and there we were, standing on our island with our thermos and little white sign. I never felt more of a fool. On shore a whole gang of police officers waited, presumably backed up by frogmen preparing to search the river for our bodies.

'I'm so sorry,' I shouted out, 'to cause all this fuss.'

Soon boats began appearing from all over the river. First a party of canoeists who, surreally, had been floating around the river in the pitch black, came across.

'We saw the flare,' they shouted at us from offshore. 'We've come to rescue you.'

I thanked them, apologising endlessly, but before they could mount a rescue mission, the coastguard from Sheerness arrived, backed up by a small lifeboat.

'I'm so sorry, I'm so sorry,' I started in again, feeling like a prize idiot for causing all these people to be dragged away from their comfy evening to rescue me.

'There's no way to get on shore,' the lifeboat called. 'We'll wade out to you.'

A man and woman clad in bright-yellow rescue suits jumped into the icy waters and waded out to us and then half carried me to the boat. Once on board the rib, we were wrapped in blankets and zoomed to shore.

Back in Gillingham Marina, the whole rescue party was there, police, lifeboat crew, coastguard, an army of people. They all surrounded our bedraggled forms and took details, name, address and just what were we doing out on Copperhouse Marsh in the dark. I felt weak with exhaustion and embarrassment and had no idea how I was to get back home until one of the lifeboat crew took pity and offered us a lift.

The next day, I cycled back through the Country Park to meet Jack. In the sunshine things seemed different.

'We would have been fine,' he said. 'The tide wouldn't have got that high.' Despite his assurance, he handed me a present. 'To say thanks,' he mumbled. The card read. 'For having a mobile phone when it counted.' Inside was a book called *River* by Dave Wise; I appreciated the irony.

I cycled along the river and found Copperhouse Island, a low-lying piece of saltmarsh. I looked at the white sign from the safety of the shore. I didn't share Jack's confidence that we would have been fine. The coastguard had told me that the whole island would have been under water a few hours after we had been rescued. The staff at the Country Park blamed Dave.

'He was in charge. He was responsible,' they said. I didn't agree. I hadn't felt right about the plan to get back along the causeway but hadn't spoken up, not wanting to look soft and lose face in front of the men. 'It's no good Carol,' I told myself. 'It's about time you took some responsibility for yourself.'

Dave and I had gone out again on the estuary; these were happier trips, during which we had enjoyed calm bays and inquisitive seals. Dave loved the estuary, although, as I spoke to the lads who had been inspired by his film, I wondered if this was the legacy he had wanted to leave behind. Boys coming to the island with motorboats and beer, believing that the estuary should be a place of free access for all? Campers pitching up on fragile bird-nesting colonies and no one being able to stop them?

Soon after my solstice trip to Darnet, I caught up with Dave. I hadn't seen him in several years. He had been travelling, met a Canadian girl and got married. As he opened the door I thought he looked browner, slimmer; as I talked to him, I felt that the change in him was more than skin deep. Dave had always been a man with an edge, an outspoken critic of a multitude of authorities, a man likely to get embroiled in an argument he couldn't win, but something had changed. We spent some time sitting in his sister's garden watching the koi carp swim round the pool. He showed me how they like to be stroked. Fish tickling, we got onto the subject of Darnet Island and Dave's film.

'When my relationship with my girlfriend broke up I had nowhere to live,' he said candidly. 'So I packed camping equipment into the canoe and came to Darnet. Many of the islands in the estuary look inhospitable, but Darnet has the fort and the sloping beach, it looked welcoming. I thought I could either see the break-up as a disaster or an opportunity to spend some time by myself and learn something.'

'But six weeks on Darnet,' I said. 'Didn't you get bored?'

'I wasn't the least bit bored. I could spend hours just watching the tide come in and with each tide the landscape changed. Things would happen at the same time every day, the seal would come by in the morning and just stare at the island, a whitethroat would sing in the scrub. I could tell the time by watching the trains running on the mainland.'

I'm aware how his words echo those of Stephen Turner. Both men hadn't tried to enforce their will on the island; instead, they had tuned into a different pace of life.

'My days soon settled into a routine,' Dave said swirling his hand in the garden pond. 'I'd get up, do some exercise, have breakfast, sit and read, walk to the end of the island, spend time thinking about and cooking my dinner.'

The island for both men had provided somewhere they could escape, not only from the outside world, but maybe in some ways from themselves, as well. It was a place where you could let the public image drop and not have to live up to anyone's expectations. For Dave the island had also been a test to his ego.

Dave had taken his dog Juno to the island, but one day, following a thunderstorm, he found the dog missing. Dave's film documents his increased agitation as he searches the island and slowly realises that his dog must have swum away.

I had spent enough time with Dave's dog to appreciate the desperation of this act. Juno was terrified of water. As a puppy she had come with Dave and me across to Darnet, cowering in the boat. On later trips, she would run back and forth along the canoe, practically standing on my head as I tried to paddle.

For hours, Dave thought that Juno must be dead; then he received a call from his ex. Scared by the thunder, the dog had swum the river and been picked up by staff at the Riverside Country Park, which lay along the shoreline. Dave was not on good terms with the Country Park staff, who had opposed his plans to stay on the island, thinking him reckless, and he struggled not only with the loss of his companion but also with the thought of his ex and the park staff laughing at him. In the past, Dave would have fought back against this ridicule; on the island he could do nothing.

'Darnet helps you let go of things,' he acknowledged.

'After Juno left,' Dave said, 'I thought I would really struggle to be on my own, but it was actually company that caused me the most concern. Friends would turn up at weekends and we would sit by the campfire drinking. Before they came I would feel one way and after they left I would feel different. The island would feel different. When I was drinking I didn't like the way the island became just a backdrop for our pleasure, but when I was alone I was part of the island, not superior to it, just a part of it. It wasn't just there for my benefit.'

This was a different Dave to the one I used to know. On one of our previous trips we had canoed past the bird reserve of Burntwick Island. The guys had wanted to get photos and in order to do so had canoed close to the shore. It was the height of the breeding season and the ground-nesting terns and gulls had risen into the air, leaving their nests unprotected. I had felt uncomfortable with this and said so. It was as if the need for a photograph was more important than the lives of the eggs and the chicks that were now easy targets for gulls. The Dave fish-tickling in the garden I don't believe would have acted in the same way.

I asked him about his film, which had 33,000 hits on You Tube. I told him about the guys I had met. 'Do you feel some responsibility for the people who go to the island inspired by your film?' I asked him.

'It's difficult,' he said, 'if you love something. You know you should ignore it, never talk about it, because if you do you will kill it. I am not a strong enough person not to use this place I love for inspiration for my photographs and films. I think the best you can do is to give a true account. You can't control what someone else wants to use the place for.'

Was this the solution – not talk about the estuary and hope no one came? Or was it better to show people the beauty, explain its fragility and encourage people to care? Dave's was a dilemma that many writers and artists had faced about landscapes they loved. Maybe with more people using the estuary in a harmonious way, it would be easier to regulate the behaviour of those who didn't.

Back on Darnet, Dave's fans asked me to join them.

'Thanks, but no,' I said.

Instead, I lay in the sun and watched the tide recede further. Mediterranean gulls yelped their catcalls overhead, a plane left contrails in the sky, I could hear the distant slap of water against broken barges. I lay on my back reading. The afternoon was burning hot and I slapped on suntan cream, a hat and long sleeves, being the type who will burn to a crisp in minutes. I was being intensely lazy. It was delightful.

The island had proved to be therapy for Dave as well.

'For me, the stay on the island helped me process the break-up of my relationship,' he had told me before I left. 'I could see that if I didn't do something I could go down the road of getting depressed and drinking in order to blot out my thoughts, but Darnet made me confront my fears of where I was going to live and where my life would go from here.'

My rescue from the estuary by the lifeboat had a similar effect on me. The day before my first trip to Darnet with Dave, I had visited the houseboat office to talk through the possibilities of buying a boat. The day after my rescue, I began looking into buying a house.

I reached for safety and security like never before. This latest trip to the island had also helped galvanise my thoughts. Dave Wise had said it best: 'Darnet made me feel, I can do this, I can be on my own, there is no reason to fear. It made me realise how good life can be.'

A distant buzz of an engine roused me. Phil had arrived on the hovercraft. Dave's admirers sat up in excitement as this tip-top boy's toy made its way towards them.

'My chariot,' I called out.

Phil dismounted. 'Do you want to go straight back?' he said. 'Or would you like a tour?'

I had always wanted to see the fabled submarines nestled in the marvellously named Humble Bee Creek and told him so.

Soon I was flying across the water away from the envious boys on shore. Seagulls reluctantly scurried out of our way. On the other side of the island we encountered two seals hauled out on a mudflat. They writhered into the water in a ripple of belly fat and splashed out of sight. Salt spray brushed my skin, a welcome relief from the intense heat on land, bass leapt from the water like flying fish. We flew on the aerial quad bike across the glistening mudflats, leaning into the curves, cutting sideways along the edge where the tide meets the water. Nowhere was inaccessible with the hovercraft.

Seeing what the hovercraft was capable of made me all the more sure that open access couldn't be a good thing. Phil said the hovercraft didn't disturb the wildlife but, if I needed ear defenders on to sit in it, I couldn't see how the noise wouldn't shatter the afternoon peace for a seal. Although some of the hovercraft owners would undoubtedly act responsibly, others wouldn't, and with this machine, you could access all the islands of the estuary even at low tide. The estuary was now everyone's playground and I couldn't see how that could co-exist with the wildlife. Surely, there had to be 'No Play' zones.

Within seconds, we reached places that I had long wished to explore. The pier of Kingsnorth Power Station, snapped and broken by the hammer blow of a storm, looked as I imagined Southend Pier would look after a nuclear winter. We stopped to view the wreckage of two German submarines, broken up for scrap after the war. Twisted metal lay scattered across the estuary, hoops of iron, like strange corals rising up and dressed with seaweed. A third submarine was still largely intact. It lay on its side with its ribs exposed like a beached whale. The U-boats had been sold by the defeated Germans after the war and dismantled in the estuary. The metal, Phil told me, had been used to make razor blades; a fine bit of propaganda – the German war machines reduced to shaving the faces of British officers.

I felt slightly disappointed at finally reaching Humble Bee Creek and later realised that it was for the same reason that I didn't want takeaway deliveries on Darnet. I wanted to earn this fabled place. I wanted to struggle with the tides. I wanted to exert effort to reach it, but with the hovercraft it was all too easy. If you could get there in seconds it somehow reduced its value. Like so many things in life, easy wasn't always better. The things of real value had to be earned and I hadn't earned Humble Bee Creek. The hovercraft was undoubtedly a clever bit of kit, but overall I think I preferred the quiet dip of a canoe paddle.

We headed back to the mainland, nipping crossways through the sailing traffic, passing a sailboat which had misjudged the water depth and receding tide and become stranded in the mud. The woman on board looked supremely unbothered. She was birdwatching with a small pair of binoculars and sipping a glass of wine.

Back on land, I helped Phil winch the hovercraft onto a trailer, shook his powerful hand and reattached all my bags to my bike.

I made my way past the crowds at Gillingham Strand looking windblown and feeling sticky with the combination of salt spray and suntan cream. It was a beautiful Sunday afternoon; women with stay-press hair and massive sunglasses were out strolling in maxi dresses on the arms of men with bulging biceps in tight white t-shirts. I tried not to care about the open-mouthed stares my appearance excited. After all, I was the girl who had just arrived on shore with a chunky brown man on the back of a tricked-up hovercraft.

The bike was badly loaded, the bags repeatedly trying to escape off one side. I was too hot and tired to bother to re-tie them and instead stopped to haul them upright at intervals. The air was fragranced with the smell of the first blooms of buddleia.

I stopped in the shade of some black poplars opposite Copperhouse Marsh. The signpost that I had planned to cling to when the tide rose had been swept away. Now there was nothing to hold onto. It was a sunny afternoon, not a winter evening, and the island should have looked benign, but it didn't, it looked... flat, not an island, just a salting, the kind of place lost at high tide. I never could look at it without being thankful that I had been rescued and hadn't had to experience what it was like to hold onto a metal post in the dark as the cold water swirled around.

NINE

Rainham – Upchurch – Lower Halstow – Iwade

I T WAS MID-AUGUST by the time I set out again, leaving behind
my two-bedroom terraced cottage that I had bought four years
ago. The fact was that after years of fighting a mortgage, as if
getting one would mean I would cease to exist, I had slipped into
the adult world of house ownership quite easily. Slipped into it!
Who am I kidding? I had run towards it with arms open. For years I
thought that 'being settled' would signal the end of any excitement
in my life. I had longed for change, for something to come along
and shake things up and hadn't I got what I wanted? In two weeks
at the end of 2008, my life had become anything but settled. I had
been made redundant from the RSPB and found myself single at
the age of thirty-six. I moved from the farmhouse into a 'freezing-
cold flat with damp on the walls' as The Jam had once sung. Not
only that, but the back door of my freezing-cold flat overlooked a
pub car park where the patrons took great delight in hurling abuse
and occasionally mud and beer cans at me when I emerged.

The experience of being rescued from Copperhouse Marsh had
been the final straw. I had returned to my flat after my rescue
covered in mud, flopping up the outside stairs, ignoring the drunken
crowd in the beer garden and had stripped off in the icy bathroom.
I had phoned my parents, sounding normal, telling them I'd had
a nice time, not wanting to worry them with the truth, and then

I sat, on my own, feeling sick and cold with no one to talk to or make me a cup of tea. I didn't want this. Life had just become too unstable, I had no firm footing, and if I continued to look at buying houseboats, or chalets I never would. I wanted the ground to stop moving underneath me. I wanted solidity, I wanted settled.

So I bought the house using all the money I had saved up while living in the caravan. Connor had spent his on new computers and film cameras and cars, but mine had been packed into high-interest bank accounts. I learned a lesson, which many a cast-aside woman has learned over the years: when all else falls away, money can help. It wasn't a vast sum, but enough to put down a deposit on a modest house and become a property owner. I was proud of myself, I was proud of the house and I was surprised at feeling this way. Owning the house didn't make me feel suffocated. It made me feel strong and independent and safe. Unless I royally screwed up, I owned this and no one could step in and rip it out from underneath me.

My house is situated just a short walk from the Medway River. A few doors down, the housing gives way to scrublands and pony paddocks, places with vulnerability written all over them. I wait nervously for the day the scrub is ripped up and a sign appears saying, 'Coming soon, Hawthorn Towers'. But at the moment my road still ends in a rural world where little owls sit on lampposts searching for beetles and hedgehogs snuffle for snails.

I set off past the scrub and into pear orchards. This was edge-of-town countryside: tatty hedgerows, hung with plastic bags, overgrown footpaths full of dog poo, farmland hanging on alongside fly-tipping. The orchard gave way to an industrial site. St John's wort and buddleia sprouted from cracked pavements as nature reclaimed the tarmac.

At the end of the road I passed a yard full of ancient trucks, their rusting cabs proudly displaying the words FODEN in a long-lost font. An enamelled Union Jack, its white stripes mildewed, its colours blistered by years of sun exposure, was secured to each truck's flank.

A man and a little girl were busy tending the trucks. I asked if I could take a photo.

'Are you interested in Fodens?' the man asked hopefully. I pleaded ignorance. He told me the ages of the trucks ranging through the sixties and seventies.

'It's a British make,' he said. 'The best. I'm doing them up for shows.'

His granddaughter, Nancy, aged six, was his budding mechanic.

'She holds the grease gun and finds the punctures,' the man explained. Nancy moved around the trucks in a professional manner wearing wellies and pink rubber gloves.

'I have my own truck,' she told me proudly. 'My granddad made it for me to ride on.'

I left them to their morning and followed the footpath up an ivy-covered hillside.

I emerged back onto a road full of blind bends and prickly hedgerows, which I had to leap into to avoid rushing cars. Between gaps in the traffic I felt myself slowing down, my mind unwinding to the speed of walking. The traffic careered past at a frantic pace, but even if I stormed up the road with the kind of speed I reserved for crossing Victoria Station in rush hour, I would still be relatively slow. My mind accepted it. I would cover maybe ten miles all day and there was no need to stress about it. I said hello to a man working in his allotment, picking runner beans for his Sunday lunch. I was back in the season, back in the rhythm of nature.

A man and his girlfriend cycled past. He bellowed instructions at her: 'Pedal, pedal, use the momentum.'

The woman's legs pumped frantically. I experienced that occasional rush of happiness I got at *not* being in a relationship. I love men. In the last few years men had mainly been excellent to me. They were my mates and, yes, sometimes more, but I didn't feel inclined to swap that for a Sunday morning bound to a man who felt he could shout instructions at me about something I could do perfectly well without his assistance.

The Yes and No of Pete's question had been swirling in my head since we had met. I had spent the spring delighting in the company of a lovely but unobtainable man. This was a story I knew well and could deal with, but in the last few weeks a long-term friend had declared his feelings for me and had totally sent my head into a spin. I had thought I was ready to put the past behind me, but this offer had made it rear up in front of me once again; fears of losing myself, of being told that what I was and what I wanted was all wrong, had resurfaced. I was happy, I was enjoying life and suddenly I wasn't at all sure that I wanted to exchange my single status for the mixed bag of a relationship. If Pete had asked me his question now I would have still said 'Yes and No'. Yes, I was happy, No, I wasn't ready.

I mentally elbowed this issue out of the front of my mind. I had two days of walking ahead, plenty of time for it to swill back and forth across my thoughts as background noise without actively thinking about it. I concentrated instead on climbing a steep hill along with a migrant hawker dragonfly who made it look so much easier.

The spire of St Mary the Virgin Church came into view, situated at the crossroads of Upchurch village. The double spire looked as if one peak had got washed out of the heavens and landed on the top of the other. The top one sat a little off-centre making me want to give it a knock and set it straight. The strange spire was supposedly used as a navigational aid for shipping out on the river, fitting for a church which once had Sir Francis Drake's father for its vicar.

As I entered the church, the clock chimed the quarter hour. I walked down the side aisle passing a line of chalk carvings of green men with petalled flowers growing from their mouths and bat-eared demons looking cheeky and mischievous with their tongues sticking out. I picked up a leaflet and a book called *The Quiet Life* by Ray Ashford from a stand with a sign telling me the books were free to take.

The quiet of the church descended upon me – that particular shadowy hush only to be found amid the white-washed walls and pews of a village church. There was the feeling of an unseen presence, not so much that of God, but of the many ordinary people who had sat and prayed and pondered there. I added my thoughts to this accumulation of human cares palpable in the air. Life had become way too chaotic lately. I was working long hours in my job and packing my weekends with freelance work just to make ends meet. Requests from friends and family to see me had begun to feel like demands, one more thing To Do, and this was all wrong. I was getting to that tipping point. These two days of walking had come at just the right time. For two days I was 'out of contact', unable to do 'just this one thing' for anyone. I had slipped off the face of my life, escaped to the estuary and couldn't be found.

A family entered and I headed out of the door as the rain began to fall. Outside, I struggled into my waterproof trousers and walked through pony paddocks and then along a dark tunnel of vegetation hung with plums. I marched across a football pitch in heavy rain, my broken and leaking boots giving little protection. By the time I reached the other side I was squelching along with damp socks, but blue skies were opening up promisingly behind me. Clouds touched the top of Kingsnorth Power Station, a hulked barge stood on the muted horizon like a dash in a long sentence and swallows skimmed the field. I began to sweat inside the waterproofs and I unpeeled myself, watched by the golf ball eye of Motney Sewage works.

Emerging at Ham Green, I walked beneath an avenue of spreading oak trees, their hands stretching to clutch fingers across the road. Plums were everywhere; bullaces, damsons, tight yellow balls of sweetness, bloomy and downy, black and juicy. I made up songs about them. I wanted to gorge myself but feared the consequences. Dragonflies hawked in the growing warmth of the air, goldfinches twittered overhead and the chatter of orchard workers rose from behind a poplar hedge. Boys and girls with fizzing Eastern European accents teased and flirted their way back to lunch, as fruit pickers of all nationalities had always done.

Out of the orchards I walked along Shoregate Lane, picking blackberries along the way and being delighted or disgusted in turn, depending on whether the berry of choice was watery sweet or sharp-eyed and poisonous on the tongue. It was slow going, this walking and eating, but eventually, I turned down an alleyway and emerged onto the expanse of the estuary.

I was back in the world of mud and broken pier heads, of tussock grass and gulls. The ark of the Sheppey Bridge rose from the flatness into a limitless sky. The grass buzzed with the radio static of cricket communication.

I passed the houseboats of Twinney Wharf. A marmalade cat lay at the foot of a pot-bellied stove but no human life stirred. I didn't hang around. The sky had become slate-grey and marbled with hail. Rain was streaking down across the river. I quickened my pace. Colour-saturated birdsfoot trefoil coated the path, glowing against the gathering gloom. Two Red Arrows circled above through the storm clouds on their way to a weekend air show. The cranes of Thamesport in Essex became blotted by the rain sweeping across the river. The breeze picked up; the sheeting of the boats, lying on the mud at Lower Halstow, clanged like bells foretelling the coming storm. Dogs were barking, the swallows had stopped flying, the stems of dried hogweed rattled in the wind.

As I passed the *Edith May* barge, the storm caught me, clattering down in a deluge. There was no time to get into the waterproofs again. Within seconds I was soaked. I jogged to the door of the Three Tuns pub and burst into the Sunday lunchtime crowd, getting startled looks.

I am never aware of how odd I must look until I am surrounded by what passes for normal. There I was with harlequin trousers, one half dark and soaked by rain, the other half miraculously dry. I was wearing an oversized hat to keep the sun off my head, big boots and a bag overflowing with head torches and chocolate bars and bits of clay pot I'd picked up from farmers' fields. My hair was ridiculously windswept and my face quite possibly streaked with blackberries. I elbowed my way to the bar beside men with rolled-up shirt sleeves, showing off their tanned biceps, and women perched on wedge sandals. These people were polished and shiny and urban and I was a creature from the hedgerow dropped in among them. I ordered a pint and a burger and spied a party vacating a squashy couch in the corner. The pub was at standing room only; I dived into the seat and, strangely, no one else came to join me, except the pub cat who, clearly recognising another feral being, sat on my lap drying my jeans.

I lurched from the pub sometime later feeling a little drunk and swayed down the road and onto a footpath, once again sandwiched between fences and brambles. It was 3.30pm; the beer had got to me. Outside Funton Brickworks I parked myself in the lea of an oak tree and fell asleep, my hat pulled down over my eyes, a bag of fruit and nut mix propped on my stomach. I woke to a view of the Swale, a blue streak across the desert of Chetney Marshes, where I was to walk the next day.

Back on the trail, I passed the brickworks; one large chimney dominated the yard with a fringe of fancy bricks near the summit. Until recently, Funton had produced bricks with names like Old Chelsea Yellow and Orchard Mixture, using the earth dug from the surrounding fields. The bricks were used to restore Georgian buildings and the company had been busy with restoration projects all over London. Now the works looked derelict, warehouse roofs ripped and windows broken.

It was getting to that time of day when the walking got hard. I headed through more plum orchards and lost my way. I was forced to backtrack. I stumbled about in a stubble field, tripping over clumps of grass because I was tired. The modern estates of Iwade appeared on the horizon, looking as if they'd been dropped from the sky into the marshes. I turned right towards the village and began to put on my public face. I was here to dig out the story of the Cobham hermit.

I had first heard about the Cobham hermit through a local history website. 'Man who lived in the woods,' the title said. It struck me that every community has a 'man that lives in the woods'. Growing up in Essex, we had a local tramp who would hang around outside the baker's each morning, hoping someone would buy him a pasty and a coffee. He had long hair and a beard and would stand there talking to himself. He hadn't always been that way. There were rumours that he had been a doctor, that his wife had left him and he had fallen down the rungs of the ladder. We can all fall down this ladder, when life whomps us with a series of tough blows. If you're lucky, you catch a rung on the way down or someone grabs you and stops you falling further, or something in you enables you to climb back up from the bottom. My childhood Man in the Woods had fallen and found no safety net. He lived rough on a ridge overlooking a disused Second World War airfield.

The stories I read as a child were full of these figures. There was Tammylan in *The Children of Cherry Tree Farm* by Enid Blyton, a man who lives in a cave, a kind of 1930s version of St Francis of Assisi, taming the wildlife. Smokoe Joe is another figure in the marvellous *Brendon Chase* by BB, a charcoal burner living deep in a woodland, not wanting to bother or be bothered by the world. The children in both these books are drawn to seek out these characters and, frankly, disturb their peace.

I, too, wanted to track down the 'Man Who Lives in the Woods'. I would lie in bed at night thinking about him living under the trees, with just the noise of the leaves and animals. As a child who hated school and being indoors and spent most of her time sitting up an apple tree in the garden reading nature books, this, to me, seemed the perfect life. If a careers advisor had popped up at that moment in my youth and asked me what I wanted to do when I was older, I may well have told them I wanted to be a man (yes probably a man as, at that age, being a girl seemed such a drag) who lived in the woods.

Finally, I plucked up the courage to pay him a visit. Instead of going to school, I headed for the airfield one Tuesday morning and, fearful of being caught by either a teacher or a pervert, scurried towards the woods. The place where he lived was not much of a woodland, more a remnant of oak trees and scant bluebells overlooking the River Ingrebourne, a silty, rat-infested river, full of shopping trolleys. But this to me, at eleven years old, was the wilds. In a part of the woods, tucked away from marauding youths, I spotted his camp – a tent, a sleeping bag and cooking pots hidden in a thicket. However, I couldn't find the courage to approach, warned off by stories that 'he might be dangerous,' but more because of the crippling shyness I suffered at that age. I backed away, angry at myself. I wanted to be the kind of child I read about in books; instead, my life seemed full of chances not taken. My chance of meeting this man was gone and I was back in school by first break.

Our culture, our stories are littered with Men of the Woods. What is our fascination with them? Is it a feeling of 'there for the grace of God?' Partly, I guess, but maybe it is also admiration for their self-sufficiency and possibly just a little bit of envy. Not the envy of an eleven-year-old girl wanting to live among the hedgehogs, but the adult envy of not having any responsibilities. What is it like to be someone with no ties? Whose life does not belong to the bank and the boss, or the wife and kids, but wholly to themselves?

There have always been people who consciously choose this lifestyle, such as Emma Orbach, an Oxford graduate who left her family at the beginning of this century and took to the woods, built a hut out of mud and lived without water or electricity, claiming she wanted to 'help people come back to a sense of balance with nature'. Or David Glasheen, the Australian businessman, who lost ten million dollars in a stock market crash and went to live on a tiny island with only his dog for company. 'On the island,' he said, 'I started to value what is really important: trust, honesty, respect.'

But my favourite story has to be that of the original drop out: Diogenes, a former banker, who lived in Greece in 400BC. In a tale which still has resonance today, he became embroiled in a banking scandal, was exiled from the city and lost all his material possessions. However, unlike many a modern banker, he made a virtue of his poverty. He took to living in a clay wine jar and used his simple lifestyle to demonstrate that wisdom and happiness belong to the man who is self-sufficient of society.

Maybe occasionally we all feel like these people, that modern life pressurises us into valuing all the wrong things. We spend our money on acquiring a lifestyle we have to work hard to maintain. I do it myself, fleetingly worrying that my bathroom taps are not contemporary enough, that my car, which functions perfectly well, does not give out the right image. TV bombards us with property programmes, fashion shows, even gardening programmes, which make us feel inadequate and that we must buy more in order to fix ourselves. We know it's a farce, a ridiculous game which we can't possibly win, but still we feel powerless to resist the urge to play.

Maybe these people fascinate us because they have stepped out of the game entirely; they have chosen not to play and therefore have a freedom we don't.

Andre, the hermit, had certainly stepped out of the game. News clippings told a familiar tale: 'The hermit of Cobham Woods lost his twelve-year battle to stay in his woodland home.' Even these bare facts told a story I could relate to. Another person who had tried to keep his head down and caused no one any harm had been caught by the authorities whose rules allowed no options to opt out. I wanted to find out more. In the local studies centre I scanned microfilm of newspapers from the Eighties, full of bad fashion and even worse moustaches. There I followed Andre's battle until my eyes were raw.

Andre Van Beest had come to Cobham Woods sometime in the Seventies, it seemed. He had bought a one-acre plot of the type that Lord Darnley, the owner of the woods, had been dishing out for years. In Lena Kennedy's book, *Away to the Woods,* she talks about the ex-servicemen living 'in their own small world, without the necessities of modern life. No electric, no mains water, a bucket for the loo. They built their shack and lived on the produce of their land.'

Maybe Andre had heard these stories, maybe he bought his plot from one of these ex-servicemen. Either way, he came to the woods and built his shack and kept chickens and goats to provide fresh eggs and milk. It appears that everyone knew about Andre, but turned a blind eye until the mid-Eighties, when some New Age travellers moved into the woods. The council set about evicting this group and obviously felt obliged to evict Andre, too.

Andre put up a good battle. He found a solicitor to fight his case, had his story broadcast on local news and went to the high court where a judge finally ruled that Andre's shed was in contravention of planning rules and should be demolished. In July 1987, he was served with an eviction notice giving him the standard twenty-eight days to leave his home and find a new one. He didn't leave. Where was he supposed to go? The council suggested he go into bed and breakfast accommodation and his animals would be taken by the

RSPCA, but still they didn't move in. 'The council will do what it sees fit when it sees fit,' one spokesman said when questioned by the local newspaper.

Finally, in early August the bulldozers moved in and Andre's home was flattened. For a while he camped rough in the woods and vowed he wouldn't leave, but then David and Julie Benfield from Iwade stepped in. They had seen his story on television and were angered at the heavy-handed approach of the council. Determined to allow Andre the option of keeping his independence, they offered to let him live in a caravan on the land that they rented at Chetney Marshes.

'Officialdom seems to take such great pains to squash one man's spirit,' the landowner, Ted Edwards said.

Here the story in the newspapers stopped. I wasn't satisfied; it was like following a great drama which had ended at a cliff-hanger and I wanted to know what happened next. It seemed like a happy ending. After all, Andre had found a new home, but I feared what the outcome of this move had been. I knew what it was like to suddenly find yourself in the open landscape of the marshes. It wasn't a comfortable place to live. I worried that he would have found it hard, to be cast out under those endless skies after living under the canopy of the woods for so long. I wanted to know how the story turned out.

A chance encounter with a parish councillor from Iwade led me to people who had known Andre after he left the woods. Once I reached the village, I phoned Sally-Anne Heathfield and she drove down to meet me. Sally-Anne had known Andre when she was a little girl and had become fascinated by the mystery figure living on the edge of town.

'I was curious about him,' she said as I settled myself in her car and asked her how she met him. 'You would see him walking into town. Some of the kids would be horrible to him, throw insults at him, call him a smelly old tramp, but I worried about him and his animals. I wanted to know if he was all right.'

So, without her mother's knowledge, she jumped on her bike one day and cycled out to see him.

'I'd bring cut-price biscuits and bread for the animals,' she told me. 'We had to say it was for the animals, as he would never have taken anything himself.'

I could still see this little girl in Sally-Anne, a braver little girl than I had been. Sally-Anne would not have hidden on the edge of the woodland, too scared to approach the camp, she would have breezed straight in full of questions. She is one of those people who is immediately your friend. She had agreed to drive me out to Andre's old home on the outskirts of the village and on the way she told me about her new job and the problems with her mother-in-law's health as if she'd known me forever. We passed a man cycling back into town.

'Uncle Nigel!' She stopped the car and called him back. 'You knew Andre,' she said. 'Can you follow us down to his cabin and tell this woman about him?' Nigel was ready to oblige and turned his bike round and pedalled back the way he'd just come, into a headwind.

It was another example of how welcoming and giving I had found people on this trip. It had surprised me: the basic goodness of people to a stranger and their willingness to give me their time. Not just their time, but their stories, their food, even offering me their homes to stay in. It made me feel that no matter what pressures are put on us from outside to turn us into selfish and money-oriented machines, in some people at least, the basic goodness of humanity can't be squashed down.

Sally-Anne and I, with Nigel tailing us, travelled down Raspberry Lane and then off along a side track which bordered a travellers' site. We arrived amid old broken-down concrete dwellings once used as an anti-aircraft gun site during the Second World War. A dilapidated static caravan stood at the end of the track surrounded by a pool of water with a magnificent view across Chetney Marshes.

'I think that's it,' Sally-Anne said. 'Uncle Nigel, is that Andre's caravan? I haven't been down here since he left,' she explained. 'He just vanished one day and we never knew where he'd gone. I think he had a son; maybe he'd taken him somewhere.'

I could see the intrepid little girl that cycled out to find out about Andre re-emerge. In ballet pumps and leggings, Sally-Anne clambered over rubble to look into the window of the caravan.

'I can see his pots,' she shouted, teetering on a boulder and peering in the windows. 'His stuff is still in here,' she cried, as if she could reach back and touch the past and conjure this man up again from the jumble of personal items strewn across the floor.

Nigel hung back.

'Maybe we can force the door,' Sally-Anne said, eyeing the blocked-up doorway.

'I wouldn't,' Nigel said.

I'm pretty sure if she had been here on her own, Sally-Anne would have been crowbarring the door open and taking back a souvenir.

'When were you last out here?' I asked Nigel.

'I came to shoot Andre's goat,' he said. 'I would see Andre walking into the village every day. He stood out, as he always wore a pair of wellingtons and a woolly hat, like Compo from *Last of the Summer Wine*. I would see him carrying these really heavy paraffin canisters along the road. I was curious about him and offered him a lift, but he was very independent and wouldn't accept any help. I got talking to him. He knew I was a shepherd at that time, so he came to me one day and asked me to put down this big old billy goat he had; it had something wrong with it and had gone crazy. He had lost a lot of his animals when he left the woods. They had taken them away from him, but he still had some out here.'

'He was devastated when he had to leave Cobham Woods,' Sally-Anne said. 'He used to tell me he was following a long tradition, that there had always been a hermit in Cobham Woods.'

He may well have been right. Although the original hermits were often people who sought isolation by withdrawing from what they saw as a corrupt world, it later became fashionable for rich men to have a hermit in the back garden. Landscape designers began to include plans for picturesque hermitages among the shrubbery and suitably scruffy individuals were employed to live in them and come out at dinner parties to do a spot of preaching for the guests. Maybe Andre was indeed following in the footsteps of some seventeenth-century Cobham hermit.

I asked Sally-Anne if she knew how Andre came to be living in the woods.

'You didn't want to pry,' she said, as she drove me back to town, 'but sometimes he would talk about scrubbing floors when he was in the orphanage. I would love to know his story. If you find out then I would love to hear it.'

I said goodbye to Sally-Anne and headed towards my car which I had left parked in the village the day before. Originally, I had planned to sleep in a caravan belonging to Sabby Lawrence. Sabby's family had encountered Andre a few years after he left Iwade.

The Lawrences owned a small-holding tucked away in a valley not far from Sittingbourne. When they first met Andre he was living in sheltered accommodation in Milton Regis on the outskirts of Sittingbourne.

'He was still hoping to buy some land,' Selwyn Lawrence, Sabby's father, told me as I sat round their kitchen table in the farmhouse a few weeks after my trip to Iwade.

His wife, Ernestine, chipped in, 'He would go into estate agents and ask them if they knew of any land for sale. Of course, he couldn't afford anything, but one of the estate agents contacted us and asked us if we could help.'

'This was a man who liked being outdoors, they told me,' Selwyn said. 'They knew we had a bit of land and they wondered if we would be willing to let Andre come out and help. We agreed and Andre started coming out to look after the animals. Not long after his first visit we were visited by a policeman, Graham Avery,' Selwyn said. 'He had been part of the operation that evicted Andre from Cobham Woods, but Graham never felt entirely right about the whole episode. He looked after Andre and came to check us out.'

'To make sure we were the right kind of people for him and we weren't going to rip him off,' Ernestine clarified.

'When Andre first came to us we had an idea that we would build a cabin on our land for him to live in. We even began digging the foundations,' Selwyn said. 'However, it soon became clear that he couldn't survive another winter outside. So instead, he would just come to work. He was very independent, would always get the bus or walk, never accept a lift.'

I asked Selwyn if he knew how Andre came to be living in the woods.

'He told us his dad had been a soldier in the First World War and had two children with a woman from Belgium,' Selwyn said. 'He brought the children back to England, but couldn't look after them, so they ended up in an orphanage. Andre had a harelip and whereas his sister was adopted, Andre remained at the orphanage. The harelip caused a speech impediment and he was bullied. He would tell us stories of how they beat him and threw him in cold baths. One year on his birthday we made him a cake and sang to him. He cried.' Selwyn paused. 'It was the only time I ever saw him cry. He said no one had ever celebrated his birthday before. When the Second World War started, he ended up working as a Bevan Boy down the mines. I think it was sometime after the war that he bought the land in Cobham Woods from Lord Darnley. He always said he had been misled and thought he was allowed to build a cabin on it.

'It must have been a hard life in the woods,' Selwyn said. 'He told us how he would hang strings from the leaves and the dew would run down and collect in a cup. He had a goat called Bambi and a dog which he claimed was half fox.' Selwyn confirmed my suspicions that after his eviction Andre found it hard to adjust to life on the marshes.

'When he had to leave and live in Iwade, he found it difficult,' Selwyn said. 'People were kind, he said, but it wasn't the woods.'

Here there is a blank in Andre's story, a period between him vanishing from Sally-Anne's life and entering the Lawrence's. I can only speculate that it was a difficult time. What makes a man like Andre Van Beest give up his independence and move into sheltered accommodation in Milton Regis? Here it seemed Graham, the policeman, may have been an influence.

'Graham got him into model trains,' Selwyn said. 'You would visit him in his home and the whole room would be a train set.'

Selwyn disappeared and returned with a bag of trains, carriages and handmade items that Andre created for his railway scenes. I took a train from Selwyn and turned it over in my hand, admiring its black and red livery. It was strange to handle this thing which once belonged to Andre. He is long dead. Even though I never met him, I felt a connection with this man who lost a home he loved and searched to replace it.

Andre died in his sheltered accommodation around the millennium. 'After he died we took his ashes to Cobham Woods,' Ernestine said. 'Andre had taken us there once to show us where his cabin had been. When we returned with his ashes it was so overgrown we couldn't even be sure we had found the right spot, but we saw this weird growth on a tree. Our daughter, Sabby, thought it looked like Andre, so we scattered his ashes there.'

Once again I was struck by the kindness of people. Here was a man, a stranger, whom some saw as a 'dirty old tramp', but whom others took the time to get to know. He was a man that no one was responsible for but who had come into people's lives and had been looked after. Sally-Anne, Uncle Nigel, Graham the policeman, the landowners in Iwade, the estate agents in Sittingbourne and the Lawrence family were examples of people who held the values that the original hermits had gone into the wilds to find: kindness, charity and generosity.

Sabby Lawrence, Selwyn's daughter, was a further example of this generous spirit. I had spoken to her on the phone about Andre and my journey.

'I want to help,' she said. 'Where are you going to stay when you visit Iwade?'

To be honest I didn't know. 'Maybe camping,' I said.

'Go and stay in my caravan. It's in the garden of my parent's home. It's not too far from Iwade. I'll send you the key in the post and you can spend the night there.'

Here I was, a woman whom Sabby had never met and had one chat with on the phone, but she was willing to give me the key to her property, so I would have somewhere safe to spend the night.

I was humbled by this act of kindness and feared that in similar circumstances I would not be so trusting.

As it happened, I couldn't take her up on the offer. Selwyn explained he had been at work on the land and the caravan was surrounded by trenches and had no floor. They were very apologetic; it just wasn't possible to stay.

The idea of sleeping in the car had occurred to me as I had driven out to Sheppey one day along the road which swept along the very edge of the estuary, past a wide bay formed by Funton Creek. The area had the amazing name of Bedlam's Bottom. It is a beautiful stretch of road, though a motorist's nightmare, as you are forced to pay attention to the narrow twisting tarmac while, from the corner of your eye, you see a panorama of calm, satin water with flashes of twisting dunlin flocks. The road is full of laybys, cut into the saltmarsh edge by countless drivers who have pulled off the road, unable to resist the urge to gape at the spectacle.

Partly, I was excited by the idea of spending the night in my car. If you can do this, I told myself, a whole world of possibilities opens up. I could drive into the countryside and write and when darkness fell, just curl up in the back of the car to sleep. No need for expensive campervans or boats or chalets. This journey had got my mind churning again over such possibilities in a way it hadn't since Connor and I had split up. During our days in the caravan, while Connor would pore over house prices and mortgage deals, I would write lists of what I wanted from my escape pod. An outdoor fire pit, a covered area to sit under when it rained, good security and the ability to listen to music were a must, but running water and electricity, I figured, I could do without.

The fact that I needed an escape pod had always been evident, and over the years I had compiled stacks of magazines on campervans and books on how to build a log cabin. I had roamed the internet, drooling over gorgeous wooden chalets set amid woodland, but my plans had always been thwarted by cost. I had crept close in the past to both campervan and chalet ownership, but the reality was that anything I could afford was broken down and full of filler.

With Connor gone, my need for the escape pod had dwindled, but walking the estuary had made me realise that the need to get away from daily pressures and take off somewhere out of reach for a few days of simplicity was still there. Maybe, I told myself, my Nissan Micra could provide all I needed. I practically lived in the car anyway in the summer, driving out each morning to some remote site, spending all day conducting surveys on the marshes, eating lunch and tea in the car and having a kip in the back before heading home.

Down at Bedlam's Bottom I opened the car boot and surveyed the equipment I had squashed into the back the day before. I pulled out the camp cooker and brewed myself up a much-needed cup of tea. While the water boiled, I was treated to a mass flypast in the bay: lapwings, low-flying across the surface of the water, gangs of juvenile redshank skidding along in their slipstream, and outrider gulls patrolling above.

I felt so tired that I could have fallen asleep right there, which, I thought, might not be a bad idea, as I rather suspected that, when darkness fell, I would feel differently. I ate a meal of gnocchi and pasta sauce and a few squares of dark chocolate, sitting in the footwell shielded by the open car door from the breeze and the inquisitive stares of passing motorists.

The sun began to go down and I set to work rigging up the car as I'd practised the day before. I pulled out two rolls of insulating paper, the kind of shiny stuff you put behind the radiator to reflect the heat back in, and unwound it around the back windows, sticking it into place with gaffer tape, then strung a washing line between the doors. Onto this I hung a curtain held in place with clothes pegs.

I rolled out my camping mat across the seatbelt clamps and pulled a woolly blanket across my sleeping bag. On the parcel shelf I laid out my head torch, ear plugs, phone and bedtime reading. Inside it was snug, like a little car tent, and I felt surprisingly sheltered from prying eyes. I left the window with a view of the estuary uncovered and sat up, watching the lights of Grain oil depot twinkle on and gulls paddling in the mud pools left behind with the receding tide. A short-eared owl flew past.

The traffic faded away; occasionally a car roared past the layby, inches away, and sounded its horn as if to say, 'we know what you're up to,' imagining, I guess, something steamier than a lone girl reading a book by her head torch. The blaring horns gave me a shock, but didn't really unnerve me. After all, I rationalised, if they thought I was with a man, then they were unlikely to pull off and investigate. Soon peace descended and the only sound was the noise of oystercatchers and curlews calling out on the mud.

Sometime after ten, I settled down in my sleeping bag for the night. For the first two hours I found it hard to switch off, my senses on constant low alert, like a cat dozing in the sun. I dreamt fitfully, imagining noises outside and people trying the door handles. I woke at midnight to see a half moon rising, lighting up the road. All was silent. I felt safer and fell quickly back to sleep.

TEN

Iwade – Chetney Marshes –
Elmley, Isle of Sheppey

I SWEAR that there is nothing you can't fit into a Nissan Micra, and have proved so on several occasions. In the past I have transported bikes, tools and huge bundles of coppiced twigs in the back of a car that is only really meant for pottering around town in. But I have to say, that even for someone of 5ft 2, the back of a Micra makes for a rather cramped bed. Throughout the night, I had woken every two hours, forced into consciousness by excruciating pains in my legs. I'd roll onto my back, lifting my legs to the roof, trying to stretch my hamstrings. It provided little relief, though the pains subsided enough for me to drift back to sleep.

Eventually, the sound of early morning traffic jogged me awake. I faced a grey and blustery morning as I stood outside the car brushing my hair, eating porridge and cleaning my teeth, while passing commuters cast me curious looks.

By 8.30am, the sun was coming out. I finished my cup of tea and watched an egret land on the marsh below me. I felt proud of myself. I had been scared of sleeping in the car. Although I had told myself that the chance of anything bad happening was tiny, still, deep down, I felt that for a lone woman to sleep in a layby was risky. However, I had done it and been ok, and if I had to, I could do it again. But maybe the dream of freely camping around the country was not yet a reality. It was no longer fear that prevented me, only the size of my car.

Back in Iwade, I left the car in a side street and headed out of town. Today the rucksack was loaded with three meals, a change of clothes and a sleeping bag and felt a lot heavier. I squeezed between blackthorn hedges onto the footpath, and the view of Chetney Marshes exploded before me. The huge bay was one sweep of subtle light, with paint daubs of dark barges down by the waterline. The upward finger of Kingsnorth drew the eye as it faced off with the power station at Grain. I liked the power stations – not for what they did – but for their height in this landscape of flatness. Their days were numbered. Kingsnorth had closed and its insides had been gutted. I tried to imagine the skyline without the chimneys, one vast flatness of dykes and creeks, the only signs of man the remains of barges and grain silos. I couldn't help but feel that the grandeur of the view would be diminished by their loss.

Across the sweep of Chetney I could see to the Isle of Grain, where a lorry was making its way along the low road and, beyond, a ship was heading out to sea. In the far distance I could see a house isolated on the charmingly named Ladies Hole Point. I could see the route I had taken across the Hoo Peninsula weeks ago; I could probably even see Alex's houseboat down near Hoo if I really tried.

I continued downhill to the waterline. Down on the level everything was different; I wasn't viewing the marshes, I was in the marshes, among the detail of dry grass and rabbits' hip bones and windblown gatekeeper butterflies. The verdant, decaying smell of the marshes reached me, a smell of warm, cooked samphire, all heat and salt and greenery.

I felt a sudden wave of loneliness hit me and was surprised. I was someone quite happy with solitude. My job involved days on my own walking the marshes. I loved it. If I came across a dog walker or a farmer on my travels I felt as though they were intruding. Out on my own in the countryside, I could switch off, stop being polite and sociable and be myself. Why, today, was I missing someone?

I thought about the two men who had been occupying my thoughts for the last few weeks. Which one would I have wanted with me today? One was an introvert, a loner, who wanted to be out there in the wilds. This man shared many of my own views. He was also years younger than me, and so beautiful he turned me into a pool of water at his feet. This man would have delighted in the views and the camping and the nature, but he would have walked along in silence.

The other man, who also wanted me, was easy company. With him the miles would go quickly. We would talk and laugh and time would run away with us. He too would have loved the views and the wildlife, but he was not the man to camp in a car or build a shack in the woods. I had known loneliness when alone and I had also known it with heart-breaking certainty in the middle of my relationship with Connor. My gut instinct told me that this man wasn't right for me, that I could find myself right back where I had been. These days I listened to my gut.

Enough of these thoughts, I told myself. '*Solvitur ambulando*'; work it out by walking. I passed a graveyard of barges, fractured and seaweed-hung, their hulls filled with mud, broken-toothed struts dissolving into the saltmarsh.

The wind blasted across the marshes, sending an early warning of autumn on its way. I reached a pinnacle of land overlooking The Shade, an inlet of water coming off the Medway from Slaughterhouse Point. Chetney Marshes were not the best place to feel light-hearted.

I thought about the alternative to being here on Chetney. On a normal Monday, I would have been sitting in the office under the eye of my boss, feeling like a pinned butterfly. I was all ready to jerk that pin free and fly out of the window and away, to what, I didn't know. If this journey had taught me anything, it was that there were alternative ways to live.

For the last few years, I had wallowed in the safety net of my house and my job. Both had been a blessing. I had needed security and they had provided it. Now that my confidence had returned,

I felt ready to take a gamble again. In the past, I had never been scared to quit a job; in fact, I had been spectacularly good at it. Saying my piece and flouncing out with a swish of my skirts had been my speciality. To hell with what lay beyond the P45, it would all be ok. Some days the temptation to revert to form and tell my boss to stick his job had been hard to resist, but my hand had been stayed. I was no longer in my twenties and I had a mortgage. However, right from the beginning I was determined that owning a house would not be a trap. Instead, the house, would be an escape route. I would decorate the spare room, rent it out, cut back on the day job and build up the freelance work to a point where I felt I could go it alone. I had followed this plan to the letter and was proud of myself. I was there, but still I hesitated, fearing to take that leap with no safety net to catch me.

I suddenly realised that I could hear not one man-made sound, only the wind and the birds. The source of my worries was many miles away. The sun was shining, shelduck flew across the bay. I lay on my back, ate a square of chocolate and felt any lingering unhappiness melt away.

It was time to leave the Medway behind and head across the marshes to the Swale. The Swale is a channel which separates Kent from the Isle of Sheppey. It had once been a river, but when the water rose and filled the valley, Sheppey had become cut off. Red-legged partridges scattered as I walked the old counter wall. An egret floated along a ditch then rose, croaking, and circled me, trailing long black legs and ballerina-pointed, yellow toes. I scared a marsh harrier from among the sedge; it scurried into the air, then floated, V-shaped, away towards Sheppey.

The land was a prairie of windswept grassland and broken windmills. The windmills were once used to pump water around the marshes to raise and lower levels in the ditches and provide drinking water for livestock. It was easy to get confused on these flatlands. I came to a junction, unsigned, and followed a track north. I thought I had gone wrong and was miles from the river, but suddenly I saw a ship's mast moving, seemingly across the land. I climbed a slight hillock and I was there, on the banks of the Swale, with the Sheppey Bridge rising up ahead.

The uncomfortable night caught up with me and I collapsed on the bank to doze, and woke at the sound of voices across the channel: a dog barking, two boys on a scrambler bike, but there was no one on my side. I was quite safe and sank back into a soporific daze. This luxury of time was such a pleasure. Today my time was my own. I said it to myself again as it was such a rare feeling: 'YOUR TIME IS YOUR OWN'.

I struggled up from my comfy bed of grass and heaved the pack back on once more. A clouded yellow butterfly blew along the wall. It was an autumn butterfly, a migrant alighting on a thistle to drink. Twites and wheatears scattered in front of me as I walked. They were waiting all along the coast for the signal to go south for the winter. A buzzard took off from a post and rose high into the warm air.

I could see a herd of Gypsy ponies down by a wide fleet. Cantering and fighting, they made it look like a prehistoric vision of the steppes. They spotted me and came careering up, all flying manes and feathers. I jogged to the safety of a gate, but then spent time fussing and petting them, scratching withers and patting necks, pulling burdock claws from greasy manes until the lead mare got bored and snake-headed her troops away amid a fury of fighting, bucking and whinnying. I delighted in seeing horses act like horses instead of automated armchairs for our pleasure. The ponies cantered away and I walked on.

A bait digger was collecting lugworms on the foreshore as the tide came racing in. I felt the time, rather than knew it. It was late afternoon.

Under the Sheppey Crossing the world suddenly became all twenty-first century. On the bridge high above, lorries transported new cars from Lappel Bank. Lappel Bank shows what happens when economic growth is placed so much higher than all other considerations. What had once been an important area of saltmarsh and a wintering site for around 50,000 birds was now under miles of tarmac and surrounded by razor wire. The surrounding area had been designated a Special Protection Area, one of the highest levels of protection we have in Britain, but the Government decided to leave Lappel Bank unprotected so that they could build on it. It is now possibly one of the ugliest places in the country.

The Government claimed this destruction was in the 'national interest,' that somehow the country was going to sink to its knees unless the bank was destroyed, but Lappel Bank was not destroyed to build a hospital or create green energy, or even help the supposed desperate shortage of housing. No, an important and beautiful spot was eradicated to stack lines and lines of new cars. I fail to see the 'national interest' in this; so did the European Commission. When the RSPB took the Government to the European Court of Justice, the court ruled that the Government had acted illegally in withholding Lappel Bank from the protected area for economic gain. Unfortunately, the ruling came too late; Lappel Bank had already been lost.

I strolled under the new bridge and towards the more pedestrian-friendly old one, although getting onto it proved a challenge, involving scaling a nettly embankment and climbing over a crash barrier. I walked along the road looking for the footpath sign which would lead me under the railway, but there was none. Suddenly, I realised that the only way across the railway was to walk under the bridge, along the river's edge before the tide rose too high. I raced back as fast as my tired legs would allow and found there was only about a metre of dry land left. I squelched through the mud and climbed a steep embankment over a pillbox to safety.

From behind, a siren announced the lifting of the Kingsferry Bridge. I turned to see the middle section suspended in the air. A container ship appeared, the *Faustina*; it churned upriver, flying the ensign, and turned towards the gravel sorting depot on the opposite bank. The sounds of industry leaked out across the river. This was the way of it in the north Kent marshes – on one bank, a landscape little changed in a thousand years and, on the other, noisy industry. In between, lay the decay of the last century. It shouldn't have worked, this jarring contrast, but on a small scale it did, the industry and rural landscape making for a stirring mix.

I was now on Elmley Marshes. From my viewpoint on the sea wall the whole of the Isle of Sheppey stretched away, the hills rising from Queenborough to Minster and falling from Warden Point to Leysdown. The rain was coming in again. A rising wind blew at my back, cooling my sweat. I walked past saltmarsh sculpted into pillars and curves. There was something untamed about this land; the sea and the wind still governed a landscape carved by tides and eddies. In his book, *Changing Corners of North East Kent*, the artist B. E. Beach described the coastline: 'There was something hauntingly primeval about it all. The sprawling, oozing expanse of mud and tufty random patches of saltmarsh. The horizontal streaks of receding islands, things half submerged, half discernible, the scene of emptiness and space all contributed to a strange feeling that here one was among the earliest glimmerings of things, the slimy beginning of the world.'

I crawled along through the 'slimy beginning of the world', long grass tore at my dragging feet, spiders' webs full of dead creatures clung to me. The rain began to fall. I reached Dan's Dock, now just a broken jetty at the end of the ruins of the Elmley brickworks. The brickworks once covered about 25 acres of Elmley Island and included cottages, drying sheds and kilns, but the industry itself lasted only ten years before making way for cement.

I flopped down at the dock on a piece of yellow, lichen-covered driftwood, with a blank-eyed, desiccated rabbit at my feet. I was caught in that now familiar end-of-the-second-day slump, when my brain and legs had become jelly. Storm clouds heaved towards me, sharpening the light, slivering the sedge and casting blackness into the ditches. Marsh harriers drifted across the track, a wheatear sat bobbing on a fencepost before flitting away, flashing the white rump that had given the bird its original name of 'white arse'. The air smelled of molasses from a paper mill.

I walked on, past the remains of Elmley village, once a thriving community of 150 houses, a school, a church and pub called The Globe, built to house the staff of the Elmley Cement works. Now all that remained were a few headstones and the broken schoolhouse. The cement works closed in 1900 and every year there was less to see. The roof of the school had collapsed in the previous year's gales, taking with it the high vaulted windows. Prior to that, the building had still had elegance; now it was a broken ruin like so many other buildings on the marshes, finally succumbing to wind and rain and the changing fortunes of industry.

An indignant little owl burst from the ruins and landed in a tree, glaring at my intrusion. Haws were ripening in the hedgerow as I walked up the track towards Kingshill Farm. I had fond memories of Kingshill. The Bromhey Gang had broken up not long after I had left the farmhouse. Mike emigrated to Australia and Gordon came to be the warden of the RSPB's Elmley Marshes reserve, the last RSPB warden to live there, as it turned out.

My friend Gordon had died on the marshes. That is the stark fact. I had known he was ill. We all had, in various ways. Gordon had told bits of his illness to everyone, but no one pieced it together, to work out what it really meant. I guess Gordon wanted it that way.

He died one winter's night, with the snow thick on the ground, in his bed in the farmhouse where, it was rumoured, James II had spent the night after being captured in a boat on the Swale while trying to escape to France. Kingshill farmhouse had to be one of the remotest places in the South East, two miles down a lopsided track across Elmley Marshes. You could tell someone who knew Elmley well by the speed at which they could drive the track, dodging lapwings and hares on the way. I had once waited for Gordon at the end of this track, watching as his battered Fiesta flew along, music blaring. 'Now,' I thought, 'there is a man at home in his territory.'

Gordon had always wanted to return to Elmley, where he had been assistant warden many years ago. He had been in exile during his years at Northward Hill, waiting for the then warden, Barry, to do something crazy and get the boot. In the end Barry had done something both crazy and enviably sane; he had married a girl twenty years his junior, for whom age difference was not an obstacle. They were eminently suited and went off to live on an island in Scotland.

Gordon installed himself in the back of the farmhouse. It had to be the back, as the front, which looked so sturdy, with its five windows gazing out towards the Swale, was actually a condemned wreck with cracks running up the wall large enough to stick your fist into. Gordon didn't care. He was back where he belonged. He held a party every summer and invited an assortment of friends. The friends represented the two sides of Gordon: the clean-cut RSPB birdwatchers and the outspoken, unkempt, bohemian guys whom Gordon had known when he was younger. Invariably, by the end of the night, a barrel of Gordon's home brew would be cracked open. It was awful, undrinkable backswill. I don't feel bad about saying this. I told him enough times.

Gordon was a true friend, although maybe I never appreciated it fully until after he died. When I bought my house he had promised to help me move but, on the morning of the move, I arrived at Kingshill to find him grey and sweating with hardly enough energy to leave the house.

'Look Gordon, don't come,' I said. 'You can't come, you're too ill.'

'I don't want to let you down,' he said.

'Don't worry,' I said. 'I'll find someone else.'

Frantically, I rang around and people came good and turned up to help. So did Gordon.

'I promised you,' he said, and carted boxes up and down stairs all day.

After he died, the friendship of this act broke my heart, as I never got the chance to repay him.

A week before Gordon died, I went out to the farmhouse to see him. He wasn't in, out somewhere on the marsh, rounding up cattle or counting birds.

The farmhouse was open, it always was. I walked into the kitchen, a typically Gordon, grease-stained mess of teabags, dirty frying pans and leftover curry. I left a note: 'Next time I return I'm stealing your record collection.'

The following week, I got a phone call, first from Trevor, then from AJ, telling me that Gordon had been found dead. I was stunned. He was only fifty, he was my mate, the pal I went to gigs with, who stood at the back, nodding in appreciation, while I fought my way to the mosh pit.

The man who discovered him had known that something was wrong when he found the generator still running. Kingshill had no electricity, so the warden had to go out just before they went to bed and turn the generator off. Snow had fallen on the Sunday night and the man thought it was odd as there were no footprints in the snow on Monday morning. He found Gordon in bed.

At the wake, a friend of Gordon's summed him up as 'shit and shirts'. We all laughed. This was Gordon, going to meetings in London wearing the same pair of Doc Martens with the woolly red socks he had sorted the cattle out in that morning, and then there were the shirts. I have a picture of Gordon and me at a *ceilidh*. He is wearing a 'Gordon goes out' combo of a bright-red shirt and black waistcoat, along with a pair of shorts and the cow-muck boots.

His father gave a speech at the wake. He said that he wanted to spread Gordon's most loved possessions among his friends. I knew what I wanted and what he would have wanted me to have. So a few weeks' later I made my way out again to the farmhouse to steal his record collection. It was a corker. In a fit of sentimentality I also took a barrel of that hideous home brew.

Outside I bumped into the man who had found Gordon. I wanted to ask, 'Did he just die in his sleep, or at least quickly?' but I didn't. I didn't want to know any other truth. This was what I wanted to think, that Gordon had died peacefully or quickly in a place he loved. I pushed away the awful thought that maybe he hadn't; that maybe he knew there was a problem, but was too ill or too much a man to call for an ambulance and that they wouldn't find him anyway out there on the marshes in the dark; that maybe he realised that he was dying in this isolated place, and he was on his own.

This was where the part of me that wanted to batten down the hatches surfaced – the part of me that wanted to stay in the towns, surround myself with friends and neighbours and keep out the cold wind of the wild. It had been the same after my rescue from Copperhouse Marsh. I had wanted safety and 'normality'. Isolation, wilderness, a basic existence close to nature were all very well, but not when it came to dying.

Someone else who was facing this reality was Steve Gordon. Steve was the farm manager for the Elmley Conservation Trust. The trust had leased land to the RSPB, and when the lease expired it had taken back management of the whole estate. About a year after Gordon's death, Steve was diagnosed with an inoperable brain tumour. He was enduring chemotherapy and endless other terrible cures and, despite all medical advice, had chosen to stay in his bungalow on the marshes. Steve knew he was quite possibly going to die in a remote place, but he was choosing to stay. In some ways that comforted me.

At the top of the track to Kingshill Farm I passed Steve's bungalow and went to knock on the door. I knew Steve a little. I would encounter him occasionally on the marshes during my visits to Elmley. I came across him once on a quad bike with a woman on the back who looked just like Princess Diana. Steve was a handsome, charming man with the most beautiful cut-glass accent, and it seemed oddly in-keeping that he would be transporting a Princess Di look-a-like.

In Steve's kitchen I found two men and a woman.

'Is Steve around?' I said.

They looked at me with suspicion. 'No, he's not here,' a man said in an Italian accent.

I was surprised. I had spoken to Steve only days before to arrange the visit.

'What a shame,' I said. 'I'm here to interview him.'

The man amended his story. 'He is here, but he is unwell. He is resting, he is not to be disturbed.'

'I am staying here for the night,' I told him. 'Is it OK to come back tomorrow?'

'Maybe,' he said. 'But not early.'

I was dismissed and walked away unsure as to what to do. I did not want to be like some tabloid journalist, harassing a sick man, but I knew if I didn't get to speak to Steve now, maybe I never would.

I walked across to another bungalow and knocked on the door. Gareth Fulton came out. He and his wife Georgina are the current managers of Elmley Marshes. Georgina is the daughter of Phillip Merricks, the landowner who had farmed Elmley since the Seventies. We found her in a field next to the farmhouse; she was dusting the floor of the shepherd's hut, where they had offered to let me spend the night.

'The writer is here, G,' Gareth shouted. They both looked like they had just walked away from a polo match. I felt like a piece of chewed meat in comparison. I apologised for my state.

'I slept in my car last night and have walked across the marshes all day,' I explained.

'You look remarkably fresh,' Georgina said with perfect diplomacy.

They showed me round the shepherd's hut, a little green cabin with a corrugated-iron roof and iron wheels. The shepherds' huts were newly installed, situated to give views across the marshes to the Swale, allowing visitors to enjoy a little of the beauty of the reserve after hours. I approved. I have been very privileged to live in beautiful places and am happy that others can experience a little of what I have. Inside, the huts were beautifully decorated with white-washed walls, a shower and a wood burning stove. There was even an antique telescope, with which to spy on passing ships. Within half an hour, I felt my life had gone from rags to riches, as I sat on the steps of the hut sipping a glass of homemade sloe gin and enjoying the view across the water.

I cooked up more pasta and returned to my seat to eat from the saucepan. I felt for one moment that overwhelming sense of happiness that I used to feel when I lived in the caravan from a simple act like sitting on my back step, eating my food straight from the pan, and watching the light fade and the world of nature tuck itself away for the evening.

A barn owl emerged from the nest box on the tree below me. It sat on a branch, watching me, wobbling its head to focus and determine my threat level. A stoat bounded across the grass, the reed warblers chattered. A rush of wings and an autumnal starling flock vanished overhead. Below, I could hear the paddling of coots on the reservoir.

I carried my pots and pans across the lawn to wash them in the outdoor sink and felt back in my rightful place. For some reason, a world with less made me a happier person, bringing a sense of stillness that the world of technology took away. Time slowed, the light changed on the clouds in wedding-dress hues, from ivory to cream to eggshell. I sat on the step of the hut, too tired to do anything other than watch the turning of the wind turbines and an egret patiently fishing the shallows.

As the light left the sky, I ventured inside only to find a daddy-longlegs hanging over the bed. The first of the season. With a bravery only the truly phobic can understand, I caught it in a glass and threw it out the door. I visited the loo and came back to find lights scanning the marsh, lamping for foxes. Nowadays, it seems that nature reserves are really game reserves, protecting increasingly threatened breeding birds such as lapwing and redshank from all manner of predators. Crows, gulls, foxes and in some circumstances even hedgehogs and badgers are shot or removed to ensure that these birds' breeding attempts meet with some success. It is a controversial practice. It is gamekeeping, make no mistake, and it is not that the problem for these birds is really the predators; the problem is the lack of suitable land on which they have to breed, and this has driven their numbers down to a level where predation becomes an issue. As an animal lover, I used to find nights living at Northward Hill difficult to deal with. Bright lights would sweep across the windows of the caravan and the phtt phtt of shots would go on for hours. Without the shooting though, the ground-nesting birds would have had little chance of fledging their chicks. At Elmley, they had installed predator fences to protect the birds, but few other landowners could afford this.

The marshes darkened. It was a natural dark. I'd forgotten what it looked like, to lose the light. How the land becomes muffled.

Darkness doesn't fall on the marshes, it hums down to black. Faversham glowed sulphur bright across the water. It looked like it was burning and conjured up images of Samuel Pepys writing about the Great Fire of London.

I turned in, but woke at 3am and went barefoot outside to see the gauzy streams of the Milky Way spread across the sky. I had never been frightened of walking across Northward Hill at night, despite the clanking dark hollows of the barns scattered around Bromhey Farm and the scrub-enclosed paths of the reserve. The reserves felt like separate worlds, enclosed communities, and it seemed unthinkable that trouble from the outside would penetrate that far.

At Northward Hill we had been our own community, not quite occupying the same century as the rest of Kent. We went out on occasion to see all the shiny things in the shops, but were jolly glad to retreat back to the slower pace of life. Northward Hill had been a sanctuary for me, a place where I could look out on a natural world and pretend life was what I wished it to be.

In the morning, I walked across to Steve's house again. He greeted me at the door. The drugs he was taking for the tumour had not been kind to his appearance, though could not take away his beautiful voice or manners. He kissed me on each cheek. 'Come in,' he said.

In the kitchen I found the Italians. Somewhere between the previous evening and the morning I had obviously been deemed OK and they happily made me coffee and fed me panettone which, they told me, should really only be eaten at Christmas but this year, for some reason, had been available all year.

I asked Steve what had first brought him to Elmley.

'I came to work with the animals,' he said, sipping coffee. 'I remember when I first drove over the cattle grid, I thought this is the place I want to be.'

'It's not a landscape for everyone,' I said, thinking of Andre. 'What is it that you love about it?'

'It is that mixture of land and sea and the skyscape, that 180 degrees of sky which you have here,' Steve said. 'I loved the work too. I had been studying to be a vet in Italy where I met my friends,' he said, indicating the two men and a woman who were busy clearing up after breakfast. 'I came here to work with the stock. I loved the seasonality of things. I wasn't a naturalist to start with, but I knew I loved being in the lambing fields in the spring and seeing the birds coming back, the changes in the light as the season progressed, the winter colours of silver and ivory and the changes of texture in the land throughout the year. The seasons seem slower here than on the mainland,' he told me. 'You have to be more attentive to what's happening.'

'Don't you ever feel isolated down here?' I asked him.

'No, never,' he said. 'It is isolated but never bleak. Here you are framed by the downs and the industry, but it is a world in itself. It is a big effort to leave, you grow so attached to the place,' he said. 'Gareth and Georgina are finding that too. I felt this as soon as I came here; it felt like home. I felt that I should be paying them to be here, not the other way around.'

This is a rare thing nowadays. Wardens no longer live on the marshes, at least in north Kent. The days of the Bromhey Gang are over. These days, the only people who live on the reserve at Northward Hill are interns, on short-term gaps from university. Tied accommodation was always one of the perks of a job in conservation, so although the wages were not enough to support a flea, at least you didn't pay any rent. Now, there is no more tied accommodation, the wardens live elsewhere, sometimes in towns far removed from the marshes, and commute along the motorway to work. I asked Steve what he thought of this.

'It does make a difference,' he said. 'You are not attached to the land in the same way. You don't know it intimately, you don't have that same feeling for the land.'

'Wouldn't you consider moving to a town?' I said. 'Not even now?'

'When this illness was first diagnosed,' Steve said, 'Phillip Merricks offered me anything I wanted. He has offered to send me anywhere in the world for treatment. He said anything I ever wanted to do on my bucket list he would pay for. But I told him the best therapy is being here.'

Everyone I knew had always respected Steve, and during his illness respect for him had grown. Steve was clinging onto the life he loved, still going out to talk over the work with the estate staff, refusing all advice to leave and move nearer the hospitals.

'I'm so attached to this place,' he said before I left. 'I still have that same feeling every time I cross over that cattle grid. There is nowhere else I want to be.'

I walked away from Steve's house. The morning sun was rising over the marshes, the grazing cattle backlit, the lapwings swooping down over the fleets. It was good to see this place as Gordon had seen it. I had wanted to talk to Steve, not just because of his life on the marshes, but because he held the key to a question I had long wanted answered. 'Do you think if Gordon had known he was dying he would have made the same choice as you, to stay?' But no one can answer that. In the end I hadn't needed to ask. Steve told me what I needed to hear and he was right. Looking out across the expanse of the marshes, I knew he was right. It was a good place to die.

ELEVEN

Elmley – Eastchurch

TREVOR CALLED for me early on a Sunday morning at the beginning of October. He was driving me out to Elmley to begin the next leg of my walk and was being rewarded with two bottles of homemade cherry beer.

'I can't vouch for the quality,' I told him, as we sat at Swale Halt waiting for the bridge to lower.

Down at Elmley we knocked on Steve's door. Reports were not good. He was losing his balance, I'd been told, getting confused. Once again, the house was full of guests, protecting him and shooing unwanted visitors away. An unofficial doorman asked us our names.

'Wait here,' he said.

We stood on the doorstep. Steve came down. He was as before, despite it all, charming, friendly, a gentleman.

'It's a beautiful day for your walk,' he told me.

Yes, it was. It was a golden and glorious autumn morning. My heart, however, was full of fear about the miles of horror that lay ahead. It was a sunny day after rain, the absolute worst conditions. I had no idea how I was going to make it across the marshes. Already I could see them, ranks of them, lined up on Steve's pot plants, spindly legs and click-clacky wings. It was the height of daddy-longleg season. I could spy at least ten on one plant; how many more were out there?

I couldn't put it off forever. I said goodbye to Trevor and

Steve and retraced my steps down to Dan's Dock. Flocks of twites crossed the path. 'Seed, seed, seeding,' they seemed to call, speaking their avian minds. A wheatear balanced on the crumbled remains of the brickworks, splattered with lichens. An excitable heifer came charging towards me across the tussocky grass; more cows perked their heads up in interest. There they were, my two great autumn nemeses: daddy-longlegs and herds of frisky teenage cows. 'Why have you chosen to do this walk in October?' I asked myself. The heifers came rumbling across the field. I veered left and headed towards Elmley Hill, hoping this would slow their charge, but suddenly, they seemed to take fright and struck off through a gate in the opposite direction. I hoped in vain that the daddies would do the same. As I climbed the hill, the grass shivered with them. The day was warming up, they were feeling perky, one belly flopped across the sky in front of me, arms and legs splayed backwards. 'Wheeee', its whole body seemed to say, 'here I come, for your face'. I felt the fear rising, the adrenalin levels shooting up, all common sense leaving me as the phobia took hold. I made myself walk on. I knew the view from the hilltop was spectacular. I had to make it, I had to go on, because what was the alternative? Run back to the car park and call Trevor to take me home?

At the top of the hill daddies leapt up around my legs. A fine limb brushed my hand. I squealed and shook it off. I heard rustling in my hair and flung off my hat and sunglasses, jumping around on top of the hill as if I had been stung by fire embers, shaking my hair out frantically. 'I can't do it, I can't do it,' my mind buzzed. I was on top of the hill with millions and millions of bodies writhing around me and I couldn't enjoy the view of the Swale sweeping around the island and the glass-smooth water of Sharfleet Creek. But now I was on top of the hill I couldn't just teleport myself elsewhere, I had to get off, I had to walk through them. 'Look up,' I told myself. 'Look up and enjoy the view, ENJOY IT CAROL, DO NOT LOOK DOWN. You are going to have to do this today. This is likely to be the worst test you will ever face but you are going to have to face it.'

I prepared myself as best I could, tying back my hair, arming myself with my map case and mini tripod and then I walked, because I had to, through clouds and clouds of these creatures. They touched my hands, hit my face, clattered in my hair and I just kept walking, I have no idea how.

In the previous few weeks people had said I was brave for all sorts of reasons. Brave for leaving my job and going freelance, brave for walking in the countryside on my own and sleeping in my car, brave for staying at the homes of people I had never met. I knew different. You cannot be brave about things you don't really fear. I knew that out of all the acts of bravery I had supposedly performed, this walking through long grass on an autumn day, facing a creature which had previously sent me into meltdown, this was the only thing that was really brave.

I think in some way it helped that it was so much worse than I had imagined. Is that weird? It was just that with so many of them, I couldn't concentrate on individuals, so they became a different creature. 'They are not daddies,' I told myself, as they sprang up from the grassland all around me. 'They are just massive mosquitoes, or skinny butterflies.' And there were some background aspects to the experience I enjoyed. I liked the way that my progress affected other wildlife. Dragonflies followed, taking advantage of the harry-scarry, unthinking flight of the daddies towards them. Birds flittered in the reeds. The daddies had a purpose. They were a glut of goodness for other creatures before winter set in.

I came down from the sea wall at Welmarsh Creek and headed along the path with the morning birders. A hundred oystercatchers circled the crystalline bay, their bodies reflected in the mirror-calm water. Clouded yellow butterflies floated along the sea wall. The glasswort threw up fiery tongues from the saltmarsh. Skeins of geese flew low across the surface. It was a world of reflection and sparkle. It was like a dream, translucent, blurred, too beautiful to exist. I would not, could not, be frightened away from such a morning.

Murmurations arose and segregated in mid-air, starlings to the left, lapwings to the right. They cast a net across Cod's House, an isolated and ruined farmhouse on the marsh, and settled down to gorge themselves on insects. The morning light gave the colours of the grassland an added intensity; fluorescent sedges with chargrilled edges, an iridescent shimmer of dragonfly wings. I passed two women with long lenses, sucking on the back of their hands to create a squeaking like the noise a rabbit makes when it's dying. I guessed there was a stoat hiding somewhere in the grass which they were trying to fool into thinking, if it only returned the way it had just come, it would find a juicy bunny for the taking. The stoat was presumably unimpressed and failed to reappear. I walked on beneath a cobalt-blue sky, through a landscape of burnt ochre and sienna; the world had become a child's paintbox of autumn loveliness.

The world, my world, had turned since I had last set out across Sheppey. I had handed in my notice to The Boss and I was one week into self-employment. Six years ago I had been made redundant by the RSPB. It was a fairly soft redundancy. My job had come to an end. They no longer wanted a community officer but a press officer. Even though I was offered the job, I decided it was time to move on. I planned to set up a wildlife tour company but hadn't thought it through. Following the eviction and my dad's illness I was thinking nothing through too clearly. In the weeks before I left the RSPB I began to feel that what I was doing was wrong, yet I ploughed ahead, blindly confident that I could make it work. Little did I know that two weeks after I left my job, I would find out about Connor's affair and everything would change.

For the first few months I had tried to continue with the idea of working for myself, but it soon became clear that on my own I would never make ends meet. I had so many worries about my future; money didn't have to be one of them. I saw the job as a countryside officer for the council and went for it. For the past six years, I had been in a holding pattern, circling over my life, taking all the safe options, building my life and finances back up. I was not in the same fragile position I had been in when Connor had left. I had a house I could afford, I had friends and contacts that had already found me work. My confidence in myself was restored. I was ready to step out again on the road of self-employment.

At Welmarsh, the birders left me, heading off to the nearer hides. I turned right and walked the long route to Spitend. The little block of Cod's House stood away to my left through a shimmer of heat haze. The marshes were once home to many such isolated settlements. B. E. Beach had walked the marshes in the mid-Forties, drawing the remains of the isolated farmsteads and abandoned cottages. He described Cod's House as 'strangely arresting, perhaps almost forbidding. It stood in total isolation with no reasonable access and clearly none of the facilities of modern life. The house had been left to the marsh winds.'

Many of the houses Beach painted were swept away in the floods of 1953. The land I was walking across was inundated and the army came to blast holes in the sea wall to let the water off the fields. Sheppey, however, fared better than many other low-lying places with, amazingly, no loss of life. I passed a flock of sheep. Their ancestors had suffered far more than the human population in the flood, I suspected, and I commiserated with them aloud.

'Sorry for your loss,' I called. They looked a little perplexed and scurried up the sea wall to watch this crazy fool from a safe distance.

Spitend Hide appeared, a tiny dot on the horizon. Three bearded tits pinged their way overhead. A late blue butterfly crossed my path. Finally, I reached the hide and could sit down to enjoy the breeze, drifting through the slotted windows and carrying the sound of curlews feeding out by the tideline. There can be few more peaceful places in the south-east of Britain than this outpost of Elmley. A house once stood here as well 'a small tin bungalow,' as Beach described it, 'with other buildings utterly forsaken.' I tried to imagine the people who had lived here and conjured up an image of a man like Philip Rhayader from Paul Gallico's *The Snow Goose*: 'A queer figure, dark, bearded with glowing eyes'. Or a woman like Mehalah from Sabine Baring-Gould's novel, half wild, with a spirit fashioned by the saltmarsh. Living out here, you would become part of the marshes, haunted by the curlew's call, living off the salt fish and brine weed, subject to the tides and the winds. 'But God', I thought, 'what a beautiful place to live on a day like this'. It was hard to leave, especially with flocks of dunlin flashing a smokescreen across the shore.

I didn't know the marshes beyond and was unsure of my path across them. I crossed Windmill Creek and headed into the mythical country of Great Bells. Towards the end of my time with the RSPB, there had been a lot of talk about acquiring Great Bells. As the community officer, I never had much to do with these new acquisitions, so half the time their location remained a mystery. Great Bells was 'the land across the creek from Spitend'. It had seemed fantastically remote. The RSPB had known the lease on Elmley was coming to an end and felt that the Merricks family were unlikely to renew. Great Bells was the hope for the future. Take a wheat field and turn it into another Elmley Marshes. It seemed a plan that, at the time, only the RSPB were audacious enough to dream into being. As I walked across Great Bells that autumn afternoon it was easy to be underwhelmed about where that dreaming had got them. The reserve appeared to be a world of freshly cut ditches and mown fields. However, I knew a man who could tell me of the wonders my eye failed to see.

My ex-boss, AJ, was the only member of the original Bromhey Gang still working for the RSPB. He had done well since my days with the charity and was now conservation manager for the South East. Still, he hadn't changed that much and I knew I could lure him out of his office with the offer of a bag of chips and a coke.

A month after my walk across the reserve we strolled back across Great Bells as I poked fun at his Dorian Gray ability to never age and his Stan Laurel hair, in a way only possible with a friend. It was a beautiful afternoon with the grass shimmering with gossamer webbing and flocks of geese heading for Elmley from the Swale.

Great Bells was not owned by the RSPB but by the Environment Agency, part of a complicated arrangement of creating grazing marsh habitat in compensation for land which would be lost when the EA stopped mending the sea walls and allowed the rivers to once again rush back across the land.

Rivers are meant to move, their course is supposed to fluctuate, but for hundreds of years the rivers of north Kent have been constricted into the narrow zones we have defined as acceptable. The consequence is eroding saltmarsh which can't spread inland and ever-more expensive repairs to sea walls. With sea levels predicted to rise further, it will become increasingly impossible to defend every inch of coastline. If we don't allow some places to flood we will get bitten in the tail and other places, the places with our homes and industry, are likely to flood much worse.

'Could Great Bells ever be like Elmley?' I asked AJ, as we wandered up the main track towards the Swale.

'Yes, one day, it could,' he said, 'but not for centuries. This is the problem. Developers get giddy thinking you can destroy a traditional grazing marsh and then just recreate it somewhere else. It just doesn't work like that,' he said. 'Elmley is ancient grazing marsh, it has a topography that has been created over hundreds of years, it has a soil that has never been fertilised or compacted. You can make this place look like grazing marsh, but you can't recreate the intricacy overnight. Elmley is unique,' AJ said with his trademark passionate enthusiasm. 'There is hardly anywhere that could hold a torch to it for wildlife. It's humming with wildlife, but this place is brand new. It had a crop of wheat on it until six years ago, but it's getting there. In the past, it might have had one pair of lapwings a year try to breed and fail, last year it had twenty-five pairs, and in the winter, when it floods, it is spectacular for geese and ducks.'

As if to prove him right a flock of lapwing and golden plover took to the air from the wet fields, glittering against the sharp light before falling back to earth.

'So it must have been hard when the RSPB lost the lease on Elmley?' I speculated. Elmley may well have had the 'right stuff' to begin with in its soil and its grassland, but it was the RSPB who invested in it, worked with the water levels, created the scrapes, built the hides and visitor facilities.

'We didn't want to lose Elmley because we had a long heritage there and, well, we just liked it,' AJ said simply. 'But the Merricks family managing the whole estate means we can use our resources somewhere else that needs us more. Phillip Merricks does all the right things at Elmley. He's made a huge success in terms of ecology, he uses his agricultural subsidies in the right way and he shouts about it to other landowners. He is in a better place to persuade other farmers to follow suit and turn their wheat fields back into grazing marsh than we are.'

AJ's right. Farmers listen to farmers, not tree hugging, bleeding-hearted conservationists. The Merricks family taking back the land is a good, forward-looking thing. Maybe if the Merricks can make a financial success out of Elmley then other farmers will follow suit and the RSPB can use its political sway and expertise to join up the gaps. Only in this way can we create large areas of wildlife-friendly land that will allow nature the opportunity to spread beyond reserves where it is currently isolated and surrounded by a sea of industrial farming.

I turned away from the Swale inland and walked into the world of industrial farming. Outside the farmyard I came across a sign. 'Attention Walkers, you must turn back here or face trespassing across private land'. In alarm, I studied the map again. There was my little red dotted line leading to the farm and beyond, a black dashed line, which I'd assumed marked a track that I could follow to Eastchurch village. In the distance, I spied a couple sitting on a pile of earth and headed across. They looked a little surprised to see me in such a remote spot.

'I need help,' I called out.

'Do you need water?' the woman asked. Clearly I looked rougher than I thought.

'No, I'm OK for water,' I said. 'I just need some directions.'

The couple pulled out their new, pristine map and we all studied the route. Yes, the footpath went to the door of New Rides Farm, but I was mistaken in thinking it went any further. 'How am I to get to Eastchurch now?' I said aloud.

Luckily, the couple were avid walkers. 'Try the route through the prison,' they suggested.

'Won't that have heavy security?' I asked warily.

'No,' the man said. 'There is a sign saying 'No right of way' but it is worn away, easily overlooked.' He winked.

I thanked them, and stomped back the way I had come, batting at the daddies with my mini tripod and tripping into ruts along the path as my feet began to drag. I could feel the couple watching my receding form, shaking their heads sorrowfully.

'Poor girl', I imagined them saying, 'clearly been out in the sun too long'.

Indeed I had. I was exhausted and in need of the drink of water they had kindly offered me, but I didn't want to stop until I knew for certain that I could reach the village. I found the path that the couple had told me about and emerged from the scrub into the manicured world of Elmley Prison. The contrast was a little surreal. Green lawns and flower beds bordered a tarmac road which ran the perimeter of the high prison wall. I could hear shouts from within the prison yard.

'I know what you're in for.'

To be 'in' at all on such a day was a crime in itself. More shouting voices joined in. From outside it sounded like a riot was about to break out and I hurried on as fast as my aching legs would carry me. I passed the prison gatehouse, suddenly a little conscious of my dishevelled appearance and the big knife strapped to my belt, but no one stopped me.

It was kicking out time for prison visits and I was passed by a string of women in tight dresses and false eyelashes dragging along kids for whom this may have been a normal Sunday afternoon trip to see the relatives. A line of cars flashed by, 4 x 4s with personalised number plates. Maybe crime does pay or maybe it was the desire for the trappings of a life beyond their means that had led these women's 'other halves' to prison in the first place.

I pushed on uphill to Eastchurch village, passing through a corridor of ivy flowers alive with wasps and flies, each bush erupting with buzzing insects defending their late summer hoard from this passer-by. I stopped for a lemonade at the Shurland Hotel, 'a brasserie and spa', the sign told me, an attempt to turn Sheppey into an upmarket tourist destination. However, despite many efforts over the years, Sheppey continued to defy all attempts to gentrify it. I sipped my drink and watched the Sunday afternoon traffic at the crossroads, gangs of boys walking home from their football game, teenage girls shrieking with laughter at the whinny of a horse pulling a cart carrying a fat man in a flat cap and a dirty faced boy. I fished the ice cubes from my glass and walked along, running them across my wrists and neck.

The footpath led away from the village, and a view of Shurland Hall opened up beyond the hedgerows: a beautiful red-brick manor house with two turrets and corn-twist chimneys, built in the early 1500s by Sir Thomas Cheyne. Henry VIII and Anne Boleyn once spent a night there. Henry was known to demand such banquets during his visits that no doubt the surrounding country was left as starving after his visit as when the Vikings had raided in 855 and demanded the locals slaughter all their breeding cattle to feed them. The hall gets its name from the Shurland family. Robert de Shurland's tomb lies in Minster Church two and a half miles to the west. His name is associated with a strange legend.

When a body was found washed up on the shore of the Medway at Chatham in the 1300s, the local priest buried it close to the shrine of Saint Bridget. That night, Saint Bridget came to the priest and insisted that he dig up the body and throw it back in the river because the man died at his own hand and therefore couldn't receive a Christian burial. The priest did as she asked, but unfortunately the body was washed up a few days later on the estate of Robert de Shurland. When Robert asked the priest to bury the body and he refused, Robert kicked him into the grave and the fall broke the priest's neck.

The religious community was outraged, and Robert, realising he had stirred up a hornets' nest by his actions, decided to ask for the pardon of the king, who was, at the time, in a boat on the Thames reviewing his troops. Unable to find a boat, the impetuous Robert swam his horse, Grey Dolphin, out to the boat. Having received his pardon, Robert swam back to shore only to meet an old woman on the beach who told him that his faithful horse would be the death of him. In order to outwit the woman's prophecy, Robert promptly cut off the head of the horse.

Apparently years later, while walking on the beach, Robert spotted his horse's skull and scornfully kicked it. A tooth from the skull pierced Robert's boot. He died the next day from suspected gangrene. His tomb in Minster Church shows him lying back, in couch potato fashion, with his feet resting on the head of the horse. The horse has a wry smile, having got the last laugh.

I passed Shurland Hall and plodded wearily through a stubble field; the path ended on a road. I stood in a daze for some moments trying to work out which way to turn. I made a decision. It was the wrong way but I found myself, rather fortuitously, outside the Wheatsheaf Pub instead, which was open and serving food. I ordered roast pork with extra crackling and a double whisky, then another. I had conquered my fear. I had earned it.

When I left the pub later that evening there was a nip in the air. The whisky warmed me as I weaved down the road. It was coming on for dusk, mist was growing in the fields and the smell of wood smoke came from chimneys, lit maybe for the first time that autumn.

I arrived at the chalet park where I had planned to spend the night. I had first found this place on a winter's day in 2006 when I had cycled across Sheppey to have a nose around the caravan parks out of season. The chalet parks, in the main, were not inspiring: bleak little boxes lined up in rows facing one another, peeling paint and rotting window frames, tattered St George's flags hoisted on flag poles, stickers in the window pronouncing 'if I had enough gin I could rule the world'. In summer, they became a world of over-large ladies lounging in deck chairs, with bulldogs tied to the porch, screaming kids and footballs flying. These places were anything but the peaceful writer's retreat I longed for and I almost abandoned the whole venture. But then, cycling outside of Eastchurch, I came across another park and stepped back into a world of 1950s loveliness. These chalets were set in their own little gardens, surrounded by white picket fences and looked across an orchard. They were painted pastel blue and sunny yellow.

I walked across this site now. It was growing dark, fairy lights were glowing in the gardens and people were sitting on their porches enjoying the last warmth of a beautiful day. I found Ronnie, a woman in her thirties, and Jim, her partner, sitting with their neighbours enjoying a beer. They greeted me as though they had known me forever but, in truth, we had only met that summer when I strolled in one afternoon and introduced myself. Ronnie and Jim's chalet was situated opposite the one I so very nearly came to buy.

In the period of confusion between calling off the wedding and being evicted I had put in an offer for one of these chalets. It had two bedrooms and a bathroom and a little kitchen tucked into the porch. I could live in it for eight months of the year. I didn't know what I would do for the other four months but I supposed something would work itself out with Connor. The thought of sitting on the porch with the rain on the tin roof and the kettle whistling on the stove was the one thought that made me happy during that time. I had arranged to sign the papers one Saturday and brought my parents over to show off what I was buying.

My dad was sceptical.

'Where are the lease papers?' he asked.

I passed on this question to the site owner, a young woman in a cowboy hat.

'We don't use them,' she said. 'No one needs them here. You

just hand over the cheque and it's yours.'

I sat down to sign the cheque. I wanted the chalet and besides, if I didn't buy it then, in three weeks, I had nowhere to live. I opened up my cheque book and, to my embarrassment, realised I had brought the wrong book and was looking down at a paying-in slip, not a cheque. The site owner looked most annoyed as I spluttered an apology.

'Well, can your dad pay?' she said.

'No,' I said. 'I'll come back on Monday with my cheque book.'

The thing is, when everything in your life is being blown around by the wind, small events take on significance. Over the weekend I began to question why I had brought my paying-in book with me instead of my cheque book and, besides, I didn't feel entirely comfortable about the woman who owned the park. She was too pushy. 'Couldn't you find yourself in the same position you're in now?' the voice in my head began to say. 'Owning a property but not the land it sits on? Subject to the whim of the landowner who could sell the site, put the rents up, evict you at any time?'

When I told Connor about the incident with the cheque book he said, 'Well you know what they say? There are no accidents.'

I was persuaded and pulled out of the deal.

At the time I had felt it was the right move, but thoughts of the little chalet had never quite gone away. I had visited the site once or twice in the intervening years and had always been charmed and wondered 'what if?' A friend told me recently of a quote by Terry Pratchett about the trousers of time, in which you fall into the waistband not knowing which leg you will emerge from. In this way Pratchett said, 'history occurs, in myriad, often unconsidered, minor decisions.' What would have happened to me at that time if I had burrowed down that leg and had moved here?'

I had explained all this to Ronnie and Jim over their garden gate when I had walked passed during one of my visits in the summer.

'We have a chalet for sale,' they'd said. 'It needs a bit of work, we're doing it up.'

I saw my opportunity and asked if I could stay.

Now Ronnie and Jim were ushering me into their garden. 'Take a seat,' Ronnie urged. 'How far have you walked? Have a cup of tea, or a beer. Jim, get her a beer.'

'No tea's fine,' I said, still squiffy from the whisky.

I settled down in a garden chair with Ronnie and the cup of tea. She told me how she too had been charmed when she first came to the site. Ronnie had been living in Gillingham at the time and had been looking for somewhere new for her and Jim to rent while he was working abroad. She had seen the chalet for sale on Gumtree and couldn't believe how little it cost.

'I didn't even know where Eastchurch was,' she said. 'I had only been to Sheppey a couple of times, so when I arrived I couldn't believe how beautiful it was. I grew up on the Isle of Wight and I had always told myself I would never live on an island again, but I loved the vintage feel of the park and the fact that our chalet is open plan which made it good for my dog Daisy who was half blind. I went home and counted out all the money I'd been saving; it was all in 50ps, but when I counted it all out I had exactly the right amount to buy the chalet. It was fate.'

Whereas my 'it's a sign' moment had led me away from the park, Ronnie's convinced her to buy.

'That first night I hadn't intended to stay,' she said. 'Jim was working abroad and my parents had brought me here just to drop stuff off, but Daisy curled up on the bed and went to sleep and I told my parents I would stay as well. I curled up next to Daisy with only a crochet blanket to cover us, and woke about 5.30am. I went outside and couldn't believe the night sky. There were pheasants and rabbits on the lawn. I cried. It was so different from where I'd been living in Gillingham. I was so happy to have found this place.'

I sipped my tea and asked Ronnie if she worried that they didn't own the land.

'I never thought about it,' Ronnie said. 'The chalets have been here since the Fifties, the owners won't knock them down. Some people have owned them and lived here for twenty years.'

I longed for the confidence that Ronnie felt in the set-up, but I had been burned once and couldn't ignore what I had learned to my cost, that the permanence of these places was often an illusion. They could be whipped away overnight.

'What did your friends think when you told them you were moving to a chalet on Sheppey?' I asked.

'Some people thought I was mad for doing this. They didn't get it at all. "What do you want to go and live on the island with the Swampies?" they would say.'

'Swampies?' I questioned.

'It's what they call the islanders,' Ronnie said. 'But I've met more genuine people since I moved here than I ever did in Gillingham. When I arrived, people would come knocking, offering to help, giving furniture. I couldn't get used to it at first. I was used to people ripping you off. It was a culture shock, but a nice culture shock.'

It sounded as if the retro nature of the chalet site had seeped into the people as well. There was a sense of community here that had all too often been lost from the outside world somewhere after the Fifties. As if to illustrate this, Ronnie's neighbour called over the fence: 'We're going in for our tea now, Ronnie, night night.'

'They have a place in Lambeth,' Ronnie explained. 'They stay down here for the summer and go back there when the park closes. They are going to have to shut up soon, but they hate it. I hate it too. When we used to move back to Gillingham for the winter I thought it would kill me to be back there. Now we rent a flat above the pub down the road. Last year, when my dog died I thought about selling the place. It was just too full of memories of her, but now I can't believe I even contemplated it.'

I looked down the line of chalets with their neat gardens and twinkly fairy lights and, for one minute, I wanted to hang all my reservations and buy a place. It was beautiful, it was special and if the people in the towns believed that Sheppey was a no-go zone where people ate their children then long may that attitude remain. Save it for those more enlightened.

I asked Ronnie if she had noticed any change in the people who bought chalets in recent years.

'There are a few more arty types now,' she said. 'But I don't think Sheppey will ever really go upmarket. I think the "Swampy" attitude will always stain it.'

By the time I had finished my tea it had grown too dark to see. We went inside the chalet and sat around the glowing gas fire on comfy couches. I accepted a beer and admired Ronnie and Jim's décor. Ronnie bought and sold retro furnishings and the inside of the chalet was a cosy well of flower-powered warmth and colour.

'We're doing it up bit by bit,' she said. 'We only paid £2,000 for it and we don't have a lot of outgoings,' she told me. 'I'm glad I can't afford a mortgage. Why do I want to burden myself with that? I live simply, spend as little as possible, enjoy my life for what it is, not for what I own. I don't get the whole idea of materialism and big houses. A lot of people who live on the site have what you might call an alternative working lifestyle. They don't work nine to five, they work for eight months and then go abroad for the winter. That is the way to live. If I had a normal house I would be stressed. Some weeks with my work I do well and some weeks I don't. If I had a mortgage that would put a lot of pressure on me.'

This is a world far removed from the government's idea of a productive citizen. Or rather the world that the shareholders of big businesses who really run the country want us to believe is the only way for Britain to survive. If there were too many Ronnie and Jims it would cause the establishment a few sleepless nights. This philosophy of living simply on little, not wanting to be a homeowner, a purchaser of things, is the opposite of the lifestyle we are so encouraged into pursuing. What would happen if lots of people decided not to get into the debt of a mortgage, live within their means and purchase only what they really needed? Would the country grind to a shuddering halt? Would we cease to be a world power and instead be happier, more enriched, less stressed citizens of a poorer but wiser country? Would we all regain a little of the help-each-other-out, community spirit that I had found in abundance among the people in the chalets and houseboats? These were not wealthy people. They did not have cars with personalised number plates, iPads, food from Waitrose in the fridge. They probably did not have wardrobes full of this season's clothes. They probably didn't have wardrobes, they might go without holidays, they might do without cars. They were, by most people's standards, poor, but they did not seem like poor people.

As more people fail to keep up with the economic pressures of a society which seems to value material possessions over human relationships, they are increasingly looking at other ways to make their lives a success. While governments continue to tell us that unrestricted economic growth is the answer to everything and, given time, will redress all the world's inequalities, many people are looking at the evidence and concluding that this is blatantly untrue. The rich get richer and feed on the poor like we are so many Matrix plugged-in battery cells. Downshifting is growing in popularity as people opt out of the goal of material wealth and, instead, focus on leading fulfilling lives.

As Ken Worpole says in *New English Landscape*: 'These small experiments in living act as both a safety valve and a beacon in an economic system that has almost eradicated the language of livelihood and self-sufficiency from the political vocabulary.'

If the world is changed by millions of tiny actions, downshifting may well win in the end; millions of people taking baby steps away from what they are told to pursue and thinking instead, 'do you know what, I think I won't'. But maybe the very individualism, the very pacifist, holistic nature of the downshifters is a problem. Unless those millions of little people unite and get bloody angry about the way things are, then, I fear, they will never work up the collective chutzpah to really challenge things.

Still, I am full of admiration for Ronnie's attitude, no doubt partly borne out of circumstance rather than choice, but still, she can appreciate when and how she's lucky. Ronnie and Jim are not making huge contributions to Britain's economic growth and so, to many people, they are failures, but as American philosopher Vernon Howard said, 'You have succeeded in life when all you really want is only what you need.' Ronnie and Jim feel like the enlightened ones, not those still on the treadmill.

I wondered how my life would have turned out if I had moved to the chalet park after the eviction. I think I would have been happy there, for a while. These people would have been kind to me, would have helped me out. They would have seen me as one of their own, a working-class girl, dumped by her feckless lover, with little money, making do. They would have come knocking with offers of friendship and trips down the pub. In some ways, moving there would have saved me from the long period of loneliness and isolation I endured after my break-up, but still I am not sure. I am not sure that, at a time when I wanted to lock the door and hide under the duvet, this would have been a good thing or not. Maybe in the community of the chalet park I wouldn't have gone through the dark time. I would have put on a happy face to the world and inside I would have sunk lower. I think despair to happiness can't be skipped. They are like two pinnacles with a chasm in between – with grief, you have to fall into the chasm to really, truly crawl out.

As if drawn by my thoughts, Ronnie's neighbours came knocking.

'Come down the pub,' they said.

Ronnie looked doubtful.

'Go,' I said. 'I'm done in.' Two whiskies and the beer had seen the end of me after my long walk. 'Come too,' the neighbours urged me. 'The pub does a lock-in, you can sleep in the bar.'

I declined and instead Ronnie and Jim took me across to the vacant chalet.

Jim carried a bucket of water, 'To flush the loo,' he explained. 'The water's not turned on.'

I carried the two bricks they'd given me to prop the fan heater up off the floor. Ronnie apologised for the basic conditions.

'Don't worry,' I told her. 'I am grateful for any lodging.'

They stood at the door fussing over me.

'If you're cold, if you need anything, if you are nervous, then just knock.'

I assured them I would be fine. Once inside, I pulled the cushions off the couch and made up a bed on the floor. By 9.30pm I was asleep.

TWELVE

Eastchurch – Leysdown on Sea – Harty Ferry – Faversham

I WOKE EARLY and went out to explore. Jim had told me the previous night about another chalet site I should visit on the clifftop. At the Dickens pub I turned up Fourth Avenue, a pot-holed dirt track lined with brambles. I found the chalets. They were the same boxy little buildings that could be seen all over Leysdown, with none of the charm of Ronnie and Jim's cabin. It seemed that the chalet park I'd discovered on that winter's day was unique. Anyway, these chalets would not be standing much longer. They were ringed by steel fences, some already partly demolished.

Over a morning cup of tea at Ronnie and Jim's I asked about them.

'Hoseasons have bought the site,' Jim explained. 'The guy that owned it lives in Australia. He inherited it off his parents but now he's sold it.'

'They want to turn it into one of the big family holiday places,' Ronnie said. 'They are trying to buy up a lot of the sites round here. It will be just awful when that happens.'

As I walked down the road half an hour later, I worried about Ronnie, Jim and the little chalet park. Its inhabitants seemed as vulnerable as the plotlanders once had. They had found their little bit of heaven, but it could be taken from them so swiftly. Ronnie had thought the place would never change, but I was nervous for it. Whitstable lay just across the water. How much would Ronnie's chalet be worth there? Ronnie and Jim paid a yearly rent for their plot, a modest amount, which could easily explode out of their reach if a different sort of person came here wanting to buy into the park's unique charm. And what if Hoseasons came knocking at the door of the park owner? Would the woman in the cowboy hat really resist the money offered or would she sell this piece of British history and disappear off to Australia too?

Ronnie and Jim had offered to sell me the chalet I had stayed in. There were three more on the site for sale. I wanted to say yes, turn round, buy one and enjoy it while I could, but even ignoring the fact that every penny I had was going towards getting my business off the ground, I knew that the chalet would not be the writer's retreat I envisaged but a DIY nightmare that would leave me in despair.

I walked away, heading through a strip of woodland full of blue tits, jays and fly-tipping. The last vestiges of the countryside gave way and I emerged to a view of bungalows crawling down dirt roads. I was back in the remnants of the plotlands.

Frederick Francis Ramuz was one of the driving forces behind plotland development on Sheppey. Originally from Leytonstone in East London, Ramuz climbed the social ladder, partly on the back of sales of cheap agricultural land to plotland holders. As far back as 1906, Ramuz's company, The Land Company, was declaring that 'land nationalisation is coming' and speculating that, in this way, a garden city could be built without the help of outside philanthropists. Despite the rhetoric, land sales on the cliffs of Minster and Eastchurch were slow and, even today, there are undeveloped plots to be found on the steep dirt roads.

There were few undeveloped plots to be seen on the road I was now walking down. Instead, it was the usual sorry tale of characterless red-brick bungalows, block-paved driveways, high walls and metal railings. It was little different from the prison I had passed the day before, only with less greenery. Still, there was an air about the place of a lost Britain, conjuring up a world of kids with brightly coloured plastic buckets, excited to be beside the sea, any sea, even this cold grey murky one, of women in minis and men sure of their role in the world as breadwinner and master. Down on Beach Approach a few remnants of the original plotlands remained. Across the road stood The Chimes, a two-storey stuccoed house with a sloping roof and diamond-shaped windows. A 'for sale' sign stood in the garden. I thought about the man who had originally built this house by hand. How proud he and his wife would have been at their achievement. How much clever resourcefulness they would have shown to pay for and build it. Soon The Chimes would be demolished. There was no doubt it would turn into The Beeches next door, red brick, double garage, lollipop hedge plants in pots, not a beech tree in sight.

At Warden Bay I climbed the sea wall and followed it round to face the grey, rain-streaked sea. I sat on the beach among the mermaid purses and razor shells, a black-backed gull sat on the groyne watching the rising tide. A flock of turnstones alighted and worked their way down the beach flipping the stones, looking for sand hoppers and other delicacies. A dog walker appeared with no fewer than nine yapping terriers around his heels. The turnstones made a dash for it but I was too slow. The dogs stood round me barking.

'Is she on your beach?' the owner said to the dogs. 'Does she need a permit?'

'No, I bloody don't,' I felt like saying as his dogs crapped freely into the sands, 'but you should.'

I walked on, into Leysdown. The holiday season had come to an end and Leysdown was shutting up shop. Beyond the low sea wall lay holiday parks, thousands of caravans and chalets, stretching back for miles. There was little protecting them from the sea should there be a storm surge or levels rose in the way they were predicted. Given a bad winter, a high tide, an onshore breeze, many people could return to their little kingdom to find it floating away to France.

A huge domestic had exploded outside the door of one caravan. A woman in a white tracksuit was dragging her mother into a car, while a man alternately yelled abuse at the women and hugged his mother-in-law, wailing, 'How long have you known me, Dot?'

The woman succeeded in manoeuvring her mother into the passenger seat of the white four-wheel drive and roared away from the park. Their weekend break had not ended well.

It was time for second breakfast and I popped into the Talk of the Town café and ate a large fry-up amid the builders from the site opposite. Another chalet park was being demolished to make way for a row of 'executive flats with sea views'. In the toilet of the café I startled a woman who found me cleaning my teeth in the washbasin. She took one look at my windswept hair, my sleeping bag wrapped in bin liners strapped to my back and the toothbrush in hand and gave me a look of pity.

'Don't mind me,' she said. 'You've got to do what you can when you can.'

I smiled a toothpasty grin.

Outside it had begun to rain. I walked through town, passing amusement parlours with no one to amuse and shops shut for the winter. Cards littered the shop windows. It seemed in Leysdown everyone had a chalet or caravan to sell. In the summer it was a different story, The Rose and Crown heaving with customers, blasting music onto the pavement, queues forming outside the tattoo parlour and the shellfish stall. Leaving Leysdown, I passed a road sign. 'Sea and Sky, Pitch and Putt, Eggs and Bacon, Birds and Bees'. A large arrow pointed the way to these many and varied delights and I followed, passing a man in a red Reliant Robin eating coleslaw and staring out to sea.

I trudged along beside the grey water, humming a ditty to the fish: 'Whiting and pouting, codling and grayling, dogfish and topknot, turbot and plaice, wrecks upon the Goodwin Sands, deep-water piers and rough ground marks, warm weather, calm water, tidal race'. This is what happens when your only reading matter is a tide timetable from the local fishing tackle shop.

The rain was falling heavier now in fat drops which stung my neck as I turned to face the sea. I pulled up the hood of my waterproof and the weather became an outside thing, the rain crackling in my ears like Space Dust sweets. I walked down to the beach and picked my way through the yellow-horned poppies and sea holly, passing the occasional dog walker, and strangely enjoying myself. The waves were spitting up the concrete sea defences, which were a triumph of practicality over aesthetics. I walked the tide line of slipper limpets and cockleshells, climbing through the holes in burnt-out groynes. Ringed plovers chased me up and down the beach. Bags of fetid dog poo hung from the broken teeth of washed-out groynes; why was a mystery to all but the dog owners.

I reached the line of beach huts. A wet dog came leaping from the beach, jumping up at me, sending me stumbling back under his large soggy paws. He showered me and my camera with sand as his owner screeched in the distance to no effect. The dog bounded after me as I pounded on. The owner seemed to have no control, but I soon realised that, when said with the right tone, 'Down' was a word this hound could understand. He sat at my feet, long forelegs splayed, hind end held up and wagging furiously. We eyed each other from our stand-off. Despite my sometimes intolerance of their owners, I don't always dislike the mutts themselves, and this wire-haired lurcher, with his yellow eyes, rock 'n' roll looks and Union Jack collar reminded me slightly of Keith Richards. The woman came rushing up and, without apology, gathered in the dog before I could run off with it and teach it some manners.

I walked on along a deserted nudist beach to Shellness, a private hamlet. On my map, which had hung in my cellar all winter, I had placed a post-it note on this spot. 'Who lives there?' I still didn't know. It was a place about which I could find precious little. A man I met on my walk told me that Pink Floyd's first guitarist lived there but, as this was Syd Barrett, who died in 2006, I found it unlikely.

The hamlet was beautifully situated on the edge of Sheppey. Looking out to sea, the houses sat low behind the wall, cobbled with brick. A two-storey beach hut rose up above the rest. On the beach was a pile of pallets, perhaps awaiting a bonfire night flame? Sheppey was a place of mystery and this place might be the most mysterious place on Sheppey. I had hoped to find someone out and about to talk to, but on this day of autumn gales, the hatches were down and if any eyes did watch me walk the perimeter, they were not curious enough to venture out and investigate.

At the end of Shellness I found a sheltered spot out of the wind and sat down to drink some water. The tide began to recede and curlews landed on the shore. A late-flying sand martin flitted past, having perhaps left it too late to follow its fellows across the channel.

Beyond the hamlet I discovered a beautiful stretch of coast line. A wild beach full of oystercatchers and brent geese vanished into the dune grass and marshes beyond. I hid in the shadow of a pillbox with a fantastic mural of a hen harrier painted on the side and looked out to the sea. Curlews flew low across the bay, joining the growing army of birds feeding on the wet mud exposed by the receding tide. Inside, the blockhouse was a mess. I walked in warily, fearing a dead body or the waste of too many live ones. It was a two-room hut with a little tower with skylights. The slit windows showed views of the bay on every side. I entertained a fantasy of presenting this as a project to George Clarke who could help me turn it into an 'Amazing Space' with hidden storage. This was what I wanted: an isolated hut on an undamaged shore, a place with just me and the wildlife. I thought of Stephen Turner's quest for a place where he could 'choose to be sociable or not'. I understood that need. In the last few years, friendship had been the thing that had sustained me but, still, I felt the need to withdraw occasionally, to be on my own. It was part of who I am, and more and more I felt that being who I am was not something I had to apologise for.

Further along I passed a series of strange, elliptical shapes scattered along the path, a public art project now being taken advantage of by gangs of hibernating snails who were finding the cracks and crevices to their liking. Later, I discovered that these had been created by Stephen, inspired by the pillbox where I had sat and contemplated our shared need for solitude.

The sun came out, briefly lighting up the sea. My path ended in a muddy creek and I had to retrace my steps. I didn't regret the diversion.

The wind picked up again as I found the right path and began the four-kilometre walk to Harty Church. A marsh harrier and a kestrel patrolled the saltmarsh. Pools of brackish water wriggled with wind waves, the samphire was burnt crimson amid the faded heads of sea lavender. It was hard going, fighting my way through snagging grass along the rutted track. I began to feel like I was in *Wuthering Heights*, walking a lonely path into the wind across the desolate wastes. I entertained a fantasy that I was pale and interesting in long black skirts, instead of the red-cheeked reality in muddy waterproof trousers.

I saw a box on the horizon and prayed it was a bird hide, somewhere to get out of the ceaseless wind. I trudged on. It was a hide, I could see it now, standing on stilts, with its slit windows looking out over a fleet. My legs ached to stop. I needed a drink. The rain began again, the reeds shushed in the wind, the sea wall curved round and round. I wanted to stop, but the little wooden box beckoned me on. I could barely keep walking against the wind. It seemed intent on hurling me into the ditch below. My shoulders ached from carrying the pack. I reached the hut and climbed down one flight of steps and up another. 'Let it be open,' I thought. I tried the door handle and it turned. Blessed be the birdwatchers and their little wooden huts.

I scattered the contents of my bag around the hut and pulled out the egg mayo baguette I had bought that morning. I munched my way through it in no time and followed up with two squares of Bourneville chocolate. I bounded along the rest of the sea wall, fired up by the egg and chocolate mixture. Four brent geese met me at the end of the reserve. They rose into the ashen sky like four pieces of charcoaled wood, blown from the fire. Away on the marsh a water pump twirled furiously. I fought my way into a head wind and passed a wooden sign which told me I had only a kilometre to go.

The track emerged onto a long path between a line of poplars. A covey of grey partridges whirred away across a stubble field.

Harty Church appeared on the horizon, a long low building with a little bell tower set on a ridge overlooking the Swale. I reached the church and found it open. I collapsed on a pew in the darkened building while the wind swirled outside.

A guidebook informed me that the church was much admired by the poet John Betjeman, who described its 'splendid isolation with seabirds wheeling by and the Thames so wide as to be the open sea and air so fresh as to be healthier than yoghurt (unflavoured)'. I was slightly sceptical about Betjeman's taste in yoghurt but liked the sentiment.

At one point in my planning, I had thought about sleeping in the church; I was now glad I had reconsidered. The church is a sanctuary and beautiful with its carved rood screen, intricate oil lamps and stained-glass windows depicting barn owls and farming scenes throughout the seasons, but the pews looked a little hard and I wasn't sure how I would have felt about the unlit, unheated building come nightfall.

Outside, I continued along the avenue of trees and cut off through an overgrown hedgerow onto a footpath. The rain continued to fall heavily as I reached the Ferry House Inn. I had booked myself 'The Spa room'. After two days of walking, I reckoned I could justify this one luxury. From the window of my room I could see the slipway leaving Sheppey and the other rising up at Oare. If I had to canoe or row my way across that water in a gale tomorrow then I felt I might be more up for the challenge after a good night's sleep. I dumped my bag on the double bed and fished through the contents for the one luxury I had carried for this moment. I found the bottle of lavender oil and tipped it into the Jacuzzi bath. As I lay back in the steaming water, pummelled by jets, and looked out across the windswept Swale, I felt I had spent my money well.

I woke after ten hours' sleep punctuated occasionally by the shrieking wind outside, but, when I looked from the window, the storm seemed to have passed and the morning looked hopeful. I ate enough for an army at breakfast and then walked down to the slipway. The old winch for the chain ferry was still standing, although no ferry had regularly used the crossing since the mid-1940s.

The tide was still a fair way out. It was shaping up to be a beautiful day, though the wind across the straight was icy. Over the preceding weeks I had contemplated many ways of crossing the Swale. There was only one bridge from Sheppey to the mainland and no footpath to get there, so there were few options but to take to the water. Originally I had planned to cross in the kayak I had found dumped in some bushes during the spring. It had seen better days and had several holes in the bottom, but after some experimental patching, involving waterproof duct tape and a hot spoon, it seemed watertight. True, it had only been tested on the far less daunting waterbody of the Stour in Canterbury, but I was fairly sure it would hold together for the crossing. However, the kayak technically belonged to my now ex-workplace and getting it to Harty would have involved breaking into a, admittedly unlocked, building, ferrying it across the county and organising someone to pick it up at Oare. In the end, the logistics proved insurmountable and I began to look at other means. 'Maybe I can swim,' I thought. I am not a strong swimmer, but the distance looked tiny on the map. Dave Wise had swum this part of the river and said there was nothing to it.

'At low tide you can practically walk across,' he'd told me.

Now, standing on the shore, the Swale looked an awful lot bigger than it had on my map. I had heard tales of the treacherous current and passing boats sucking people down. With a chilling wind coming off the sea and chopping up the water, I was mightily glad I had seen sense and looked for a third option. Glynn Roberts was my third option. As was the way with this trip, I had talked to a friend, who had talked to his sister, who had talked to her sister-in-law, who had talked to her partner, and that was how Glynn, a man I had never met, came to volunteer to be my boatman.

'Rescuing a girl from an island,' he said. 'Sounds like quite an adventure.'

Glynn phoned. 'I won't be able to make it across till high tide,' he told me. 'I was going to bring an inflatable canoe,' he said, 'but it is quite choppy so I have found something a bit bigger.'

With a lazy morning ahead, I went back to my hotel room and promptly fell asleep again. I had developed an amazing capacity for sleep while undertaking this trip, breaking all my previous records.

I awoke at 11.30 and shuffled back into my many layers and by noon I was down on the jetty once again. I watched two boats coming towards me. One looked like a fishing boat and the other a yacht. I was not sure which to expect. The fishing boat appeared more interested in a wrecked barge and headed towards it, frightening a roost of oystercatchers who piped a protest into the sky. The yacht sailed on. A motorboat now made its way towards me. A man waved at me from the deck and then, with the help of the rest of the crew, launched into a rowing boat and fought his way across the chop.

I watched helplessly as he got blown off course. I tried to follow him along the shore, not sure where he would land. I could see him fighting with the oars, straining as he wrestled with the wind. The boat veered back to the jetty but, despite his work at the oars, Glynn just couldn't get the boat onto the slipway. In the end, he gave up and jumped overboard, dragging the boat behind him. I balanced on a mudflat and managed to get into the boat without toppling it over. Glynn climbed back in and the crew on board the motorboat hauled us in with a rope.

I clambered aboard and found myself amid my three-man, one-woman crew, consisting of Mr Mac our skipper, Fergus, Glynn and Linda. They all had the deep-etched wrinkles, salt-blown hair and ruddy cheeks of people who spent a lot of time on the water.

'To the jetty or up the creek?' Mr Mac asked.

I opted for the soft option and we headed across the Swale and into the mouth of Faversham Creek, passing oyster boats and a curious seal. As the crew stopped to search for Glynn's hat, which had blown from his head on the journey across, I got talking to Linda, an artist, about the boatyard we were heading to.

'I met a man earlier in the year who used to live on the boatyard,' I told her, 'in a converted tour bus.'

'Do you mean Jason?' she asked.

'Yes,' I said.

'I know Jason well,' Linda said with enthusiasm. 'The bus he lived on is still there. I'll take you to see it when we land.'

At Iron Wharf we moored up alongside a Thames Barge. On the quayside was a line of railway freight cars with a blooming garden outside. Apple and hazelnut trees grew in pots besides bushes of lavender and rosemary. Freshly picked apples were lined up on a table outside.

'Who lives there, Linda?' I asked.

'A girl, who turned up years ago on a boat with a German man.' She pointed out the bleached hull of a wooden boat alongside the freight cars. 'They lived in the boat to begin with and then had a son and bought the first railway carriage, and when he grew up they bought another freight car for him to move into.'

'What happened to the German man?' I asked.

'He died,' Linda said. 'He was a lot older than her.'

'And she's there on her own now?' I said in awe. 'How old is she?'

'Sixty-three,' Linda said, which required some radical shift of mental image in my head from a young blonde hippie to a somewhat older 'girl'.

'Do many people live on the wharf?' I asked.

'Yes,' Linda said. 'They're not meant to, but they buy a boat and begin doing it up and then buy a caravan to shelter in while they're doing the boat up and then gradually the boat stops being built or they run out of money or they just like living on the wharf too much and they never move away. Fergus lives on the wharf,' she said, indicating the short, smiling Irishman with salt-glued hair, tying up the boat we'd just disembarked from. 'I think he's stopped building his boat now.'

We walked through the yard and Linda pointed out an ancient red and white Vega Major bus. It stood, wedged between piles of tyres and bricks, brambles growing around its wheels, its sides covered with mildew, its windows blocked out by raffia blinds. In the windscreen was a sign. 'No Dogs Allowed in the Club House'. Next to the steering wheel, the white legs of a shop dummy were perched upside down, wearing pedal pushers and a rather natty pair of grey suede shoes. On the side was painted in red letters, SMACK ALLEY. Smack Alley were a folk group, named after a lane in Faversham. They won a 'national wine bar entertainer of the year' title back in the Eighties with songs considered 'too dirty' by Southern Television, who had interviewed them following the win. This was their tour bus, a legendary vehicle as far as I was concerned after meeting Jason.

I had met Jason through my friend Will. Will had told me of a woodcarver who had lived in a bus on Cliffe marshes. As it turned out the story had got slightly twisted in the retelling. Jason had indeed lived on Cliffe Marshes for six years in a caravan but had also lived for four years in the Smack Alley bus at Iron Wharf. Either way, this sounded like the kind of man I wanted to meet. I had turned up at Jason's house one summer's afternoon.

Jason had sent the message: 'Park on the drive and come round the back'. I walked away from the Wednesday afternoon street with the kids playing football between the cars and into a courtyard full of sculptures. Jason came out of the conservatory. He was a Welshman, an earthy, surfer-looking guy with bleached blonde hair. He sat on a squashy sofa and asked me about my life in the caravan, maybe as a way of not discussing his, but slowly his story emerged.

Jason was now forty-six. He had lived in the caravan on the marshes at nineteen. He had studied at Thames Poly and couldn't survive on his student grant in London. In a fit of inspiration he had bought a map and looked at places from which he could commute to college. He spotted Higham Station, an hour from London by train. He drew a circle around the station and paid the area a visit. He then knocked on farmers' doors and asked if he could put a caravan in their field and pay to live there. I felt inspired by Jason's enterprise and bravery in doing this, and envious too, as it seemed somehow much easier for a man than a woman to do this.

Jason found Fred Wright, a local farmer whose family had owned swaths of the marshes for generations. Jason described Fred as 'blue to his core but a gentleman'.

'He was both deeply conservative,' said Jason, 'and on the other hand he liked rebellion.' Fred rented him a patch of ground at Westcourt Farm for £5 a month. Jason bought a 1962 Bluebird caravan. It had no electricity or running water. He heated the caravan with a gas fire, ran a lamp off a car battery and carried water in barrels across the field. He finished his degree and stayed on, helping Fred with the lambing, earning extra money knocking on doors and sharpening knives and teaching himself to carve wood.

I asked him if this life was hard. He said it wasn't.

'The caravan was so small it heated up quickly. I boiled kettles when I wanted hot water and washed myself and my clothes in a tin bath, and I was stupidly idealistic,' he said. 'I wanted to live simply. I had some romantic notion about being a Gypsy. The marshes helped with this. They have a strange ambience, a magical quality. They are a place where you can connect with an older way of life. There were parts of the marshes in those days where things had remained unchanged for hundreds of years.'

I understood this. The past was somehow very near the surface on the marshes. It was as if modern life was just a Perspex veneer over something ancient. Maybe it is because, in many ways, life is little changed here. It is still, for the most part, a landscape of mixed farming, not great wheat fields, but orchards, soft fruit, livestock; the type of farming which is still hands-on. The crop is picked by gangs of workers. They may no longer be Gypsies and Eastenders from London – nowadays, the winter fields are full of women in colourful saris and the orchards full of young Eastern Europeans – but the people are still on the land. The sheep are still on the fields too, lambs at heel in the spring and foraging the stubble in winter. It is a landscape where communities are still small, churchgoing is still strong, family names still matter.

Evidence of the people who lived on the marshes is all around, in the rotting barges, derelict cranes, unmodernised barns, small, ruined marshland houses. The people from the past still walk alongside you; they are a shadowy presence out of the corner of your eye. I don't mean in some spooky way, more like an echo. It is easy to imagine boats being unloaded at the docks, children walking to the village school, shepherds leaning against the wooden gates and women preparing supper in the kitchen. Sometimes, on the marshes, in the quiet of an afternoon in late summer, the past seems more tangible than the present. As Jason said, 'There are ancient connections there that you can still touch.'

Jason showed me some of his work, a beautiful mirror carved with wooden flowers and leaves.

'Would you have become a woodcarver if you hadn't lived in that place?' I asked him.

'I think it was always in me,' he said. 'I was just waiting to find it but, yes, the woodcarving and all that came after were based on the foundations of that caravan.'

It took Jason six years of living on the marshes before he was good enough to earn his living carving. I told him I admired his fortitude, sticking at the thing and the way of life so long, not giving up and just getting a job.

'I think I stayed there twice as long as I should have,' he said. 'I wake up sometimes from a dream in which I'm still there.'

'A good dream?' I enquired, but, unlike me, Jason had no rose-tinted ideas about that way of life. 'I wouldn't go back,' he said. 'I burned that part of me out. Life is a lot easier now and I like it that way.'

I told Jason about how I had clung onto the caravan. 'If I hadn't been evicted I would still be there now,' I told him. 'Despite the fact that staying would have been wrong for me in many ways, I would have stayed.' When Jason talked about his life in the caravan with no water or electricity, I felt lit up by the idea, not burnt out.

Now I was there, standing on Iron Wharf, looking at the Smack Alley tour bus, I could maybe understand Jason's feeling more. I wondered about the woman in the freight cars with no windows. Was she still actively choosing that life or was it that, after so long, she didn't now know what else to do? Many of the people I had met on my trip, living in the buses and chalets, houseboats and caravans did so because they saw it as the best of the options they could afford. They had chosen well. A chalet in an orchard or a houseboat on the river is much better than a flat in Gillingham. It is a sensible choice in a world where you are sometimes in and sometimes out of work, but did the two things, poverty and an alternative house choice, begin, after a while to converge? Did living in a tour bus on a boatyard surrounded by others leading similar lives make it harder to break that cycle, get a solid job, save money? The people I'd met on my journey had lived in communities where kindness, neighbourliness, helping each other out were part of the culture, but so was part-time, occasional work, fleeting relationships, late-night drinking sessions, shared roll-ups. After a while, did you choose that life or had it taken on a life of its own and you succumbed to it? Maybe if, after my break-up with Connor, I had moved to the chalet or the houseboat, I would have followed this path, with my sad story and love of whisky. Instead, I had chosen the stability of a job and house ownership. In this I was lucky. I had been the recipient of a free university education which enabled me to get a job I loved, which gave me the opportunity to live rent-free on a nature reserve, which allowed me to save up a deposit for a house. My education gave me choices. Not everyone was so lucky. In the end, the choice to leave the caravan had not been mine. My hand had been forced, but Jason had actively chosen to go.

'It was just time to move on,' he said. 'I stayed in a friend's caravan recently,' he told me. 'Just for a night, and didn't like it. I didn't want to be back there. I don't want anything to do with it now,' he said. 'It's done, it over, it's gone. That person is gone. I don't look back.'

Was I the same? Had the person who longed for houseboats and shacks gone to be replaced by this person with a mortgage and lodgers? Both Jason and I had fled from insecurity towards a more settled existence, but I still couldn't be sure which life was for me. I perched on my solid world with one eye on the door. The world of the boatyard was one of transience and maybe hard to move forward from, but perhaps its very instability made you question the dominant values of society and search for alternative way to achieve success. I still wanted the simple life, the indoor–outdoor world, a place in nature. I still believed in the values of kindness and generosity that I had seen displayed time and time again among the people I had visited, but I no longer wanted to return to the fragile world where your home could be taken from you at the whim of a developer. I had stepped out of that world and now, like Jason, I also wasn't so sure I wanted to step back in.

THIRTEEN

Faversham – Whitstable

I T WAS THE END OF NOVEMBER when I next set out. I planned to walk from Faversham station to Whitstable, a distance of about nine miles. After weeks of rain, it was a day of bright winter sun. The shops in Faversham were gearing up for Christmas. Displays of tartan, Christmas puddings and fairy lights pinged at me from dressed windows. These were the last days of calm before the panic buying descended.

I walked through the pretty streets; the road led past the twin spires of Faversham's brewery and St Mary's Church. At the end of the street was the Anchor Pub. Following my boat trip across the Swale with Mr Mack, Fergus, Glynn and Linda, we had adjourned to the Anchor for lunch, sitting outside in a little sun trap, wiling away an afternoon in a world of cider, beer and stories.

I walked back to Iron Wharf, taking a different route and seeing a more public face of arty cafés, posh garden shops and the sentinel of the Oyster Bay House, a restored warehouse, with its little turret, into which boat cargo would have been winched. It looked out over the creek towards the muted colours of the marsh. Gulls fed on the creek edge and a redshank scattered droplets of light from its toes as it lifted off the mud at my approach.

There were plans for more housing, shops and restaurants along the creek. Local people feared that the real working world of the boatyard would be lost. Currently, Thames barges came to the creek to be rebuilt. There was a thriving apprenticeship scheme offering the chance to learn traditional skills. The boats needed dry docks and sail lofts, but more development and new uses for the buildings could see this world challenged.

Already waterfront properties loomed imposingly on the other side of the wharf. Linda had told me that people in the new developments complained about the residents of the boatyard. I imagined that they felt the container homes and ramshackle sheds were spoiling the view. The hard-drinking boat owners were lowering the tone in the local pub. This was what happened when two cultures clashed. People who lived in waterfront apartments inhabited a different planet from people who lived in a container, and the two didn't rub shoulders easily in the local boozer. Which culture, I wondered, would find it easier to squeeze the other out? If the people who currently lived at Iron Wharf were squeezed out where would they go? I didn't know, but I doubted it was somewhere they could grow apple trees in tubs outside their front door, wake to a view of the marshes or live lives surrounded by a community of like-minded people always willing to lend a hand.

Fergus cycled past and raised his eyebrows in greeting, but couldn't quite place me as the girl he had rescued from Sheppey. It was still early and I was looking less windswept. I followed his tyre tracks along a narrow, muddy path and emerged into the boatyard. Wood smoke lingered in the air and the place, on this beautiful Saturday morning, was alive with the sound of sanding and hammering. Everyone I passed said hello. It was a while before I got back into my stride and returned their greetings. For the past month I had been in closed-off, fast-paced modern life; setting up my business, going to meetings, thinking about tax and whether I could make ends meet. I had forgotten that things were different out here. I immediately felt myself slowing down, relaxing, returning the smiles.

Going freelance had created its own challenges. For the first time in ages I had felt lonely. I missed running my volunteer group. I missed the social life I had made for myself in Canterbury. Long days working on my own made me feel isolated, though I had anticipated feeling this way and that helped. I set about finding an office space where I could work once a week, getting out of the house for a cycle at lunchtime and joining a networking event that met for coffee once a month. There were upsides too. I felt unpinned, no longer having to justify my every move. I was free to succeed or fail on my efforts alone and this thrilled me. So far it appeared I was succeeding. I had offers of work coming in, my finances looked tight but not dire. I was beginning to feel positive that I could indeed make this gamble pay off.

I paused at the boat brokers and wiped the early morning dew off the 'For Sale' board. I looked at the advert for a sailing boat called *Katie*: 'Sloop rigged, motor sailor, twin bilge keels, roller reefed, mainsail and furling jib, £3,250'. I had no idea what it all meant but it sounded beautiful. A sign next to it informed me that I could have my very own railway carriage for £10 a week, £40 a month, ten times less than my mortgage. I was torn, still, torn.

I walked away from the boatyard via a narrow bridge of rotting timber and rusty metal balanced on the banks of a side creek. It was the most glorious day to be back on the marshes; the world and all its contents were backlit by winter sunlight. Mistle thrushes chuckled in the hawthorn bushes overhung with silvery tendrils of old man's beard. Millions of winter midges hovered around the twiggy ends of the scrub, while late-migrating warblers danced about among them.

I passed a massive outflow churning phosphate-smelling foam into the river from the adjacent sewage works. The Swale, along which I was about to walk, was protected, for now at least, under European law because of its importance for wildlife, but it was also polluted. Chemicals sprayed on crops ran off the land into streams, wood preservative used on boats in the 1960s killed dog whelks and poisoned the seals. Even the prized Whitstable oyster beds were not spared and were in danger of failing to meet shellfish standards owing to the amount of raw sewage being discharged into the river from misconnected drains or badly managed treatment works. If this smelly foam was anything to go by, then we were still doing far too little to change things.

I crossed a flatland of wheat fields and reached the banks of the Swale. I climbed onto the concrete embankment and sat down. The river was luminous with winter light, smoke drifted up from the factories surrounding Milton Creek further upstream, across the water I could see the Ferry House Inn. A wire-haired, golden-eyed, lurcher came along the wall. She stopped and looked unsure of what to do with this blockage in the way. We made friends and she hopped across my legs and continued towards Faversham.

I took off my boots and spent a merry few minutes, picking the stones, mud and gravel out of the holes with my knife, but then realised the holes went right the way through the soles and the stones were acting as a damp course. I put the boots back on and ate a handful of festive nut mix with cranberries and chocolate chips and took a swig from my hip flask of homemade elderberry elixir, a mixture of elderberries, spices and dark rum.

Despite its pollution problems, fifty-one square kilometres of the Swale were being proposed as a Marine Conservation Zone in 2014. These were being set up to provide protection for some of our most important coastal areas, which are degrading at an alarming rate. Originally, the Government pledged to protect 127 areas, but somehow they had managed to lose one hundred of these along the way and even protection for the final twenty-seven was not yet agreed. The Swale Estuary was hanging on in there, but could be dropped at any time if protecting it was deemed too costly. As the RSPB pointed out: 'It is much easier for industry and commerce to put forward a balance sheet to show what a marine conservation zone might cost them, whereas the enormous benefits provided by the marine environment are much harder to quantify.'

Even when the Swale received Coastal Zone status in 2016, the law still had enough loopholes in it to create a crochet blanket. Only named features and habitats would receive protection within a zone. If your name wasn't on the list you were out of luck. Dolphins, sharks and sea birds hardly featured on the lists because they didn't stay in one place. Without some provision for ocean predators and protection of the whole site, the health of the Swale and our seas in general could still freefall.

I followed the sea wall through the South Swale nature reserve. Stonechats flew along behind me, flitting between patches of bramble. The wall was graffiti-sprayed with daubs of yellow lichen. Gulls, flecklings of white, like splattered bird droppings, speckled the tideline for many miles. Out at Castle Coote bird sanctuary the action of the tide had sculpted the gravel into sinuous curves and spirals. Widgeon whistled out on the mudflats and skylarks played a game of chase across the marshes, fluttering up from the grass and speeding after each other in circles.

I spied a blackthorn bush and put on a burst of speed, in need of a little cover for a sudden call of nature, but it was no good, the day was just too beautiful and hordes of people were heading out from Whitstable along the wall: joggers, cyclists, birdwatchers.

'Hello, beautiful day,' they all called heartily at me.

I reached the bush only to find two people lingering next to it, staring out across the river with a pair of binoculars. I started to curse them, but then realised one of them was my friend Mansel, out for a stroll with his wife.

'Have you seen the seals on the far bank?' he asked and lent me his binoculars. I could just make out the pebbly blobs lying on the Horse Sands. 'There are about thirty,' he said.

'That's marvellous,' I told him. 'It's lovely to see you, but could you please now scurry along so I can nip behind this bush for a wee?'

He tactfully departed and I rushed down the embankment before anyone else could appear.

After months of walking the marshes and seeing no one I was not used to so much company. I leapt the wall and escaped onto the beach where, strangely, no one was walking. I crunched my way across cockleshells and through feathery and leathery seaweeds, stopping to squeeze the bladders of bladder wrack, which burst with a wet pop.

I stopped next to some weathered groynes for a sandwich. Bait diggers were out on the mud, calling to each other across the sandflats. Their voices travelled a long way and they chatted easily as they pulled bristly ragworms from their lairs. Sheppey rose up on the other side of the Swale. I could see the stretch of beach along which I had walked. Before, when I had looked at it from across the water, it had always been an unknown place, but now I knew it: the shingle spit where the geese landed, the pillbox with its painting of a hen harrier, the marble globes on the beach. It was weird to see my route laid out on the horizon, like looking back into my past. I felt that, if I'd had binoculars, I could have gazed across the water and seen myself, making my way through the Swale reserve, huffing and puffing and trying to reach the bird hide.

Looking back on my past was something I no longer wished to do. I wished to look forward, but I still didn't know to what. The business was going well, I thought. I had work and money coming in. My lodger helped pay the mortgage. I wouldn't starve before the spring. I knew I could only do this because I had good friends, work contacts, a good support network, but there was still that need for one person in my life to come home to, to talk it all through with at the end of the day.

The Man of the Spring had gone and the Man of the Summer? More and more I could see that this man felt too much like Connor. I was easy and relaxed with him. He made me laugh, I could tell him anything, but there were other things that made me wary. I didn't always walk away from this man feeling good about myself and besides he didn't want any kind of commitment, he wanted to continue to live separate lives. I think, in the past, I would have leapt at this, but I was not the same person I had been with Connor. I was not even the same person I had been a year ago when I had started this walk. I wanted more.

So there was the Man of the Autumn, a man out there on the horizon, another whom I could never have, but who represented something that maybe now I wanted. This man was kind, he had supported me and been a cheerleader for my plans to go freelance. He was someone to rely on, he was someone who took responsibility for his actions. He treated me with respect. Was that really now what I wanted? Steady, reliable, solid. Really, me? The commitment-phobe? Did I really want safety?

The bait diggers were heading home. There was a nip in the air as the day turned. I was conscious of losing light and, although I could see Whitstable crawling over the hills and ridges to the east, I knew I still had a fair walk ahead. I evicted the sandflies from my lunch box and walked on. My shadow grew long across the beach, my feet walking on sand, my head somewhere out in the pools, my hair wiggling into the mud rivulets. Mist grew from the sea and the light glowed blue around me. Blue sky reflected in blue pools, the blue haze of the grazing marsh on Sheppey, the shadows, blue, the mussel shells, blue, the little blue sticks of a million cotton buds flushed down toilets and washed to beaches on the tide, all blue.

I reached the Seasalter beach huts and entered the invisible force field of Whitstable, the Emperor's New Clothes of seaside resorts. Whitstable, beloved by crowds of Londoners who own second homes here, so beloved that they crowd onto the pavements on sunny weekends and topple off into the traffic, fight their way along the boardwalk by the beach with their shiny-haired infants in strollers, wielded like swords, and have endless barbecues on the beaches, setting fire to the beach groins in the process.

The Seasalter beach huts, once tumbledown and eclectic, were slowly being gentrified. Now there was a patchwork of peeling paint and felt roofs next to glass-panelled frontages and brand-new decks. In contrast to the boatyard, the people working on these properties did not greet me. Instead, notices informed me that I was crossing a 'private beach'. I trudged down to the tideline to walk below the high-water mark on land owned by the Queen, who, I felt, was less likely to give me grief.

The beach hut hadn't always been so exclusive. In the past, it was somewhere an ordinary family could rent out for the summer and enjoy long, cheap days in the sun, while the kids played for free and dug for crabs. 'How could an ordinary person afford one of these beach huts now?' I thought, 'and would they fit in if they could?' I knew I was nostalgic for a past that would never come back and which was never mine anyway, but still it made me angry.

Down the road from here was Seaview Holiday Park. The chalets in this park had been bought by families from poor areas of London in an era before Whitstable became fashionable. In 2007, these families returned to the site to be told that the lease for the ground that their chalets sat on would not be renewed. They were asked to either move their chalets or hand over the keys. The owners refused. The huts became ring-fenced with metal security gates and the owners were told that if they did not empty their chalets and hand over the keys their holiday homes would be bulldozed with their possessions inside and the chalet owners would be charged for the demolition. 'The old chalets were unsafe,' the chalet park told the owners, 'they were full of asbestos, and they had to come down. New chalets were being built, and they were free to buy one of these if they so wished.' The old chalets had cost the owners around £2,000, the new ones would cost £45,000. The owners of Seaview Park were as good as their word. They bulldozed the chalets with the owners' possessions inside and charged them £587 for the privilege.

I was reminded again of the words of Patrick Abercrombie, the city planner from the plotlands era: 'The preserver of rural amenities cannot allow any sort of old junk cabin to deform the choicest spots.' I could imagine him sighing in relief. 'Thank God, everyone back in their proper place, the rich owning second homes, the poor back on the council estates.'

Cold air was drifting in from the sea as I entered the outskirts of Whitstable. Away to my right stretched the Seasalter levels. Sheep grazed in waterlogged fields, reed-fringed ditches wound their way across the marsh, curlews were coming in to land. I passed a set of metal gates. A wide track led away and, in the distance, could be seen little clumps of scrub and the occasional leylandii tree, out of place on the wet grassland. This was the entrance to the Whitstable Bay Estate, the last gasp of the working-class dream of a place in the country.

The Whitstable Bay Estate consisted of 160 acres of the Seasalter Levels which were sold off, subdivided into plots in 1972 by Messrs A. R. and G. E. Darling of Cheam, Surrey. The advertisement stated that planning permission for the plots could not be ruled out. The Darlings bought the land at £30 an acre and sold it at a £1,000 an acre. By 1975, 200 plots had been sold. The Mr Darlings were not alone. Thousands of 'leisure plots' were sold throughout the Sixtiess and Seventies. Kent County Councillor, John Heddle, saw what was happening and 'deplored these unscrupulous firms trading on people's aspirations through speculation'. These businessmen saw that those from inner city areas dreamed of owning a place in the country where the kids could run free and sold off parcels of land, knowing the owners would never be allowed to build or even stay on them. When the plot owners arrived with the kids and a tent in the car they were often met by an enforcement officer from the council or a sign telling them that, under a piece of planning law known as Article Four Direction, the owners were not allowed to park a caravan, or a car or pitch a tent. If they applied for planning permission, it would be refused.

Despite this, the people who bought plots on the Whitsable Bay Estate were not deterred. They moved in, fenced their land, towed the caravans into place and set about enjoying their country retreat. 'It was a poor man's holiday,' one plotholder told Clio Barnard when she interviewed him as part of her 2008 film, *Plotlands*, screened at the Whitstable Biannual art festival. 'It's our version of country living, better than arguing with your neighbour and watching a dog shit on the pavement.'

Local people, far from seeing the site as a rural idyll, labelled it a shanty town. By 1975, front-page headlines in the *Whitstable Times* cried: 'We will kick them off the marshes,' following the news that Canterbury City Council would begin proceedings to prevent landowners staying on their land. Plotholders such as Mr Knowles, an engineer, were dismayed.

'The decision to make a living off our own land represents a big thing in our lives. We can't accept that we are going to be thrown off.'

Despite the opposition, the plotholders held on. By the mid-1980s, evictions, court appearances and fines were becoming commonplace. In 1985, at a time of mass unemployment, a man who was living on his plot with his wife and son told the court he had nowhere else to go. He was fined £25 and ordered to pay prosecution fees of £25.

In the hope of legalising their position, the plotholders invited their local MP down to visit the site and see for himself how they were trying to work the land and live a simple life. The plan failed. Mr Crouch, the then Conservative MP for Canterbury, branded the place 'an eyesore' and opposed the use of 'perfectly good agricultural land for leisure purposes'. He knew of several similar areas, he declared, 'which were properly drained and used for farming'.

However, instead of the land being drained and used for wheat growing, as Mr Crouch had hoped, in 1985 it was designated a RAMSAR site, a wetland of international importance and a Special Protection Area for its breeding and wintering birds. Canterbury City Council renamed a neighbouring piece of land that they owned 'The Seasalter Levels Local Nature Reserve', and began looking at ways of acquiring the rest of the site. The City Council felt that the way the owners were using their land was detrimental to its wildlife value. They cited things such as camping, lighting grass fires, planting inappropriate trees, fishing, erecting structures, creating roads and using boats. Natural England was brought in to advise owners on everything they were doing that was likely to damage the wildlife value of the site, and the council issued 100 enforcement notices.

Before coming here, I had looked at aerial photos of the site of the Whitstable Bay Estate. The outline of the plots could be seen; the marks of settlement, tracks, former boundary lines, the last remnants of shelters and animal enclosures. It looked like an Iron Age settlement, the people long gone but their lives etched on the ground, a human fingerprint that was not so easily erased as the people themselves. Would a future archaeologist look at these patterns and wonder what happened to these people?

The metal gate to the site was open, so I walked through and along a dirt track, passing a lichen-covered gatepost with a rusty tin sign which read 'G3'. Further along were the remains of a white picket fence. Inside, a box-shaped stand of young hawthorn showed the site of a former shack, an apple tree stood opposite what would have been the entrance gate. There was not much active management for wildlife to be seen at present, just abandoned dreams.

It was hard to know where I stood. On the one hand I thought, 'What a great place, quiet, full of wildlife, close to the sea'. I wanted to put my caravan there, but I knew that the reality may have been somewhat different. All this individual ownership could breed anarchy. I didn't approve of the fir trees, which some plot owners had planted. I didn't approve of the scorch marks which showed where fires had been lit in dry grass. Despite what I wanted to believe, the reality I felt might have been noisy football games and kids trying out mini quad bikes bought for them by their parents.

The council, and later the RSPB, who leased the site from 2007, decided that there was no way that they could manage the land effectively for wildlife while the plotholders were still in possession. They considered the options for managing in partnership with the owners, but thought that as there were so many and at least twenty percent of them could not be traced, then this just wasn't a practical solution.

In 2014, a partnership of organisations, including Swale Borough Council, the RSPB and Natural England, agreed that Canterbury City Council should put a compulsory purchase order on 242 plots of land for the purposes of establishing a nature reserve. The Compulsory Purchase Order stated: 'The council felt it could not stop damaging activities unless it owned the land.' Despite my sympathies with anyone evicted from their property, I had to conclude that they were probably right.

The Seasalter Levels should be managed for the benefit of wildlife and maybe, not least because of its vulnerability to sea-level rise, it is not the ideal place for anyone, rich or poor, to build their dream home in the country. But the Whitstable Bay Estate showed how poor people living in cities continue to dream of a simpler life closer to nature. So many of the people interviewed by Clio Barnard mentioned the effect that the place had upon the children who came there.

'The kids change here,' one plotholder said. '[It] takes three or four days to adapt, then [they become] quiet, more within themselves, thinking.'

Where would these people and their kids go now? While nature reserves can easily be swept away by governments for housing estates, it seems increasingly impossible for the less affluent to find a place where they can let their children play in the countryside and discover nature. Everyone agrees that children need to spend more time playing unsupervised outside and the plotlands allowed people to do just that. '[It's a] safe place for children to play and learn about the environment away from the roads and motorways,' said one of Clio Barnard's interviewees. 'You can't put a price on that.'

There must be some middle ground. In a society where people feel alienated and powerless, where so many young people suffer from depression and use drugs to escape reality, then the idea of the plotlands has increasing value. Self-determination and autonomy, working with your hands, being close to nature; these are things which could help many young people, the unemployed or those suffering with mental health problems to begin to grow in confidence and turn their lives around. Maybe at the Seasalter Levels there was no other way, but more thought needs to be given before we evict those who are trying to take some control over their lives.

Colin Ward and Dennis Hardy in *Arcadia for All* conclude that 'the present generation owes a debt to those who worked to protect a diminishing countryside from indiscriminate development, but ways surely can be found to allow room for modern innovation without letting in all the evils of the past.'

I left the estate, climbed back onto the beach and walked behind a mixture of tasteful, timber-clad beach homes and burnt-out shacks. I crossed a slipway behind some blue metal sheds. The air reeked with the smell of shellfish. An oyster dredger sat on the mud, another appeared to be wrecked in the bay.

The beach groynes wound their way into Whitstable like football terraces. Two oystercatchers fought out on the mud, turning in circles, piping at each other. A herring gull flew in to see if there was an opportunity to exploit.

A sign informed me that I had reached the Granville Estate and that the path and beach were once again 'private'. I walked on, passing houses growing more lavish with every step. The pages of home improvement magazines sprang to life: antique children's sailing boats, propped at jaunty angles in windows, faded ice cream signs hanging on walls, dried flowers in old milk churns standing on kitchen tables. It was all so achingly correct and picture perfect.

I passed yummy mummies gossiping on the beach, surrounded by children and Labradors. Everyone I passed seemed to have exactly the right shoes, hair and clothes, even the kids: brand-new jeans, correctly distressed leather boots with built in scuff. For one moment I considered taking off my battered walking boots full of holes and trading them in; after all, they had the kind of patina that money just can't buy. The gardens of the properties I passed were the same; the correct heritage colours, the correct fence panels, the correct kind of plants. It was all so tasteful that I felt a rebellious urge to run amok with a can of spray paint in some lurid colour and splatter everything, little Tarquin and Juniper, yummy mummy and Fido, bleached wood and lavender bushes with the wrong, wrong, WRONG shade of BRIGHT ESSEX PINK.

But then I checked myself. I had spent the last year meeting a whole mixture of society and prided myself on my acceptance of all manner of human foibles. If you were a homeless alcoholic recently released from the loony bin then I would no doubt welcome you into my home, but did my acceptance stop at those who had money? Did I feel it was OK to sneer at the wealthy because their money made them immune? Was my desire to redecorate really just a bitterness because I had to struggle for what I had and I presumed these people didn't? It was an accumulation of having to live off bags of potatoes at university, while others had food parcels delivered containing beef wellington, of having to fight my way into a career where my accent was all wrong, of having to deny myself the things that others didn't think twice about buying. I felt an affinity with the 'have nots' of this world because I saw myself as one of them, but was that really true anymore? I had a good job, I ran my own business, I owned my own house and I was a landlord. What was to stop a person struggling for cash and living in a leaking chalet looking at me and thinking 'it's all right for her'. I didn't know these people and what they had done to earn their beach home. Janet Street Porter, I was told, owned one and her mum had been a dinner lady. While second homes were clearly part of the problem and the influx of wealthy people into Whitstable had played its part in the eviction of chalet owners from Seaview Park, could I really knock people who at their core were only after the same thing as me, somewhere to escape the city and feel closer to nature?

I reached the Neptune pub. It was late afternoon, the tide was sloshing around the base of the groynes. The seals I had seen earlier would be swimming out there now, diving for fish beneath the silver skin of molten liquid. Directly opposite, I could see, through the hazy light, the cliffs of Warden Point on Sheppey. I had reached the mouth of the Swale, the end of the estuary. If I walked on, I would be out to sea. It should have been the end of the journey, but it felt unfinished.

Over the last few months, I had set myself on a new course. I was proud of what I'd achieved and maybe I now knew that I was not the woman I was when I was with Connor. My life had moved on, his life had moved on. Even if I didn't know what my future held, I knew what I no longer wanted. But where did I go from there? I didn't know where I fitted. My walk through the

Whitstable beach homes hadn't convinced me that I would fit there even if I could afford to, but neither did I quite fit in the plotlands, or boatyards or chalet parks. That life felt too fragile. Where was my place? What was my future? It was no good. The sun was going down and I couldn't walk on, so maybe, for one last time, I needed to go back.

FOURTEEN

Rainham – Lower Halstow – Upnor –
Chattenden – Rye Street

THE BLUE TIT NESTLINGS had fledged from my bird box on the day I set out on the final part of my journey in 2015. I took it to be a good sign. Spring had come again. It was just over a year since I had first set out on my walk across the estuary and I had come full circle. The whitethroats rasped and squealed from the may trees in Hawthorn Towers as I cycled along my road. A few days ago, I had written yet another objection letter about the proposed development of this area. The site was home to cuckoos and nightingales, lizards and snakes and orchids, but it was brownfield, a former brickworks, the perfect place to plant a housing estate according to the newly elected Tory government. Except it wasn't. After one hundred years of abandonment, the former industrial site had become a wildlife haven, far more diverse in botanical delights than the chemical-drenched mini orchards that surrounded it.

I felt, that with the loss of this land, my house had fallen in value, not in a financial way, but in other ways: as a place where I could sit in my garden on a spring evening and hear a nightingale sing, where flocks of long-tailed tits sailed over from this scrubland into the apple trees behind my summer house. My house had value to me because it was close to nature and wildlife, and soon this value would be stripped away.

I cycled on, down the back roads, before the morning traffic appeared, and arrived at Lower Halstow, where the *Edith May* sailing barge was moored. I was going back to the Hoo Peninsula. I had walked across it and away from it months earlier, but now it was time to go back and face the things I had run away from, and I was going to do it in style. For the last year, I had walked along the shoreline, seeing the remnants of the old Thames barges, the places they had once sailed from and their sad fate, but there were still a few of these vessels operating on the river and it seemed fitting to begin this final leg of the journey aboard one of them.

The *Edith May* had been built in 1906 and had worked the waters around East Anglia, collecting grain from Great Yarmouth and taking it into London. On board I was greeted by Ed Grandsen and his father Geoff. Geoff had bought the barge as a wreck for £5,000 ten years ago and was now doing her up, using her to take paying customers out on the river and compete in sailing-barge matches. Alongside her was *Thistle*, an oyster smack, the latest project.

'Feel free to explore,' Ed said. 'We have to wait for the tide to float us out.' I climbed aboard *Thistle* and down the steep ladder which led below decks, into a dark hull, smelling of creosote. Below, the living quarters were cramped, even for someone of my hobbit-like proportions. Bent double, I scrambled past the beds, which seemed to be covered in tan oilcloth, towards the stove with its smoke-blackened kettle and stuck my head round the door of the tiny toilet cubicle.

'Fourteen people sailed on her,' Ed's voice assured me from above.

I counted three beds.

Ed ran Sun Pier House, an arts and community centre, where I had been renting an office space since the autumn. It was a good place to go, once a week, to laugh with the other freelancers and homeworkers, a mixture of web designers, dance company managers and marketing staff for fashion designers.

The winter had been hard. The work had kept coming – river reports, flood alleviation projects – but the money had trickled in slowly. For Christmas, everyone got a handmade gift: lavender bath scrub, pickle, jam and nettle beer which was likely to explode if handled without care.

Now things had begun to get easier. I had ironed out some of the problems that came with setting up a new business. I had begun to rediscover where I lived, met new acquaintances which, given time, might just become new friends.

The other workers at Sun Pier, for instance, had welcomed me as a fascinating oddity, a girl who spent her days wading down icy rivers and looking at water vole poo. They would ask me: 'How is the tentacled lob worm today? How is the many barnacled shellfish?' Slowly, it emerged that many of them – the web designers, the mobile phone engineers, the debt collectors – had spent a childhood searching for slow worms in the quarries, or keeping caterpillars in a jar, or hunting rabbits in the scrublands near their homes. They were secret beekeepers, or Greenpeace activists. 'We're so envious of your job,' they told me. Here was hope, that these men, their childhood spent among nature, had grown to know it and love it, and hopefully had passed that on to their children. Here was a silent force, an undercurrent of people who, if push came to shove, I hoped would fight to protect the edgelands from destruction.

I emerged from the hull of the *Thistle* and climbed back onto the *Edith May*. The crew prowled the decks waiting for high water; Ed scaled the rope ladder; the kettle rang out from below. The chatter was all of laying up and bilge pumps, hard water and rigging and mostly about the barge match that the *Edith May* was to compete in, a competition which, Ed told me, had stopped being competitive but was now 'a serious business again'.

Finally, we loosened the ropes holding us to the dock and motored out into the estuary, piped away by the oystercatchers. We passed the islands of Milford Hope, streaks of saltings disappearing beneath the rising tide. The land – all the miles I had walked – stretched away. There was the path to Lower Halstow that I had run along in the rain shower, Darnet Island, where the rats danced at night, Humble Bee Creek with its German U-boat, the place I had swum with Pete. It was the river I had read about with Mr W.

Coles Finch, the river of Francis Drake and prison ships, of man-of
-wars and the Dutch fleet coming to burn them. It was the river of
dredgers and smacks, bawley boats and barges like this one.

Ed climbed into the rigging to untie the ropes which bound the
top sail. The sail flapped overhead; craning my neck to see him at
work was like looking up into the roof of a cathedral. The rust-red
wing unfurled and flapped in the wind. Ed shimmied down again
and began pulling on ropes. It wasn't work for the feeble. Using his
whole body strength, he hauled on the rope, bending at the knees
and swinging back up to snatch it and pull again. I felt exhausted
just watching him and happily gobbled down chocolate biscuits
with a cup of tea.

As we passed Hoo Ness Island, other barges could be seen,
moored up.

'They mainly come from Kent and Essex,' Geoff told me.

Ed pointed out his competitors.

'The *Edme*,' he said, pointing to a slimmer, smaller boat, manned
by boys with dreadlocks and a feisty dog that ran along the decks
barking abuse at us. 'It is the number one barge,' he said, eyeing it
with envy.

The men on board were busy polishing the woodwork.

'Too late for that,' he shouted to the crew. 'You're either ready
or not.'

The crew waved back in acknowledgement.

'No one beats it,' Ed said and bit down hard on a chocolate biscuit.

Tall masts appeared to be everywhere, moored mid-river, moored
on Alex's boatyard. I imagined his delight. How he would wander out
to tell them stories of his life on the barges and the women he had
known. There was tension in the air, the first match of the season.

'It's a fresh slate,' Ed said. 'We won in 2011 and 2013, and we
were close last year, too close; the boat went well, the crew let her
down. That's hard, we need to be better.'

We sailed towards Upnor and moored up alongside another barge
called the *Repertor*. The boats were strung with tyres and rubbed
together with a long chorus of squeals and groans. Ed's counterpart,

the son of the *Repertor*'s owner, a man with wiry muscles, hauled on ropes to level the boats. The engine was cut and water piddled out of the bilge pumps. The men stood on deck trading stories.

'Who did you see coming down the river?' The *Repertor*'s son asked Ed.

'The *Lady Daphne*, the *Niagara*, the *Cambria*.'

The *Repertor*'s son sighed. 'The *Cambria*, they should take her out. She's a different class, so much faster than the rest.'

I sensed this conversation was a familiar and long one. I took my leave and crossed between the *Edith May* and *Repertor*, climbed over the decks and leapt down onto the shore at Lower Upnor.

Once on shore, I strapped my knife on, shouldered my pack and headed away from the Medway for the final time on this trip. I was heading back, across the Hoo Peninsula, back to the beginning. I climbed a steep path through grizzled woodland, amid the calls of blackcaps and wrens, and then followed a barbed-wire fence beside an ugly compound lined with fir trees, the cuttings from which had been dumped into the woodland stream. Signs warned me that I was being watched, that dogs were loose, that the fence might electrocute me. I emerged to a sign telling me the site was owned by the MoD. All around were fortified gates and barbed wire. I followed the road, only to see a huge metal fence across my path. I feared that the footpath had been closed but, no, to one side, almost covered in foliage, was a little gate. I felt a sense of gratitude for our long history which had delivered Rights of Way, our legally protected right to pass and re-pass that even the military and big business had a hard time overturning.

Our right of way is something we take for granted, but in many other places in the world, riverside views, hilltops, meadows are all privately owned with no route through at all. The right of way is a great leveller. Many paths are so ancient that they came before everything that surrounds them; grand estates, rich people's gardens and shooting estates all have these tricky little footpaths running through them, which allow us all, riff raff, commoners, peasants and poor, to walk along and enjoy the same views.

I crossed the dual carriage way and followed the signs to Lodge

Hill. In the valley below me was the former plotland settlement of Cliffe Woods. Lodge Hill rested on top of Lena Kennedy's 'lovely hill'. The woods were still lovely, paths lined with the drooping heads of pendulous sedge led to coppice clearings which rang with woodpeckers drumming in the spring. The woods were home to early purple orchids, silver-washed fritillary butterflies and one of the largest colonies of nightingales in the South East. All of this was threatened with development. Despite its SSSI status, the MoD, who owned Lodge Hill along with its partner, the perkily named, Defence Infrastructure Organisation, were planning to build 5,000 homes on the site. The development would see most of the SSSI destroyed. Medway Council had given planning permission, but the voice of protest had forced the government to call the decision in, something which happens in only about one percent of planning cases. A public inquiry was now to be held before a government minister would make the final decision. Despite the fact that the public inquiry wouldn't take place until 2018, Medway Council continued to insist that Lodge Hill should go for housing. In 2017, they included it in their draft housing plan, ignoring the protests of local people. If Medway Council had their way, they would go down in history as the local authority that gave the green light for the destruction of protected sites.

I walked along the road past high metal fences, beyond which were meadows and woodlands ringing with chiffchaff calls. I parked my bag on a tank trap and listened. A chaffinch fell down the scales, a song thrush beat out a three-chorus stanza. Pignut bloomed in lacy drifts along the side of the road, each flower unique, like a snowflake. And then I heard a 'seep, seep, seep, seep' of exquisite, descending, liquid beauty, like golden syrup poured into the light: the rich, delicious, dark and spicy song of a nightingale. These birds were holding the front line against the destruction of this place, but still, it might not be enough.

Further along the road I passed the abandoned buildings of the Army training quarters – a big site in itself, which could easily fit a small village, a school and a shop, but the developers were greedy.

They wanted it all. They wanted to create not a liveable place, but a fast buck by squeezing in as many houses as possible: 5,000 houses, 10,000 cars on this quiet road, 3,000 dogs fouling the footpaths, 2,000 cats hunting for nightingale chicks, countless bored teenagers with no transport links. I thought of the shopping centres with vast car parks, places which sucked the life out of town centres and forced ever-increasing traffic onto our roads. I thought how much better it would be to do away with some of these eyesores and build housing on them instead, drive business and retail back into town centres to the benefit of local communities and ordinary people. But these people did not have the ear of the government; developers and wealthy business owners did. Why else would they ignore the fact that enough houses sit empty long-term in our country to house 300,000 families? Was it because opening up these houses did not fuel an easy construction boom to create economic growth at any cost, even at the cost of our greatest and irreplaceable asset, our countryside?

Yet, there I was, a freelance consultant, which to many within the conservation industry, meant only one thing: I had gone over to the dark side. Freelance consultancy firms wrote the weak environmental-impact assessments that steamrollered developments through. They looked at things at the wrong time of year, they looked at the fragile habitats and rare creatures and thought only about how they could translocate them and create a pale replica elsewhere; they greenwashed greed. This was not me. I couldn't, wouldn't do this work. Even if people got pickle and exploding beer for the next ten Christmases, I wouldn't go over to the dark side.

I was lucky in being offered enough work of the type I was happy to do. I was working for the RSPB again. Spring had come and I was out in the fields shortly after sunrise surveying lapwings and redshank, chatting to farmers and helping them make the most of their environmental subsidies. It wasn't easy work. It was easier to be at the Northward Hill Reserve, seeing only the land between Bromhey Farm and the Thames, full of wildlife, and thinking that there was no need to fear.

Nature reserves are increasingly islands for wildlife. We can go there and pretend it will all be OK, but outside of them, the working countryside is often empty of once-common species. Islands of loveliness are no good. The wildlife can't move between them. The woodland at Northward Hill lacks basic woodland birds, such as tree creepers, because there is nothing linking it to other big woods. Lapwing numbers can recover only up to a certain point if all they have are patches of well-managed habitat, such as at Elmley, while all around them the countryside goes to the dogs. Wildlife has to be able to spread if more species are to thrive, and the only way that can happen is by keeping all the links in the chain. We need them all: the beautiful places, the reserves, the SSSIs, but also all the little scrubby backyard places and hedgerows that the current drive for housing is sweeping away.

Reserves alone could never be a solution; the blinkers had to come off. I didn't want pockets of beauty; I wanted a countryside that worked for wildlife. I was determined to use whatever skills I possessed to encourage famers to manage their land in ways which would allow more birds to breed and more chicks to survive. I was back working on the marshes, back to walking the fields with AJ and ribbing him about his hair. Things had come full circle.

Earlier in 2015 I had spoken to AJ about Lodge Hill.

'It feels like dangerous times,' he agreed. 'If Lodge Hill goes, it will be like, "now what? All bets are off, nothing is safe." It is a worrying combination of massive declines in wildlife, the economic downturn and the government looking for ways of moving the economy on by supporting building and development projects. Then there is just a huge apathy in the population. People do care about green issues, but it's not reflected in the way they vote. It felt in the 1990s that we were at the start of something good, but now everything has stagnated. What is the signal that is being sent out if you can tear up a place like Lodge Hill and no one cares?'

I didn't know the answer. The sudden hard-lining of government, which made environmentalists the enemy, had taken everyone by surprise.

'A few years ago, the RSPB relied on the legal system to look after protected sites,' AJ said. 'Because we felt those areas were safe and it was better to use our resources to create new habitat from scratch like at Great Bells. Now it feels like we can't rely on the legal system anymore. Developers are sniffing around SSSIs, and the European Directives that protect these sites are under severe threat. It feels like nothing is safe at the moment.'

Since speaking to AJ everything had been thrown up in the air. The decision to leave the EU in 2016 was unchartered territory. European legislation protected many of our best wildlife sites and funded much of the work with farmers to improve the land in between. It was hard to believe that a government, which seemed determined to strip away protection from our countryside, would prioritise this work when it came to divvying out the cash. Only the kind of public outcry that ensued when the government tried to sell off nationally owned woodlands in 2010 would persuade politicians to rethink their policies.

'But do you think that some of the RSPB's campaigns are helping create apathy?' I asked AJ. 'Is ticking a box to say, "yes I support this", part of the problem? People can go away feeling they have done their bit and they don't really have to think about the real issues.'

'Then tell me what the alternative is?' he challenged. 'We've done big science, we've done dramatic films, we've tried every way possible to get people to act, but what do you do? There are so many vested interests fighting against doing the right thing. How do you articulate that message to people?'

'You need a cartoon spokesperson,' I suggested, only partly in jest. 'A Boris Johnson, a Jeremy Clarkson, a person with stupid hair who can dole out one-liners on TV quiz shows. Someone who can put across a very black-and-white message and forget the intricacies.'

'Maybe you're right,' he said, 'but we also need legislation that can't be swept away. People are not going to self-regulate. The problem is really the growing population, and the only way you can challenge that is by attacking something as fundamental as reproduction.'

AJ was right; this was the elephant in the room that no one

talked about. It was a simple equation of too many people in too small a country, but none of the solutions to this problem were very palatable.

'But if protection of our countryside goes, then what?' I said.

'If development at Lodge Hill goes ahead, we are quite prepared to chain ourselves to the gates to stop it,' he said. 'Because if protection goes, then it will all fall off a cliff.'

Here I am in agreement. The government, until the change of leadership in 2016, was hoping to weaken the laws that protect our countryside. Boris Johnson's Thames Estuary Airport had been defeated in autumn 2014, thrown out by the airport commission as being an uneconomic non-starter. In October 2016, the government indicated that it wished to expand Heathrow, and while this made the creation of an airport in the Thames Estuary less likely, no one on the Hoo Peninsula celebrated. We didn't cheer the news that communities around Heathrow would suffer increased air and noise pollution and that their local countryside was to be destroyed not ours. It was yet another example of the government backing financial growth over all other measures of quality of life.

Once out of Europe, the government will have a free hand to build a country to their liking and to the liking of the people who have their ear. As AJ said, Lodge Hill was the thin edge of an almighty wedge and maybe we all needed to consider the possibility of chaining ourselves to the gates, of not just ticking the box on the form but taking direct action and really doing something.

I feared that my country was becoming an uglier place, both physically and spiritually. There was a growing poverty in the country, a sea of people who rarely looked up from their computer screens or TV sets at the world around them, who rarely saw the countryside except as a view from the motorway. Sometimes I felt that this inertia was part of the government plan too, a dulling of the senses, a conspiracy so that we stayed lost in a world of entertainment and failed to notice what was happening.

There were people out there, however, who gave me hope, particularly young people bought up in a world of mass consumerism, social media and celebrity, who looked at the world they were told to embrace and felt that there must be more to life than this. My new assistant, Tam, gave me hope. He had come to volunteer with me that spring as a first step in getting a career in wildlife conservation. I sensed that he had a story and, on long journeys across the county in my Nissan Micra, I grilled him about his life, his thoughts and his philosophy. He didn't disappoint.

Tam had a difficult youth. Lacking confidence, he had started taking drugs as a way to interact and make friends, and then later, as his mental health spiralled out of control, as a way to escape reality and deal with depression. Tam was in his twenties, well-educated, softly spoken, from a good background. His upbringing was a world away from Andre the hermit's, but he ended up on a similar path. After reading a psychiatrist's report, which suggested he might be placed in a secure unit, Tam left home and took to living rough in the woods.

'I wanted to start again and try to live a more natural life.' he said. 'I'd always loved Ray Mears and the idea of living off the land, and that first night in the open, I built a fire and felt better. I didn't want to live on all the anti-depression drugs; they just made me feel dull and grey. I wanted to try to beat the depression without them and there seemed to be something simple in living this way. Life was suddenly reduced to the basic elements of survival. I couldn't think about all the other stuff when I had to think about how to stay warm and find food. Planning to leave and live in the woods was a positive decision for me. It was taking back some control over my life.'

Unlike Andre, Tam had left the woods behind. He returned home, took a course in countryside management and rejoined society, but he still felt that those years had taught him useful lessons.

'My love of nature pulled me through,' he said. 'I like working with my hands, making things and working with the seasons. The modern world, in comparison, seems so plastic. You spend your time watching blockbuster films on a computer screen or working in an air-conditioned office and it stops you truly appreciating the world. It does you good occasionally to be rained on, to feel discomfort, to be affected by the world.

'So much of modern life is about instant gratification, the high of being liked on Facebook, of buying the latest gadget. You get addicted to that, but it is all discardable and temporary. The natural world has more permanence. There is a timelessness about it, and it has more value because of that.'

This is a problem. A world where everything is easily reachable and quickly disposed of is without worth or meaning. If your goal in life is to always have more, you will never be replete, as there will always be something newer and shinier to have. You can gorge yourself and still feel as though you are starving, you can consume until you are sick and still feel hollow.

Tam agrees: 'I don't see that amassing things and wealth is the way to live. I don't see that more stuff is better, that more growth is better. It's unsustainable.'

He's not alone. A growing number of people are starting to look at other ways to live. Less stuff and less money means more time, more connection with nature and the people around us, and the satisfaction of growing, making or doing something yourself. The satisfaction comes from an investment in your possessions. If you have created something yourself, you are aware of the labour involved and that thing becomes precious. Conversely, if all you have done is press a couple of buttons on a computer to send money whizzing across the world, you are disconnected from the effort and energy that goes into making that object.

Connor had asked why anyone would struggle with a basic way of life when you no longer had to, and I would answer, as Tam would, because it keeps the world real, it keeps you connected to the earth and to yourself. When you become disconnected from the process of making things, from how energy is produced, from such basic acts as getting clean water to drink, you lose something essential. You lose your connection to the ecosystem and, if we lose connection with that, we suffer in ways that we can't yet define.

Quite a few of people I had met had chosen simple lives to keep them in touch with nature – human beings are part of nature after all – and in many cases, this made them healthier and happier people. One day, I suspect that people who wish to scale back and work alongside nature, not against it, will be not the outsiders but the pioneers.

A nightingale called after me as I left Lodge Hill behind and descended to the hamlet of Spendiff, passing farm cottages and oast houses, their chimneys resonating with the sound of doves cooing. I walked along the deserted lane between cow parsley and poppies humming with bees. Swallows skimmed low across the fields. This was a Britain that others had seen was worth fighting for.

I stopped in the shade of a railway bridge for a drink of water. The air hung heavy with the lemon scent of elder blossom, a cuckoo called. I passed fields of strawberries ripening in the sun and the gatehouse of Cooling Castle, and then set off through a meadow of clover and grass vetchling.

It was the same meadow which I had passed through a year ago, running away from thoughts of a past which still then had the power to hurt me. There was Rye Street Farm. I had spoken to Keith a few days ago. He had said his daughter was currently away and he would leave it open for me, but it wasn't until I stepped up and turned the door handle that I was sure. The door was open and I stepped into the caravan.

FIFTEEN

In the caravan

I WAS DISAPPOINTED AT FIRST. It barely looked like my caravan at all. The wallpaper of silver birches, which I had loved, had been painted over. There was a new carpet and lino, but the wood panelling was still in the dining room, the fake brick chimney piece remained. There was the gas boiler I had mended, now with an ominous line of black smoke issuing from the pilot light, a sign that a spider was once again living in the gas jets. There was the tiny shower where a daddy-longlegs had once sent me into meltdown among the steam. It was still my caravan, still full of memories.

I thought to myself, 'If I could choose to, would I still live here?' and knew the answer was yes. I still wanted this indoor–outdoor world, though I would never again put myself in the position where something I loved could be taken from me so easily.

A few nights before, a friend had asked me if my house was my 'forever home'. I told him that I was proud of owning my house, I loved my garden, I had good neighbours, I liked the town I lived in and the short walk down to the river; I had no plans to move. But my forever home? My dream home? No, it wasn't that. I would keep it if I could for the independent financial security it represented, but it wasn't the simple, close-to-nature existence that brought me the feeling of completeness that I had once experienced in Canada and to some extent in the caravan.

It wasn't a feeling that could be satisfied by just owning a campervan or a boat, I knew that now. It was something to do with having some settlement that worked with the surrounding land. It was something to do with returning to basics, relying on sustainable resources and your own hands and brain to provide for your needs and not giving over control to energy companies and technology giants. It was something to do with not having more than you truly needed.

I still dreamt of the shack in the woods, but next time I would make sure I owned the land on which it sat. I had learned a little from each person I had met on my travels. I had seen how people can pick themselves up from a low point of divorce or bankruptcy and make something positive from the experience. I had observed the happiness that a life lived close to nature can bring, without the burden of a mortgage and material wealth. I had learned from Steve and Gordon that a good end can be found in being true to yourself and following a life that makes you happy. Jason had shown me that stability was an achievement to be proud of, not a sign that you had succumbed. Most of all, I had learned from the plotlanders, from their determination, resourcefulness and sheer belief in their ability to achieve their dreams from a position of poverty. I wanted to take their attitude with me. There were others who shared my vision of a simpler existence. I wasn't about to create a hippie commune in the Kent hills. I was way too strong-willed to cope with community decision-making and no lover of herbal tea, but I was inspired by the stories of communities pulling together and helping each other out to achieve a common dream. I had a vision of gathering together a group of people, who would buy a piece of land, pitch a tent, cook over an outdoor fire and begin with that. That was possible, that was achievable.

I took one last look around the caravan. It didn't look like my caravan. It looked like a caravan belonging to a young woman who loved it, as I had, and laughed with her friends and listened to her music. The caravan had had a life after me. I could be happy with that.

I had needed to go back to the caravan because it was the scene of so many of the moments which had led me to this point and because part of me still longed for it and what it represented, but I had known that there was one more thing I needed to do to put the past behind me. I had to meet with Connor.

The idea of this meeting had grown throughout the winter. Taking this journey, looking back on those last years with Connor, I had seen things differently. It wasn't all him, it wasn't all me. It takes two people to break a relationship. I wanted done with it, to be rid of him, but there was so much anger and bitterness between us that I felt that, in some way, while this remained, we would forever be tied together.

Two weeks after our final split Connor sent me a message telling me his affair was over.

'It was just a fling,' he wrote, 'nothing more. Can't we meet for coffee, be friends?'

I replied that I was too hurt, it was too soon. I told him not to contact me. I needed to break myself away from him and I could only do this by going cold turkey. He returned to the girl, she got pregnant, they got married. The fling had become his wife.

Connor had chosen the ending, but now it was time for me to choose a different one, to take back ownership of the ending of the relationship. So I emailed him and asked to meet. He came back and said it would be great to 'catch up, maybe meet for a glass of wine in Rochester'.

'Catch up?' It didn't seem quite the right expression for a meeting with a woman you hadn't seen since she'd thrown you out seven years ago. It seemed a little casual. Still, I felt the only way to finally achieve some closure with Connor was to see him and say goodbye.

So I prepared for this ride out in a way that a woman does. I got a haircut, put on a dress I knew I looked amazing in, sprayed myself with perfume. We met at a café that I had suggested, set on a bend in the river. It was middle ground. From there you could look back into the town and forwards towards the estuary. Connor arrived. He was wearing a pink shirt, a pair of sky-blue chinos and suede shoes. He was nervous but, then, so was I.

We caught up. He told me about his work, I told him about my business plans. He asked after my family, I asked after his.

'So you own a house now?' he said.

I nodded.

'I guess it was just that you didn't want to get a mortgage with me then?'

I didn't know what to say. Yes, that was partly the truth, but it was so many other things as well.

'Have you got a television?' he asked.

I laughed. 'Yes,' I said.

'What about Sky?' he asked.

I looked at him. It seemed the weirdest question when there were so many possible questions to ask each other. Had I got Sky TV? Was I, in his eyes, normal yet? It seemed almost that if I had answered 'yes', Connor would have remained frustrated that maybe there had been a way to make me change but he just hadn't found it.

I put him out of his misery. 'No,' I said. 'No. I doubt I ever will reach a day when I feel I need Sky TV.'

He sighed. It was OK, I was still and always would be, in his eyes, a wacky freak.

'We should have split up years ago,' Connor said.

I agreed. 'We should have split up after calling off the wedding. I think then we could have walked away from each other with decency.'

'It wasn't like it was a fling,' he said of his wife. 'I'm married. I have two children. Do you want to see pictures of them? It wasn't like I was looking for a way out.'

I smiled. We all write our life stories to suit ourselves.

'I still laugh about that final night,' he said. 'I was telling someone the other day how funny it was, that it happened on Christmas Eve, like an *EastEnders* plot.'

I thought about that moment of discovery and what it had been like to go downstairs and face my parents on Christmas morning and tell them he had gone.

'No, Connor,' I said. 'Some things may be darkly comic, but that night and what I had to deal with the next day, really isn't.'

I had wanted to say so many things to Connor. To say sorry for making him feel bad about himself, to acknowledge how important he had been in my life, to thank him for all the great advice that he had given me and had helped me choose my career. For all the support he had given me with my parents. I said all those things to him. It was important to say them. If you can't acknowledge how important someone has been to you, then you can't let go.

'We had a lot of fun,' Connor said.

We had, but we were done here.

We parted in the stairwell of the café. 'Good luck,' I said. We hugged and he walked out through the door. After he left I realised that I had forgotten to say 'goodbye'.

SIXTEEN

Rye Street – Cliffe – Lower Higham

I WALKED AWAY from the caravan and came into Cliffe Village. When I had first come to Cliffe, it had four pubs and a post office. Now its facilities had dwindled. The village shop was still hanging on, a green corrugated-iron building where the cash register was an unlocked drawer, guarded by a tiny old woman in huge glasses. I tried the door. It was locked. 'Half day closing on Saturdays and Wednesdays', the sign said. Thankfully, the Six Bells was open and I popped inside to have a pint.

The church bells chimed 3pm as I headed out of Cliffe and followed Pond Hill towards the marshes. A Thames sailing barge could be seen out on the river, the top sail visible beyond the distant sea wall. A nightingale sang loudly from the scrub on the edge of the village and bored teenagers chucked bricks at each other.

At the end of the track I reached Cliffe Pools. Cliffe Pools had historically been a notorious dumping ground and had attracted an array of unsavoury activities. The main road leading to the pools had once been so full of rubbish it was impossible to drive down. Scrambler bikes had zoomed around at breakneck speed, the swans had been shot at with crossbows, and a Gypsy encampment had set up on the edge of the pools and burnt the copper out of electrical wire, sending noxious chemicals into the water. Despite all this, the pools were a haven for wildlife and represented two percent of the country's saline lagoons, one of the rarest habitats in Europe.

The RSPB had bravely taken on this site, fly-tipping, bikers, Gypsies and all, and had spent a small fortune turning it around. In my first week working for the RSPB, Mike, the warden, had driven me to the gate of the site to find it had been smashed open. Overnight, the price of scrap metal had risen and the seventy-eight burnt-out cars that had littered the site had vanished.

'They should have called,' Mike said. 'We would have opened the gate for them.'

I walked along the central path and saw a woman cycling towards me wearing pearls. It was Gill Moore, one half of a duo of glamorous and ardent campaigners, who run, along with George Crozier, the Friends of the North Kent Marshes, a group that have long fought to protect the marshes from developers. Gill Moore and Joan Darwell make an unlikely pair of eco-warriors. Joan is tall and slim with long, blonde hair, Gill, tiny and delicate. They are a pair of ordinary women from the village of Cliffe who were, to their surprise, thrown into the frontline of a battle to save their homes from the threat of the first Cliffe Airport proposal. They took up the challenge and, within weeks of plans for the airport being announced, Joan and Gill were campaigning outside parliament, asking awkward questions at public meetings, speaking to news cameramen and outwitting politicians with their knowledge of every argument for and against the airport. For their work to protect the marshes they were awarded the RSPB President's award, a volunteering 'Oscar' given to those who have made an outstanding contribution to the work of the RSPB.

Gill and Joan approved of my plans to bring new audiences out to the marshes. 'We love it quiet and peaceful,' Gill once told me, 'but we know that people will only care about it if they visit and see how special it is for themselves.'

I give Gill a hug now and admire her pearls.

Gill and Joan have not stopped their fight for the marshes. After Cliffe Airport was rejected, other plans came along: plans to flood the marshes, to build motorways to Essex across them, to infill the villages with houses to make one giant estate, and then, as if that wasn't enough, they had to start the airport fight all over again with Boris Island.

'Do you think the threat of the airport has finally gone away?' I asked Gill.

'Some people think Boris was only ever playing to the gallery for the people of West London,' Gill said, 'but I worry we won't ever be safe.'

She told me about the government's plans to downgrade Natura 2000 sites to lessen their protection. The Natura 2000 sites are all of those places protected by EU laws from development, but the government, in 2015, wanted to weaken the protection to allow development to go ahead in our most prized and important places.

Two women passed us and smiled. Gill stopped them. 'Will you please do me a favour,' she said to them. 'If you enjoyed walking here today, then please go onto the RSPB website and sign the petition to Defend Nature.' She gave them the address. 'Please do it,' she said. 'It's so important that we protect this place.'

The women promised to do so.

'I'm stopping everyone,' she said. 'Telling people is the only way.'

People like Gill helped generate a huge response to the European Commission's public consultation. Over 100,000 people from Britain alone backed the petition to Defend Nature and eighty percent of MEPs subsequently voted against the changes. In December 2016, the European Commission agreed that the laws protecting nature should not be changed. Once we left Europe, however, I felt worried that this protection of our wild places would be gone. The government pledged that 'where practical' all European legislation would be converted into domestic law, but I had little faith in politicians' promises. I shared Gill's fears that the Hoo Peninsula would never be safe.

There never seemed to be a let-up in the battle to protect the marshes. Airport proposal followed airport proposal, followed by new roads and bridges across the river, followed by industrial estates and lorry parks and housing, housing, housing. The marshes, for centuries prone to flooding and malaria, are not a traditionally desirable location. The Hoo Peninsula still felt remote, unconnected from the Medway Towns, with precious few facilities or public transport. Now, as London spread its feelers outwards, it was suddenly a prime location, but what would happen to all the 'undesirables', the birds, the woods and all the people who already lived there and got in the way? Would the sea fog of change sweep across us, cleansing this area and leaving behind a blank canvas for the 'right sort' to move in?

The right sort? Who were this faceless body that I feared? I pictured someone who lived in a waterfront apartment and commuted to London, who updated their gadgetry every six months, paid their taxes, took out loans and consumed freely and without conscience. In other words, who were model citizens and the fuel that kept the economy ticking along. They were coming and I doubt they would want to live next to Alex or Fergus or Tam or Ronnie or me. And what about the wildlife which needed space and to be left alone. This empty land of dykes and sheep was full of competing desires and was just too small to accommodate them all. It was easy to feel powerless, to roll over and give in, but Gill wouldn't do it and neither would I. Gill was right, telling people was the only way. I just hoped it was enough.

I watched Gill cycle away, a diminutive and brave one-woman campaign trail.

At Cliffe Creek, I caught up with the women Gill had stopped. They were standing on the sea wall, reading a notice and looking in desperation at their Ordnance Survey map. The notice was in large red letters: THE PATH AROUND CLIFFE FORT IS CLOSED DUE TO EROSION. THERE IS NO SAFE ROUTE BEYOND THIS POINT.

'What are we going to do?' one of the women asked. 'We've walked eight hours to get here.'

'No safe route makes me think there is a route,' I said to them. 'I'm heading on. The tide is out and I'm sure we can find a way round.'

We strode on, skirting the edge of Cliffe Creek, an inlet which was once a favourite place to land smuggled goods. The mud was folded in on itself like a rumpled bed. I stopped to take a photo and my two companions pushed on. I passed an old wall, an outlying fortification for another of the Napoleonic forts scattered along the coastline. The wall had been constructed from sandbags filled with cement from the nearby works. The hessian bags had long since rotted away but the outline of each bag and the imprint of the fibres could still be seen. The wall was topped with the fleshy lobes of stonecrop, and the fluorescent yellow flowers shone in the sun.

I emerged from the enclosed pathway to a sandy beach. The towering cranes and conveyor belts of Brett's Aggregates, the company that owns the fort and the footpath that surrounds it, loomed up. Another sign told me that I could go no further and should take the alternative route. The alternative route was longer and uglier, involving a walk along a road where every tree and bush was covered in dust delivered to them by the aggregate company's lorries. It was not tempting.

I walked on, stepping over a fence, broken down by many boots before me. The original route went along the sea wall but, not knowing how bad the erosion was, I decided to take a different route, a short hop round the front of Cliffe Fort, passing the silent conveyor belts and empty diggers. Mounds of sand and gravel were piled up against the fort and it struck me as odd that an aggregate firm couldn't lay their hands on the materials to fix the eroded section of pathway as a goodwill gesture to the local community who have to accommodate the lorry traffic. The path rejoined the sea wall and I saw the two women walking along.

'How was the erosion?' I asked them.

'There's a bit of the path which has completely washed away,' one of the women said, 'but people have dropped boulders and bits of wood into the gap to help you across.'

'I had to shuffle on my bottom,' the other woman told me, 'but we have walked from Upnor and were in no mood to turn back.'

I knew how they felt.

The women strode on around Higham Bight, a huge bay, again

owned by the RSPB, which understands the importance of these muddy inlets, rich in crustaceans, as refuelling spots for migrating birds travelling along the Thames every spring and autumn. I passed the *Hans Egede*, a boat which had sprung a leak many years ago and had been towed to Higham Bight to safely collapse out of the way of passing ships. Huge concrete blocks – parts of the Maunsell Forts, built during the Second World War – surrounded the boat.

A pygmy shrew ran along the path towards me, long nose down, tiny bottom up. He poked under every grass stem and pebble on the lookout for insects. He was so intent on the hunt that when I bent down to get a photo, he mistook me for a giant rock and burrowed under my leg. I could feel him, working his way along my shin, but dared not move for fear of squashing him. I stood up slowly and he scurried on.

The wind was gusting off the Thames and the clouds were rolling in. I could see my two companions from earlier fighting their way towards Gravesend. I turned inland.

Gypsy ponies with foals at heel were being scurried along by two boys on scrambler bikes. The boys raced up and down the same patch of grass, engines whining. It seemed a pretty dull hobby to me and I wondered how much more fun it would be to leap on one of the ponies and charge the others towards them.

I cut down a narrow path between scrub, where the boys could not follow. May-blossom honey scented the air. Lapwings swooped from the wet meadows beside the path. They jinked away in a tipsy flight at my approach. I remembered a time when the fields were dry and bare, but now the RSPB, working with the local landowner, had turned the place around, creating shallow scrapes, keeping the grass short, pumping water from the ditches at the right times of year. It is a simple recipe, and one which has had astounding success.

When the RSPB started managing this land in 2013, two pairs of lapwings had tried to breed. In 2015, there were forty-nine pairs and seventy-four pairs of redshank. A good news story and little patch of hope on the Peninsula? AJ felt so. 'In some ways, north

Kent is somewhere I feel quite optimistic about,' he told me. 'It feels like the RSPB is getting stronger, we have more members than ever, we are better than ever at habitat management, we are talking to farmers. I see reserves thick with birds and I think, "it's going to be alright". In some ways it feels like we are more battle-ready.'

I hoped so. In the long run, it is inevitable that nature will win. The marshes have wiped away centuries of human desires and ambitions. This landscape is a hard place to take root in. The wind, the weather and the flood will eventually reclaim the land. It is as inevitable as the tide coming in and drawing out. Sometimes this thought helps – that the marshes were there at the beginning and will be there at the end – but for now, the threats to this special place are likely to grow ever more numerous. If the marshes are to remain a sanctuary for people and wildlife then in the coming years we will need to be battle-ready.

I climbed a stile, and across the meadow lay my destination, St Mary's Church, Lower Higham.

I had returned to the beginning. Pilgrims, on completing their journey, traditionally return to the church they have set out from and give thanks, so I was back again.

In the lane outside the church was my little red car, left there the day before, packed with everything I would need for the night ahead.

I opened the boot and pulled out my camp stove and food supplies. I hauled them round the back of the church to a clearing amid the gravestones, set a pan of water on to boil and tipped in some pasta. I sat with my back to the church, drinking a glass of red wine and reading Charles Dickens' *Complete Ghost Stories*. Dickens, a greater walker and a great drinker, I felt would have approved. I ate my pasta and watched the sun become hazy and sink low.

As it began to grow dark, I walked into the church. I looked at the high-beamed ceilings, dusty oil lamps and dark pews and thought, 'I can't do this. I can't sleep here'. The little church, which always seemed so welcoming to me, suddenly appeared cavernous and full of shadows. 'I'll sleep in the car,' I thought, but then I remembered my night at Bedlam's Bottom and the pain in my back and legs.

I had come to the church the day before and had chosen a spot to stay, wedged between an old Tortoise Stove and the front pew, overlooked by a statue of the Virgin Mary. I would be lying on someone's tombstone, but if it had been me, cold in my grave for several hundred years, I wouldn't have minded. I think I'd enjoy the company. If I lay here, I would be looking directly up at the rood screen and the statue of Jesus.

I walked over to the spot and sat down. It felt okay. It felt peaceful.

I headed out to the car and pulled out the thin mattress which I had folded inside. I heard a car coming and pushed the mattress back in. I knew the church was open all night, but I didn't know if the Church Conservation Trust, which manages it, would give their support to my idea of sleeping there. I had thought to ask, though feared a barrage of rules and insurance concerns. I knew I would do no harm, come to no harm and it seemed right to sleep there. I couldn't go home because there was something I needed to do in the early morning, something I could only do by walking out from this spot and reaching the Thames for high tide. This church had long been a place of sanctuary to me and I needed it to be that now.

The car passed and I pulled the mattress out once again, followed by a sleeping bag, head torch and pillow. I carried these items into the church and pushed the heavy metal bolt across the door. The bolt could be opened from outside but it was reassuring to feel it slide into its hasp.

I set up my bed on the floor and lay down, looking up into the dark wooden rafters. A barn owl called outside the window followed by a little owl. Another car drove down the lane and stopped outside. My heart began to beat faster. The lights from the car lit up the stained-glass windows and their coloured reflection bounced off the plaster walls and picked out the limbs of the Jesus statue above. I thought how few people would know this, that when a car came down the lane, headlights on, a light show danced across the walls of the church. I listened for footsteps approaching, but the car lights went out and no footsteps came. I lay in the dark once again.

I am not a great believer in ghosts and felt the only ones likely to visit were the ghosts of the women associated with this building: Kate Collins, Dickens' daughter, and the nuns impregnated by the vicar. I didn't mind; if these wronged women wanted to look down on me while I slept, I felt I could entrust myself to their care.

The little owl called outside again.

I took it as a good omen. I felt safe.

SEVENTEEN

Lower Higham – Thames

I SLEPT SOUNDLY and woke early next morning to the sound of the wind gusting outside. The church was brightly lit, and the daylight shining through the stained glass made the white plaster glow. I felt I had never woken in a more beautiful place.

I bundled my bedding away and sat in the church porch boiling up water for tea and watched the sparrows make love on top of people's headstones.

My journey was almost at an end. I went back inside the church and placed the pilgrim shell on the wooden step of the rood screen which led to the altar. I sat on the floor and thought about what I needed to do.

I put on the ring and walked down to the river.

At the railway crossing outside the village I met a party of brightly coloured ramblers off for a day's walk, despite the threatening rain. The men put their hands out to help me down from the stile.

I headed on. Low leaden clouds were drifting in across the river from Essex. The grassland, ditches and buttercups glowed bright in the steely light. Swifts hawked the meadows. The chatter of the ramblers twittered like the linnets which flew overhead. I walked on, with the ring on my finger, towards the Thames.

I thought of the past year, of the unique lives I had been let into, of the beautiful moments of light on the rivers, of the tiny shrew and the grass vetchling and how precious each of these were, not for my sake but for their own. I thought of conquering my fear of the daddy-longlegs and of the support I had received, which had helped me step out and start my own business, and mostly I thought of the generosity, openness and kindness of the people I had met.

I crossed a stile and there was the gang of Gypsy ponies waiting for me. I touched noses and rubbed foreheads. A man on a bike cycled past.

'I'm a sucker when it comes to horses,' I called to him.

Some things about me had changed, some things never will.

I climbed the sea wall and there it was: the Thames, grey and choppy, with rain coming in. It was twenty past eleven, at the turn of the tide.

The Romans built a bridge across the Thames, in the days when the river was much narrower here and lined with sandbanks and islands. I'm not sure if anyone knows the exact location of this crossing but I knew I was close. The Romans built a bridge here and there they gave offerings to the river; they would throw precious items into the water to appease their Gods and ensure safe passage on the way ahead.

A dog walker was making his way along the sea wall, the ramblers were negotiating passage with the horses. I walked down to the pinnacle of saltmarsh that jutted out into the river. I was wearing the ring. My engagement ring. Let there be no misunderstanding here. It was not a big diamond ring, otherwise I would have pawned it and got the shack in the woods. It was a replica of a ring found in the rubble of the Rose Theatre in London where Shakespeare once performed. I had chosen the ring. It was silver and around it was printed the French: PENCES POVR MOYE DV, and there was a heart with two crossed arrows. It said, 'Think of me, God willing'.

I thought about Connor. I thought about the boy I had loved, of his joy and excitement over the simple things in life. I thought of all the conversations we had in coffee houses when we returned from university and were struggling to work out what to do with our lives. I thought of all the night journeys on National Express coaches when we were living in separate parts of the country and travelled every weekend to see each other. I thought of the games we made up, of the support he had given me. I thought of the woman who'd been a fling and then his wife. I sent them warm wishes for their future together. I could do this, send them warmth, but I wanted no more of them. I wanted it gone. I pulled the ring from my finger and held it in my hand for a long time and then I flung it through the air into the river. It vanished with a splash into the brown muddy waters of the estuary and so quickly it left me. My ring was lying on the mud of the riverbed where tides would cover it in silt, where slowly it would be rubbed clean of the words and eventually dissolve. I burst into tears at the finality of the act. It was a reaction I hadn't expected. A moment of grief at the loss of all that potential we once had. I took a deep breath and felt better. The feeling was released into the air and blew away down the river like soot dust. I would think of him no more. I stood on the pinnacle of land as the tide lapped at my feet and felt the breeze coming down the river. A boat headed out to sea.

ACKNOWLEDGEMENTS

I MET SOME WONDERFUL PEOPLE while taking my walk across the marshes who were generous with their time and their stories, most of those are mentioned by name in the text and to them I owe a debt of thanks.

I would also like to thank, Angie Murray, Lynn Yardley and my mum for reading and editing the original manuscript. Joanna Swainson for believing in the idea from the very beginning and finding inspiration on the marshes, even on a wet January day. Steve Wilkes for lending me his house when I had nowhere peaceful to write. Ruth Reisenberger for invaluable insight and editing skills and Mark Loos for endless helpful advice, inspiration and photography.

Lastly I would like to thank the RSPB and all members of the Bromhey Gang, past, present, dead or alive, especially to AJ for saying yes to the caravan in the first place.

Little Toller Books

We publish old and new writing attuned to nature and the landscape, working with a wide range of the very best writers and artists. We pride ourselves in publishing affordable books of the highest quality, which are designed and printed in south-west England. If you have enjoyed this book, you will also like exploring our list of other titles.

Field Notes

MY HOUSE OF SKY: THE LIFE OF J. A. BAKER *Hetty Saunders*
ON THE MARSHES *Carol Donaldson*
DEER ISLAND *Neil Ansell*
ORISON FOR A CURLEW *Horatio Clare*
LOVE MADNESS FISHING *Dexter Petley*
WATER AND SKY *Neil Sentance*

Monographs

HERBACEOUS *Paul Evans*
ON SILBURY HILL *Adam Thorpe*
THE ASH TREE *Oliver Rackham*
MERMAIDS *Sophia Kingshill*
BLACK APPLES OF GOWER *Iain Sinclair*
BEYOND THE FELL WALL *Richard Skelton*
LANDFILL *Tim Dee*
LIMESTONE COUNTRY *Fiona Sampson*
HAVERGEY *John Burnside*
SNOW *Marcus Sedgwick*

Nature Classics Library

THROUGH THE WOODS *H. E. Bates*
MEN AND THE FIELDS *Adrian Bell*
THE MIRROR OF THE SEA *Joseph Conrad*
ISLAND YEARS, ISLAND FARM *Frank Fraser Darling*
THE MAKING OF THE ENGLISH LANDSCAPE *W. G. Hoskins*
A SHEPHERD'S LIFE *W. H. Hudson*
THE FAT OF THE LAND *John Seymour*
FOUR HEDGES *Clare Leighton*
DREAM ISLAND *R. M. Lockley*
THE UNOFFICIAL COUNTRYSIDE *Richard Mabey*
RING OF BRIGHT WATER *Gavin Maxwell*
EARTH MEMORIES *Llewelyn Powys*
IN PURSUIT OF SPRING *Edward Thomas*
THE NATURAL HISTORY OF SELBORNE *Gilbert White*

A postcard sent to Little Toller will ensure you are put on our mailing list and among the first to discover each new book as it appears in the series. You can also follow our latest news at **littletoller. co.uk** or visit our online magazine **theclearingonline.org** for new essays, short films and poetry.

LITTLE TOLLER BOOKS
Lower Dairy, Toller Fratrum, Dorset DT2 0EL
W. littletoller.co.uk **E.** books@littletoller.co.uk